by Ciara Conlon

Productivity For Dummies®

Published by: **John Wiley & Sons, Ltd., The Atrium, Southern Gate, Chichester,** `www.wiley.com`

This edition first published 2016

Registered Office

John Wiley & Sons, Ltd., The Atrium, Southern Gate, Chichester, West Sussex, PO19 8SQ, United Kingdom

For details of our global editorial offices, for customer services and for information about how to apply for permission to reuse the copyright material in this book, please see our website at `www.wiley.com`.

For general information on our other products and services, please contact our Customer Care Department within the U.S. at 877-762-2974, outside the U.S. at 317-572-3993, or fax 317-572-4002. For technical support, please visit `www.wiley.com/techsupport`.

Wiley publishes in a variety of print and electronic formats and by print-on-demand. Some material included with standard print versions of this book may not be included in e-books or in print-on-demand. If this book refers to media such as a CD or DVD that is not included in the version you purchased, you may download this material at `http://booksupport.wiley.com`. For more information about Wiley products, visit `www.wiley.com`.

Library of Congress Control Number: 2015956887

ISBN 978-1-119-09952-9 (pbk); ISBN 978-1-119-09954-3 (ebk); ISBN 978-1-119-09953-6 (ebk)

Printed and bound in Great Britain by TJ International Ltd, Padstow, Cornwall, UK

10 9 8 7 6 5 4 3 2 1

Contents at a Glance

Table of Contents

Part III: Applying Productivity Techniques 91

Introduction

Ten years ago, the word *productivity* had no meaning for me. Apart from the fact I am the most naturally disorganized person I know, I had no inclination to make it any other way. I tended toward chaos, hence the title of my first book *Chaos to Control.* But having reached my early 30s with three boys to look after and very little achievement to speak about, the time had come for change.

I wasn't clever enough to go out and seek ways to improve my cluttered and disorganized life; a chance meeting on a sunny day in South Africa was what changed the course of my life. I met productivity expert Gerrit Cloete of Productivity Pit Stop, who sparked my interest and guided me while I learned the things that were about to rock my world and my business for the next ten years.

About This Book

This book is about all the techniques, tools and behaviours that you can adopt to change your life. Most of them have been tried and tested by yours truly. Note that some of the resources I speak about are apps and websites, and although I aim to be as accurate and up-to-date as possible, new applications and software changes happen all the time.

This book is a comprehensive guide to how and why you should become more productive, more organized and more in control of your life. Whether you're a stay-at-home parent who wants better ways to organize your day, a senior manager who is responsible for a large team or a student who wants time to fit it all in while acing your tests, this book has something for you.

I'm regularly asked the question, 'Who is your ideal client?' The answer is anyone who lives and breathes. Everyone needs help fitting it all in and planning days with the right things, the things that make a difference. Who doesn't need help with taking control of the digital world, the distractions, the interruptions and the information overload? We're all given the same 168 hours each week, which is plenty of time for work, rest and play. If you want to find out how to live your life to the fullest and maximize the precious time you have, this book will help get you there. But please remember that this book won't change your life unless you're willing to implement some of the suggestions in it. Even if you try one new thing, it will have a positive impact on your productivity and your life.

Throughout the book, you'll find sidebars (grey boxes) with extra bits of information or other stuff you may want to know. If you decide to skip these sections, you won't miss any vital facts or information.

Within this book, you may note that some web addresses break across two lines of text. If you're reading this book in print and want to visit one of these web pages, simply key in the web address exactly as it's noted in the text, pretending as though the line break doesn't exist. If you're reading this as an e-book, you've got it easy – just click the web address to be taken directly to the web page.

Foolish Assumptions

As I wrote this book, I made a few assumptions about you, my readers:

- You are a human being who struggles finding time to fit it all in.
- You pine for a better work-life balance and need some practical strategies to make it work.
- You know an easier way to do things exists, but you just haven't figured it out.
- You need to find time to be more creative, strategic or simply take on more work.

Icons Used in This Book

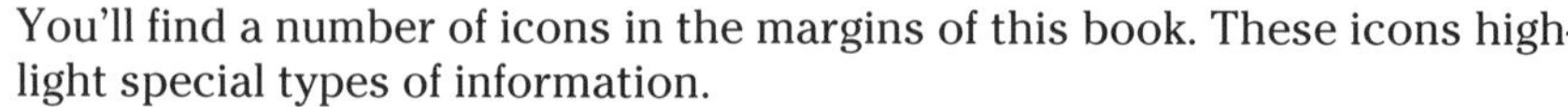

You'll find a number of icons in the margins of this book. These icons highlight special types of information.

This icon highlights points that are especially important and worth committing to memory.

Watch out for the target, where you'll find tips and tricks to help you become more productive.

The warning icon highlights potential pitfalls and things that you should avoid in order to stay in control.

This icon advises you to stop reading and try out the tip right now. Knowledge is no good unless you act on it. This icon encourages you to act now to reap the benefits sooner rather than later.

Beyond the Book

This book is chock-full of useful information to help you understand productivity and become more productive yourself. But you can find even more online! Head to www.dummies.com/cheatsheet/productivity to find ways to be more productive at work, as well as other productivity boosters. You can also find various bonus articles related to increasing your productivity at www.dummies.com/extras/productivity.

Where to Go from Here

Nothing in this book is difficult to implement. It includes strategies and techniques for even the most skilled procrastinators among you. So get started, choose any chapter or begin from Chapter 1, take action and begin to enjoy a life of calm, organised control.

Part I

Getting Started with Productivity

getting started with productivity

For Dummies can help you get started with lots of subjects. Visit `www.dummies.com` to learn more and do more with *For Dummies.*

In this part . . .

- Understand what productivity is and how being more productive can help you in all aspects of your life.
- Find the motivation to change your bad habits that hinder productivity.
- Discover all the benefits of productivity.

Chapter 1

What Is Productivity?

In This Chapter

- Discovering exactly what productivity is
- Recognising the different sources of productivity
- Understanding why productivity matters

In basic terms, productivity is a measurement of how efficiently you can convert inputs into outputs. In manufacturing terms, it's how many units of a good can be produced with a certain amount of raw materials and labour. In personal terms, it relates to how much work you can get done in the time allocated. But these definitions don't come close to explaining what exactly productivity can do for you, your family or your business. In this chapter, I explain the value and contribution that productivity can make to your life.

Productivity is simply a method to get what you want out of life. It gives you the tools and techniques to not only get the work done but to also get it done while making time for the things you enjoy and value in life. No longer is it necessary to sell your soul to your employer, nor work incessantly to launch a start-up. Working productivity can emphasise your priorities and make sure they're getting the attention they deserve while eliminating all the time-wasting stuff.

Understanding the Importance of Productivity

You've likely heard the expression, 'what you put in you get out'. With productivity, you can get out much more that you put in. You can work smarter rather than harder. You can work more efficiently rather than just effectively. Personal productivity is a subject that should be taught in schools. Teaching children simple productive habits can make the difference to their future success and happiness. Productivity transforms lives, relationships and business.

Effectiveness versus efficiency

Effectiveness is about doing the right thing at the right time, completing tasks to reach your goals. *Efficiency* is about doing these things in an optimal way. Using the fastest or least expensive method to reach your goals.

What can productivity mean to you?

The word *productivity* means the same thing whatever way you look at it. It means getting more out for what you put in. But the context in which that is done can make it mean different things to different people, including the following:

- **Reading the bedtime story:** To a working parent, productivity can mean not having to sacrifice the bedtime story to do a good job ever again. It can mean always being there for your kids' birthday or sports day or school play or whatever occasion is important to them. Figuring out how to work flexibly and fit work around your life can help you have a great work-life balance and still do a top job. See Chapter 17 for more on a productive home life.
- **Being first to market:** For the start-up, productivity can be the difference between being first to market or fifth. The more effective methods you use to get the job done each day, the more quickly you can produce what you want to produce. Cutting-edge technology or scientific breakthrough all depend on the productivity of the people to get it to the masses as quickly as possible. Waste too much time on emails, and you may find yourself at the back of the queue for recognition. See Chapter 12 for more on productivity in business.
- **Keeping the doors open:** Increasing productivity can help to produce goods at a lower cost. If you're responsible for the wages of your employees, increased productivity can mean they get paid again this month. To a business owner, productivity, can mean keeping the doors open.
- **Making the grade and the party:** To a student, productivity means making the grade *and* the party. A student wants to fit it all in – attend classes, go to the gym, have time to study, and still make it to all the best parties. These are the priorities of a student, and becoming more productive can make them a possibility. See Chapter 19 for more on studying productively.

What can productivity mean to your business?

People are generally more familiar with the business benefits of productivity – increased profits, competitiveness and less employee stress, to name but a few. But businesses today are faced with increased competition from emerging markets along with a more demanding customer who wants it all and wants it now. Forever under pressure to cut costs, and with the emerging war for talent, being in business is no walk in the park. Productivity is a powerful tool that can help you to address these challenges and give organisations a competitive edge. This section covers the benefits of productivity for businesses. For example:

- **Making the difference between profit and loss:** Most people understand productivity in its traditional sense: increase productivity and experience greater profits. To a CEO, increased productivity can mean a good year. How this difference was made could be made up of a hundred different factors. Productivity could have been increased through changes in factory processes, through the influence of a new manager who helped all employees perform at their best or through the new computer system that cut out all the downtime. The outcome is of most interest to the CEO, but his managers should know how to replicate the increase by understanding its source.
- **Reducing employee stress:** Increased productivity usually results in a reduction in stress. When people learn how to work more effectively and manage their time and energy better, they tend to benefit from a feeling of control and reduced stress. This reduction in individual stress can have a positive impact on the people, their team and the whole organisation. Stress is responsible for so many negative factors in a working environment; you can read about how to deal with stress in Chapter 6.
- **Being innovative:** Productive employees tend to have more time for strategic thinking time and innovation. Only when you're relaxed and in control of your day to day can you take the time to visualise something better. Productivity usually leads to a more innovative company culture when employees are praised for the time spent dreaming or thinking of better ways to do things.

  When an organisation is under time pressure to achieve its daily goals, any time not spent on the core activities will generally be frowned upon. If a company doesn't take the time to innovate, its future won't be so bright.

- **Creating a culture of success:** Productive organisations are more successful. Their people tend to take the lead and tend to be more proactive, more creative and more innovative. They're generally people who take responsibility for their own actions and circumstances. This can result in a culture where people are more likely to think beyond the daily remit. They'll be more inclined to have ideas and willing to share and follow up on them. Calm control breathes success.

Checking Out Sources of Productivity

Productivity gains can be felt from making changes in multiple areas of life. Simple changes to the way you currently do things can have surprising implications to the efficiency of how you run your business and your life.

The three main areas of focus where you can make a substantial difference are systems, technology and behaviour.

Productivity from systems

Creating new systems and processes in your day to day will help you see great improvements in productivity. Standardizing the way things are currently done usually leads to a decrease in the amount of time being spent on the current process.

Standardising daily processes

Many companies don't have a formal process designed for each job role. New employees learn on the job from whoever is there to train them. Along with the previous employee's habits, good or bad, new employees create their own way of completing the work. Some people are naturally faster, more organised and efficient, but others take more time – more time to learn and more time to do everything. Standardising the process, how the workflow ideally is managed, is important for any company; following are some of the reasons daily processes can be beneficial.

Quicker workflows

The first benefit of standardising procedures is the obvious time saved. If you can cut down the number of steps involved in completing a job, you'll gain hours each week. Working out what is involved in completing a job is important to be able to improve the process.

Establishing quicker workflows is a simple exercise that can help you improve every part of your job. Map out how the work flows from the first task until the last. Then you can see whether you can improve the process and make any adjustments to make it more efficient.

Increased quality

The quality of the service you offer will be improved due to fewer mistakes and more time available for customer service. You can follow a checklist to ensure that each part of the process is completed in the correct order.

When you introduce checklists, you ensure that the process is adhered to perfectly. This is very important when it comes to customer service because you can be sure that every customer gets the same quality of service and see what the results are from a particular procedure. You can then change procedures and measure the impact more accurately when you have something to follow.

Reduced handover time

When new staff come on board, it's important for them to learn the existing process. They need to know how things are done. If they can follow a written procedure, they'll learn more quickly, reducing the amount of time required to train them and the downtime of the person responsible for training them.

Reduced loss of intellectual information over time

When you fail to capture your processes and procedures in a sensible manner, you risk losing intellectual capital each time a staff member moves. To prevent this loss of knowledge that one employee may hold, you should keep your processes documented and saved electronically or on paper. You can simply record these processes in a Word document or as a checklist in a programme like Excel or Evernote. I use a website called Process Street (`www.process.st`), which enables you to create checklists for the different processes involved in your role. I have a training checklist and a blog posting process. Process Street has a number of templates that you can choose from and personalise to suit your own processes.

Exploring productivity techniques

You can use many techniques to create a more productive environment. In this section, I list tried and tested ways to up your game and get into the driver's seat. Some of the better known ones include GTD, inbox zero and using your calendar to plan your day.

Getting Things Done (GTD)

Getting Things Done is a workflow management system devised by management consultant David Allen. Allen wrote a book in 1997 called *Getting Things Done: The Art of Stress-Free Productivity* (Penguin). In the book, Allen outlines a system for managing all the work that comes your way each day. It has become a widely adopted and popular technique for getting organised and becoming productive. You can learn more about GTD in Chapter 10.

Inbox zero

Inbox zero is a technique conceived by writer and speaker Merlin Mann of the website 43 Folders. Inbox zero involves taking control of your inbox and processing your email – planning the work rather than using your inbox like a to-do list and completing the work in each one as it comes in. This technique is an efficient way of managing your email and your time. I cover email management in detail in Chapter 15.

Using your calendar

Using your calendar is an effective productivity technique for managing the time available to you. By planning your work, you make decisions about priorities and commit to completing the work that needs to be done. This technique is a powerful way to get a good overview of what you need to do and to see the time you have to do it in. There's more on using your calendar effectively in Chapter 14.

Productivity from technology

Technology is the big game changer for getting things done more quickly. Computers can do the work of hundreds in a minute percentage of the time. With both software and hardware, the world of business has seen massive changes and advancements. I cover technology in Chapter 15.

Software

Hundreds of different types of software have been created to make life easier for the modern worker, but two pieces of software that have radically changed their field and can be found in every business are accounting software and sales or CRM software.

- **Accounting software:** Few people still use paper to manage their accounts. For some years now, accounting software has become the norm for most businesses. You can use software to record all income and expenditure and to manage invoicing, payroll and any other financial transaction that a company may have.

- **Sales, marketing and CRM:** Many great software packages hit the scene in the last decade, improving the way sales and marketing are carried out. With the customer relationship management (CRM), it became possible to understand more about your customers' preferences to be able to market to them effectively. These software programmes, along with many others, have transformed the way people do business. They've reduced the labour input required and the cost of running a business.

Hardware

Having the right hardware is important to keep things efficient. Old computers or devices that take longer to turn on or process information waste time and often cause frustration.

- **Computers:** If your computer takes longer than a minute to boot up, give it a kiss and say goodbye. Each minute you waste waiting on a reaction from your computer adds up to hours at the end of the year. You'll save time and money in the long run if you invest in fast equipment that does the job it was designed to do.
- **Tablets:** Tablets are great, but unless you have the right applications installed to allow you to access all your documents and files, they can be a frustration and a time sap. Spend some time connecting your cloud-based software to your other devices for ease of file sharing.
- **Phones:** It's a good idea to have a phone that has the same software as your tablet. All Apple or all Android devices make file sharing a lot easier. Phones should be used to your benefit and not a source of distraction or frustration.
- **Printers:** I don't know many people who haven't gotten frustrated with their printer from time to time. If your printer is older than your car, you may want to consider an updated model. If it requires any jiggling or banging to get things going, it's time for a new one.

Make sure all your hardware is up-to-date and helping you stay productive.

Productivity from behaviour

Your attitude is everything; the way you think about your work will have a big impression on how efficient and effective you can be. If you feel like a victim where others control how productive you can be, you'll never get ahead. You will only become productive when you acknowledge the fact that your life is within your control. Nobody else has responsibility for making things easier or better, only you.

After you become accountable for your own life, then you can start to make the changes required to soar. Along with your attitude come your habits. You're an accumulation of all your daily habits. There are three types of habits that add to making you a productive superhero: productivity habits, physical habits and mental habits. The following sections – and Chapters 7 to 11 – cover these.

Productivity habits

Productivity habits are all the routines, processes and procedures you do to get things done. Techniques or systems – whatever you call them – help to get things done more efficiently and usually more effectively.

- **Systems/processes:** Creating systems for the regular work that you do is a positive habit to adopt. Whether it involves a checklist for preparing training workshops or a process for contacting new customers, all should have a process designed to maximise time and quality or service. Systems for processing email or managing your tasks will also benefit you and make life easier to manage.
- **The two-minute rule:** If you can do something in less than two minutes, do it now. This is a great tip for avoiding clutter or procrastination. Get into the habit of clearing some things from your to-do list and your desk by doing them straightaway.

  Look around and see what you can do in two minutes to help you clear your workload or to make your surroundings more organised and clutter-free.
- **Regular declutter:** A great habit to adopt is a regular declutter. Rather than the once-a-year spring clean, a weekly declutter will keep things feeling organised. Fix a time every week to declutter your environment, both at home and in work, and feel the better for it. I roll my sleeves up for a bit of decluttering in Chapters 4 and 18.
- **Clean-desk policy:** Commit to a clean-desk policy. When everyone in the office is responsible for keeping the standard, it makes it a lot easier to do. Having a place for everything in your office will help you to maintain the policy more easily. Look at the desks of those around you and see what solutions they have come up with to stay organised. I talk about the joys of a clean desk in Chapter 4.

Physical habits

The physical habits you have are just as important as the productivity habits. If you plan your life well and organise your work in the right way, you'll become more productive. But if you're tired and sluggish from lack of exercise and poor nutrition, you'll see the effects in your work. Chapter 5 covers these physical habits.

- **Exercise:** Daily exercise increases your productivity without you realising it. Exercise gives you energy, makes you feel happier and more positive about life and keeps you healthy. Maintaining the habit of exercise is probably one of the things that will have the biggest impact on your ability to focus and get things done.
- **Nutrition:** Feeding your body the right nutrients combined with your daily exercise and plenty of water will give your body all the ingredients it needs to work at its best. People often fail to nourish their bodies when they feel stressed or overworked. This is the time when you need good healthy food the most. Good habits for shopping and planning your meals can help to make eating heathy a natural part of every day.
- **Regular breaks:** Regular breaks help the body to re-energise and renew. They also act as a great reminder to take some deep breaths and drink more water to stay hydrated and focused throughout the day.
- **Breathing:** Most people take breathing for granted; it's an involuntary action that happens to keep you alive. Breathing is a great tool for relaxation and managing stress. Regular deep breaths can help oxygenate the body and the mind.

Stop reading and take a deep breath. Focus on your breath moving down through your body until it reaches your diaphragm. Take a couple of breaths in, following the breath each time.

Mental habits

The way you think about life and work can affect the quality of your daily life. If you have a can-do attitude, one where you expect good outcomes and want to have a positive impact on the world, you'll undoubtedly achieve more in life.

- **Positive thinking:** It all starts with positive thinking. Everyone has strengths and weaknesses, behaviours that your friends and families like and dislike. When it comes to friends, people often focus on the good points and drown out the bad with the good. When it comes to enemies, they do the opposite. Some people choose to always focus on the negative, justifying their thinking by the fact that they're being realistic.

  Sometimes negative thinkers are right, such as when bad things happen and they don't get the results they hoped for. But without optimism, you'd never start a business, get married or even have a child. Focusing on the positive is essential to achieve anything in life. So think positive and create the life that you want.
- **Can-do attitude:** With positive thinking comes a can-do attitude. This is believing that anything is possible and with a little effort you can do whatever you want in life. If you want to be more productive, you must believe in your ability to make the right decisions and employ the right techniques to make your life better.

- **Mindfulness:** Living mindfully can greatly help you to focus and do your best work all the time. Living in the now avoids the time wasting involved in worrying about the future happenings or thinking about past failures. You can, and should, of course, plan for the future and learn from the past, but holding your attention on the here and now will help you to focus and get more done. Chapter 5 has more on mindfulness.

Create a reminder on your phone or in your calendar to 'Focus on the Now'. Set it for at least once a day to remind you to come back to the present moment.

Discovering Why Productivity Matters to You

So why do you want to get productive? Is it to increase your performance at work, to deliver more and better? Or is it to have a better quality of life and improve your work-life balance and be happy? The following sections include some of the main reasons people want to improve their productivity.

Improving work-life balance

Probably one of the chief reasons people buy self-help books is to improve their work-life balance. They feel overwhelmed with too much to do or not enough time to spend with family or friends. Productivity and this book are the perfect solution for improving your work-life balance and figuring out what merits your time and attention. When you understand what is important to you in your life, you can work toward changing the things that need to change. (See Chapters 4, 6 and 17 for more on work-life balance.)

Reducing personal stress

Increased productivity usually results in a reduction in stress. When people figure out how to work more effectively and manage their time and energy better, they tend to benefit from a feeling of control and reduced stress. Feeling organised means you no longer have to worry about things you need to do or would like to do. You'll have a system to look after all of your tasks and dreams and goals. Taking charge will help you to feel like you're driving your life forward rather than being pulled in too many directions. See Chapter 6 for more on stress management.

Doing a better job

Productive employees tend to have more time for strategic thinking time and innovation. Only when you're relaxed and in control of your day to day can you take the time to visualise something better. Productivity usually leads to more creativity, innovation and enhanced performance all around.

Making time for creativity

Many people think that productivity and creativity are at opposite sides of the court. They think that organised, productive people aren't creative. This is not the case. The more productive I become, the more peaceful my mind becomes. If I have all the boring stuff organised and taken care of, I can free my mind to be more creative. Stress caused by disorganisation will negatively affect creativity. Productivity paves the way for creativity to bloom. Chapters 8 and 12 have the detail on stimulating creativity.

Making time for strategic thinking

Many senior managers complain of not having enough time in their day. The problem is that they prioritise badly, giving the daily tasks priority over the more important big-picture work. Managers need strategic thinking time. If you're disorganised and stressed with your workload, this time will rarely come. When you get organised and start to prioritise effectively, you'll have more time to focus on the important stuff like strategic thinking.

Improving your quality of life

Many things may need to change in your life – your relationships, your work or even the time you spend with yourself. Getting organised is a great first step to making changes in your life. Getting organised helps you to see clearly what you want from your life. When you have this clarity, you can introduce systems that will help you to achieve more order. With the right attitude and habits, you can maintain a relaxed, organised calm in all areas of your life. If that sounds good to you, read on.

Moving Forward – Ready, Steady, Go

After you become aware of your reasons for being productive, you can move forward toward creating a solution that works for you and your life. Of course, you need to invest some time to make the changes, but this investment will be repaid tenfold if you commit to making the changes. This journey isn't for the faint-hearted; there will be ups and downs, you will soar and you will fail, but that is the journey of life. This is what makes it sweet and sad and precious, and the destination is totally up to you.

Chapter 2

Finding the Motivation to Change

In This Chapter

- Discovering why change is important
- Finding out how to set goals
- Achieving your goals

I was once asked in an interview, 'What if you don't want to change; what if you are happy just as you are?' Then you're a very lucky person. Being happy just as you are is a wonderful thing, but it's also a rare thing. Not to have anything that needs a little work or improvement is unusual. Most people could eat a little healthier, do more exercise or drink more water, and I don't think there's a person alive who wouldn't want to get more done more efficiently, leaving more time for the fun stuff.

Discovering Your Reasons to Change

Everyone has different reasons for wanting to be more productive. People's lives differ, as do their motivations to change. Whatever your motivation to change, becoming more productive with your time and actions will help you to achieve your goals in life. Knowing what your reasons are and understanding your own motivations will be valuable to you when you meet the blocks and barriers to making those changes.

Doing more with your own time

Each week is filled with 168 hours. You can't change this fact, nor can you choose to ignore it. What you decide to do with those hours determines how happy and successful you are. If you choose to spend your time waiting for the weekend or until the next big occasion, you'll essentially waste that time and never get it back. Opting to make the most of your time each day, each hour and each minute will help you to succeed regardless of what success means to you. This doesn't mean that you can't spend some of that time relaxing, chilling or simply being, as long as this is your conscious choice and you're not in default lazy mode.

Earning more with your time

Some people are motivated to become more productive by the need to earn more money. If you're self-employed and the hours that you work add up to money that you take home, there's a big motivation to get more done each hour that you work. If you can get more tasks done each hour, you can bill more by the end of the week. The challenge of getting paid per hour has always been an issue for the self-employed. You can only do so much, so the obvious choices are to either hire people to do the tasks for you and pay them less than you charge or to limit your income to the amount of hours you can do. The following sections highlight a few other things you can do to earn more with your time. If you work for someone else, tune in to the later section 'Doing more on other people's time' to find out how you can make the most of your time as an employee.

Eliminating tasks

Create a stop-doing list. This list will help you see the things that you're doing that really don't need to be done. Maybe you're using Facebook as a marketing tool, but Facebook hasn't given you any return on investment. If you stop spending time on Facebook, could you be earning more money with the time saved? Check out Chapter 7 for more on creating a stop-doing list.

Re-evaluating tasks

Write a list of all the tasks that you do each day, and take the top two that use up most of your time. First, ask yourself: 'Do these tasks merit the amount of time I spend on them?' If they are valuable tasks, make sure you are scheduling time for them. If they don't merit your time and attention, make the decision to delegate or outsource them or stop doing them altogether.

Addressing email

If one of these tasks is addressing email, ask yourself how much time you want to spend on emails. Most people want to spend substantially less time on emails than they currently do. Refer to Chapter 15 for details on how to process your email more effectively.

Don't open your email tomorrow morning until you've completed at least one important task. Observe how good it feels and how productive your day becomes.

Working on the right tasks

Lots of people don't spend nearly enough time on what they actually get paid to do. People allow administrative tasks, distractions and interruptions to get in the way. It's important to be conscious of where your time is going. When you know how you currently spend your time, it empowers you to make a change and be more productive.

What is a virtual team?

A virtual team is a team that is acquired through the Internet. You don't need to meet these people in person. If you have a requirement for a job role that can be completed without face-to-face interaction, a virtual employee may be the solution. Virtual employees are self-employed individuals who work remotely from a home office anywhere in the world. The cost of hiring a virtual member of staff is a lot less than hiring an employee.

Take your major task, and document how you get the job done. Write the steps out as if someone with no experience is having to do your job. Detail every step and how that person would go about doing that step. Write as if you were explaining it to a child. Use this document the next time you're doing your job, and see how accurate it is. Can you do anything differently and more efficiently?

Take the time to think about how you do your job. Most days, people are too busy doing things the way they've always done them to notice whether there's a better way. You may be able to eliminate a couple of the steps to how you get things done when you take the time to look at your role from a different perspective.

Hiring a virtual team

One of the best ways to make better use of your time is to hire a virtual team. Get other people to do the nonessential parts of your job. A virtual assistant can help you with your admin and accounts. Other types of assistants may be able to help you get more out of your day. Check out Chapter 16 for more tips on hiring a virtual assistant and getting more done at home.

Don't wait until you're earning lots of money to hire a virtual assistant; you just need enough to cover her costs. If you free up your time by allowing someone else to do the work that doesn't need you and your exact skill, you'll rapidly increase your earning potential. Otherwise, you may always be waiting to earn enough – and not getting there.

Making your life easier

Becoming more productive is a clever way to make your life easier. Getting your work done more quickly and efficiently means you work fewer hours and can use the extra time saved to have more fun. Simple changes like the way you process your email can help you save up to an hour a day. An hour saved each day adds up to 5 hours a week, 20 hours a month, and almost a week and a half each year. Or, in work time, that's six work weeks each year that you can use to either earn more money or to relax and make your life easier.

Spending more time with family

There's a popular saying that says one of your regrets on your death bed will never be 'I wish I spent more time at the office'. A more common regret is not having spent enough time at home with the family. Many people neglect to spend enough time on the things that really matter. Their family, their friends or doing the things that make them feel alive and happy. Work often takes over. Mountains of work that never seem to get done. You find yourself buried in a never-ending circle of work, letting life happen outside the circle. This is not the way to live your life.

Make a list of the things that really matter to you in your life. Prioritise them from 1 to 10 – 1 being most important, and 10 being least important – then write beside each item how much time you're spending on it weekly. Most people find a great difference between what they'd like to be doing and what they're currently doing. Now is the time to readjust it and do the right thing.

Understanding that work will always expand

It took me some time to realise that my to-do list would never be empty. I spent years frantically trying to tick things off only to observe myself adding more and more. Accepting this fact and understanding what can be left to another day are keys to creating the life that you want. Take control of your workload today, and get done what you can get done, ensuring that there is time left over to be who you are and to do the things that are important to you.

Doing more on other people's time

When you work for someone else, your motivations will be similar to those in the previous sections but not so much in your control. You may want to be more productive, to earn more money or to spend more time with family, but none of those outcomes may be directly in your control within your work environment.

What you do have control over is making your life easier, happier and stress-free. Also consider that the more effective you are with your time, the more attractive you are as a potential employee if you do find that your success at work isn't getting the recognition it deserves.

Living stress-free

One of the biggest improvements to my life after learning to be more productive was the reduction in stress. I felt more in control of my work and my life. Living stress-free is crucial for a happy life, and simple changes, such as using your calendar and getting everything out of your head into a system, will have the biggest impact. Removing the stress from your life is a big motivator and also empowers you to see that the quality of your life is within your control and not at the mercy of your employer. (See Chapter 6 for more on managing stress.)

Being in control

Creating a work environment where you feel in control of your day greatly enhances the quality of your days. To achieve this feeling of control, simply take time each day to plan your work, and be sure to declutter your environment and work with a clear desk. Having a clutter-free space allows you to focus on what you need to do, and planning your day helps you to feel that the work you're doing is priority and merits your focus. (See Chapter 12 for more on managing stress.)

Setting Goals to Get What You Want

The most powerful way to get what you want out of life is to set goals. Goals create a clear picture of where you want to be and help you work out the steps to get there. Goal setting is a habit of many successful people, from sport personalities to business giants. They have achieved their greatness by creating goals.

Why goals are important

Goals are important because they give you focus. They motivate you to take action and to move toward the change that you want and desire for your future. Goals don't have to be big, hairy, audacious goals, like author and motivational speaker Anthony Robbins suggests, but they can be small improvements you want in your life. Whether it's running a marathon, writing a blog post or just changing a bad habit, all are goals of differing kinds.

Goals help you to achieve what you want and feel the satisfaction of self-improvement. Professional goals help you be more productive in work. If you're clear about what your goals are, you can focus on priorities. It's easier to know what to work on and what merits your attention. If you spend your days working on the right things, the things that add value and help you achieve your goals, you'll achieve the goals more quickly.

When to set goals

You can set goals at any age and any stage of life. My 9-year-old son set a goal to win the 100-meter sprint at school; my husband undertook to get the garden in order before the end of the month. My mentor aims to increase his turnover by 25 per cent this year. You can set goals for any reason at any time of the year. You don't have to wait until the New Year to make a change. Goals are also ever-changing and dynamic. You may set a goal on the 1st of January that no longer excites you in June. If that's the case, by all means change it. Many people set a goal each Monday to eat less but never quite make it to the weekend.

Monthly goals

The start of each month can be a good time to set goals. Most yearly goals need to be broken down into smaller chunks, and monthly goals can help you do this. The length of time required for each goal determines when to set your goals.

Yearly goals

The most common approach is to set yearly goals. A year is a long enough time to achieve most things. Of course, this depends on what you want to achieve and the length of time required to achieve it. If you want to write a book, a year should be sufficient time, but if you want to swim the Atlantic Ocean, you may need more time to plan and train.

Ten-year goals

Ten-year goals are the big-picture goals, covering the big things you want from life. Getting a house by the sea or a yacht, or becoming a bestselling author – ten years gives you sufficient time to make it happen and to gradually work toward its achievement.

You can set goals at any time of the year. Start today by writing down how you want your life to be in ten years' time. You can then gradually work out what you want to achieve in five years, three years, and one year.

How many goals to set

One of the first questions I often get asked about goal setting is 'How many goals should I set?' When it comes to ten-year goals, you will have goals in all areas of your life so you may have quite a few things that you would like to see differently. The closer the time frame, the number of goals should decrease. When it comes to yearly goals, the fewer, the better but enough that you feel like you're making progress. Five seems to be the optimum number for yearly goals: many more and you won't remember them, and any fewer and it may feel like you're not making enough progress each year. If you have only one goal, that is fine, too.

How to set goals

Many approaches to setting goals exist. You can focus on what you want in the future in many ways, but the truth is that for goal setting to work, you have to focus on what you want as opposed to what you don't want. Setting the goal is not enough; you must take action daily toward achieving the goal in order for it to manifest.

Setting SMART goals

A widely used process for goal setting is the SMART process. SMART is an acronym that can be interpreted in different ways. For a goal to be SMART, it must be

- **Specific:** Your goals must be clear and specific, identifying exactly what you want to achieve. 'I want to get fit' is not specific; 'I want to be able to run 5 kilometers' is. What training method will you use? Are you just going to run, or are you going to walk and swim as well? Deciding upfront what method you'll use will help you put the plan into action as soon as possible. When will you train or work out? Making a time plan will assist you in getting started. Know when you will work out, how many days a week and what time of day. Schedule time in your calendar to ensure that you're reminded daily of your fitness intentions.
- **Measurable:** You need a way to know when you've mastered the goal. 'Earn more money' is not measurable; 'Earn 1,000 more per month' is. Having a quantifiable amount will help you achieve more.
- **Attainable:** You must have a goal that is attainable. You can't set a goal to win the lottery, because winning the lottery isn't within your control. A goal should be something you can achieve through your own blood, sweat and tears.
- **Realistic:** Your goal must be in the realms of what is possible. A goal must be realistic, but it should also stretch you. Easy goals are not motivating; goals must push you outside your comfort zone. 'I want to win Wimbledon next year' is not realistic if you're 40 years old and never played tennis before. 'I want to learn to play tennis', on the other hand, is realistic.
- **Time bound:** A goal should have a time or date associated with it. If you don't give a time limit to your goal, you'll have no motivation to complete it. Each goal that you set should have a deadline associated with it.

Using a vision board

Some people like to use a more visual means of goal setting by using a *vision board.* A vision board is a visual representation of the goals you want to achieve in your life. You can create a vision board by cutting pictures out of magazines and pasting them on a board or by creating an electronic vision board of images online. Creating a vision board can be a stimulating and magical process. It can be a powerful way to imprint what you want onto your subconscious mind. You can add to your vision board over time or change it if, for example, you decide you no longer want a Lamborghini and would prefer a Porsche.

Mapping your vision

A vision map is another way to create a visual representation of your ideal life. You can map your vision in the form of a mind map with different branches representing different areas of your life. The more images, the better because your subconscious brain likes images.

Developing a vision chart

An alternative way to record what you want is to make a chart with all the different areas of your life noted – for example, career, family, money, work, fun, friends, spirituality and health. Take time to think about what you want your life to look like in ten years in all these areas. You can then bring it down to three years and one year. This can help you to see which areas of your life need attention and which ones need some work. It can also help to score each area out of ten. Then, in a year's time, you can revisit the chart and score each area to see how much has improved in a year.

Focusing on experiences

Sometimes trying to be too exact and specific about what you want isn't ideal. Some goals require you to be specific and very clear about what you want, such as losing weight or improving your fitness, while others rely on the experience you want out of life rather than the exact goal.

Have you ever set a goal to attain something and not liked the outcome? Or has something happened in your life that you hadn't planned for and become one of the best things that ever happened? Sometimes, it's more important to be clear about the feelings and experiences you want from life rather than be too specific about how you get them.

Here are some examples of different goals and how you could approach them:

- **Buying a house:** If you want to buy a house and fixate on a particular house, you may not be buying the right house for you. Do you want a house because you want security, or is it because you want to live in a certain area of town? If you decide you want a four-bedroom house in a good area with a great school for the kids, would renting be an option? There are different routes to happiness that you may never have considered.
- **Writing a book:** Sometimes the book you want to write is not the book you should be writing. In my experience, sometimes the book I set out to write is not always the book I end up writing. It doesn't make me any happier to write the book that I had planned. Finishing and publishing a book that people will benefit from is the goal, and being too specific won't make me any happier.

  Perhaps a better approach is to focus on writing a book that people need or want to read and not write the one you want.
- **Getting a job:** Sometimes the job you want isn't the job that will make you happy. I have often thought I knew what I wanted from a job or a company and ended up unhappy or dissatisfied.

  Try focusing on getting a job that uses your skills, rewards well and makes you happy.

This is one approach to setting goals that has worked for me in the past. Instead of assuming I know what's best for me, I focus on the experience

I want to have from achieving the goal rather than be too pig-headed about achieving the actual goal itself.

Understanding your motivations

Regardless of the method you use to set goals or to get what you want out of life, understanding your motivations for change is important. Why you want a certain goal may seem like an obvious question, but knowing the real reason will help with motivation if it fades.

Understanding your true reasons for going after your goal is essential to its success. Do you want to do more exercise to lose weight or for health reasons? By being honest with yourself, you'll greatly increase your chances of achieving your goal. Looking at how you'll benefit from achieving the goal will help you to connect with the why. Note what emotions you'll feel when you achieve your goal and all the direct and indirect benefits that will result. You may need to be reminded why you're going after this goal at times, and if you're clear about what you will gain by achieving it, success will come easier.

Doing the essential steps

You can read plenty of differing views on how you should set goals, but in this section, I cover the things that everyone agrees on.

Writing down your goals

You should write down your goals to increase your chances of success, and there are some interesting reasons this is useful:

- **Committing to your goals:** When you write down your goals, you're committing to yourself to go after them. There's something more official when you write something down. It feels like there's no way out; you have written it, so you must carry it out.

  A public commitment is the best form of commitment. Research shows that people are substantially more successful with goals when they commit to carrying them out to a third party. You could use a training buddy if you goal is exercise or a coach or a mentor for personal or professional development. The more public your commitment, the better.
- **Enabling measurement:** When you write something down, it enables you to be able to check back over your goals and review at intervals. Writing it down gives you a means of measurement and a reminder for what you once said you want to achieve.

Self-fulfilling prophecy

People are prone to a phenomenon called the *self-fulfilling prophecy.* The self-fulfilling prophecy claims that people's beliefs about themselves and their abilities determine the outcomes in their lives. If you believe you'll be successful, it is highly probable that you will be. People who have negative self-belief have a hard time breaking the patterns of negativity and most likely will have negative outcomes.

Reviewing your goals regularly

Regularly reviewing your goals is crucial for keeping your goals in both your conscious and subconscious minds. Reviewing your goals helps keep you moving in the right direction and helps you gradually get closer to your goals. It also helps you to keep on track and make your goals part of your everyday life.

Create the habit of reviewing your goals once a month or at the end of each week to stay on track and make adjustments if necessary. Schedule reviews in your calendar to remind you, and even if you spend only ten minutes looking over your goals every so often, that will benefit you in the long run.

Sharing your goals with others

Sharing your goals with other people is a commitment to yourself that you're going to do what you've said you will do, and it also enables your family and close friends to support you. Make sure you share your goals with people you trust. You want the right people supporting you and encouraging you.

Reticular activating system

The reticular activating system, or RAS for short, is a filter in the brain that is responsible for arousal and alert. Our brains would be overloaded with stimulus from the world if we didn't have filters. These filters are designed to protect the brain from information and sensation overload. The RAS blocks out anything that isn't relevant to the brain and notices anything that is relevant.

Writing down your goals commits your goals to the subconscious mind and therefore engages your RAS to filter out what's not important and to filter in anything that is relevant to achieving that goal. Examples of the RAS at work can be

- When you buy a new car, what do you see?
- When you get pregnant or someone close to you gets pregnant, what do you see?

The RAS helps you to notice things that are relevant to you. If you write down your goals, the RAS will help you to notice opportunities that are relevant to achieving your goals.

Conquering the Obstacles

Although you may be clear about what you need to change and have ticked all the right boxes when setting your goals, there are further obstacles that you might face on the road to success. Being aware of these obstacles will allow you to overcome them with ease and grace.

Overcoming obstacles

People fail for different reasons. Some fail because they weren't very committed to start with: it was something everyone was doing so it sounded like a good idea. Some fail because they never really believed they would or could do it. You can really want something, but lack of belief will keep it from you. Many fail from a simple lack of planning.

I cover some of the most common pitfalls – and ways to overcome them – in the following sections.

Not having clearly defined goals

If you write down a goal, you should be very clear about what you want to achieve and why. If one of your goals is to 'get fit', you need to be more specific about that goal in order to achieve it. Look at the section on SMART goals earlier in this chapter to see how you can be more explicit about your goals. They should be specific, measurable, attainable, realistic and time bound.

Falling at the first hurdle

And here is where we lose most people: at the first hurdle. The truth is, you're going to fall, but that doesn't matter. What matters is how long you stay lying down. Every one fails; it's part of life. The important part is your reaction to this failure. Do you stay lying down, or do you jump back up and try again? If you're starting a new habit, know that it's probable that you will stumble, but plan to get back up again quickly. It's up to you to understand why you failed in the past and put a plan in place to prevent it from happening again. It is your life and your responsibility to make it a good one. With a little bit of effort, you can make it just how your dreamed it.

Trying too much too soon

Change can be difficult. Human beings naturally resist change. We tend to prefer the status quo, the familiarity of our habits and routines, even if they're negative or no longer serve us. Our comfort zone is hard to break through, even harder if we try to break down too much at once.

The key is to start small and persist with that small change until you feel you've made it part of your everyday life. People who try to change too much at once are more likely to fail. Don't be impatient and try to do it all at once; small changes over time will lead to great results.

Not believing you can

Are you one of those people who reluctantly takes on a new habit? Do you say you're going to do something, but inside you don't really believe it? A lot of people have set themselves up for failure before they have even started. Deep down, they don't believe they can do what they've set out to. Do you think you can or think you can't? Your beliefs will generally determine the outcome, so don't waste your time if you don't really believe it can be done.

Don't set a goal if you really don't believe it's possible. So many people set the goal of losing weight every January, but they feel so negative about the goal because they've tried so many times before and failed that they don't really believe they can do it. If this is the case for you, the first thing you must consider is, are you doing the same things time after time and failing?

Remember Einstein's definition of insanity: 'Doing the same things and expecting different results'. If you want different results, you must start to do things differently. You have to plan out how you're going to achieve your goal. Seeing it written down with a plan of how you're going to go about it will help you to start believing in yourself and your abilities to achieve your goals.

There is no reason that you can't achieve your goals if you believe you can. Immerse yourself in the feeling of success: How would it feel if you achieved your goal? How amazing would it be to have finally conquered the unconquerable?

You *can* do it if you *really* want to.

Developing habits

To make any change in life, the easiest way is to form a new habit. As Aristotle said, 'You are what you repeatedly do; excellence then is not an act but a habit'. If you want to write a book, you need to create the habit of writing. If you want to run a marathon, you need to create the habit of running. If you want to buy a house, you need to create the habit of saving money. Your life is made up of your daily habits.

Whatever your goals are, there's a habit waiting to help you achieve it. If you think of your goals in terms of habits, they don't look so scary or big.

Staying motivated

Often, when starting something new, people have a high level of motivation. For example, you may buy new gym gear or set up a new workstation, and you're full of the joys of what you're about to achieve. A couple of weeks later, you're feeling tired and bored of the new routine. You start to tell yourself all sorts of things to get free from the new routine. You create loopholes to unravel the commitments you've made, and you give yourself permission to quit, even though you'd never admit that is what you're doing. Here are a couple of ways to stay motivated and keep the new habit going for at least a little longer.

Recognise the loopholes

Human beings are experts at creating loopholes, giving themselves a way out, an excuse, a reason to not do what they said they would do. People have many ways of self-sabotaging and a dictionary full of excuses the pope would accept.

- I would go to the gym, but I forgot my runners.
- I can't get up tomorrow morning; I feel a cold coming on.
- I can't exercise today because I didn't sleep well last night.
- Just one beer won't ruin my diet.
- You only live once, so let's skip the run and go have some fun.

I'm tired, sick, busy – whatever the excuse, people have a litany of lines all expertly used at the right time, and the funny thing is these are the lines they say in their own heads to release them from the commitments they've made to themselves. It sounds crazy, but it's true. The first step is to become aware of your favourite loopholes and challenge them. 'I'm too tired to exercise' is a common one. Remind yourself that exercise creates energy. A small workout or walk will give you energy, raise your mood and may extend your life. Not a bad trade for 30 minutes of your time.

Squash negative thoughts

Often, when I'm feeling demotivated, it's because of the negative self-talk going on in my head. Bring those thoughts out into the open, and squash them. Squash them with a big hammer, and sweep away the debris. Then replace them with some positive words and thoughts. Exercise makes me feel good. Meditation makes me happier and calmer. I have done many great things; if I continue with my positive habits, great things will continue to happen.

Revisit the benefits

Remind yourself of the benefits of staying with your habits and goals. If you connect back with your original motivations and remind yourself of all the good things that will happen if you stick with your goals, you may feel that original motivation creep back in again.

Identify your obstacles

Sometimes there are genuine reasons for your motivation to wane. Perhaps your life has genuinely gotten busier, or you have family commitments that keep getting in the way. It's important to identify these issues and look to a solution. Sometimes it will be easy to solve once you're aware it is happening.

Many years ago, my habit of mediation wasn't working for me because every morning when I sat down to meditate, a little body would come into the room to disturb my practise. I started getting frustrated and tried to wake earlier to overcome my intruder, but the earlier I woke, the earlier he woke, and I would be left with the same situation. I could have given up, but I switched my practise to evening times after my children were in bed. It wasn't ideal for me because often I would be tired and find myself falling asleep, but it was the best solution for that phase in my life.

Identify your obstacles, and if you can't come up with a solution, discuss the situation with others. Many times, other people have solutions you simply haven't thought of yet.

Record your progress

Tracking your progress can be a great motivator. When you're dieting and see the progress you've made, you're more motivated to continue. You can track your progress on paper or with an app. Coach.me or MyFitnessPal.com are both great apps to help you monitor your new habits and commit to continuing to make change happen.

Make sure you are accountable

Accountability is a powerful ally. You'll be surprised at what you can achieve and how your motivation can increase when you've promised someone else you will do it. Find an accountability buddy, preferably someone whom you don't know too well. An acquaintance or work colleague can work well. Check in with him regularly to track your progress.

Don't break the chain

Another method that can help keep you motivated is to use Jerry Seinfeld's 'Don't break the chain' method. It's a simple calendar-based method where you mark off each day with a large red X to signify completion of the habit. The goal is not to break the chain and to have a red X across every day. It's a very simple but effective method to keep you motivated.

Create milestone rewards

Don't forget to reward yourself for your great achievements. Each time you reach a milestone, give yourself a pat on the back and reward yourself with an appropriate award. If you're dieting, don't reward yourself with food but with a trip to the cinema or a hot bath, or maybe some new clothes each time you go down a size. Interim rewards can help to keep you motivated when the goal takes time to be realised. But the most important thing to remember is to never ever give up. When you keep taking action, no matter how small or insignificant it appears, you'll be a step closer to success.

Chapter 3

The Benefits of Productivity

In This Chapter

- Understanding why productivity is important
- Improving work-life balance
- Identifying business benefits

Productivity is a word that can have many interpretations. For some, productivity is for governments or senior managers; for others, productivity means the difference between getting home in time to read a bedtime story or not. The reason productivity means so many different things is that it can benefit so many areas of your life.

Finding the Personal Benefits of Productivity

For many years, the word *productivity* had no place in my life. It was a word from my economics textbooks in college, but it never featured in my life after that. And when I say it didn't feature, I don't lie. My chaotic tendencies were strong: clutter, untidiness and mayhem dominated my day-to-day life. Finding productivity for me was a life-changing event, helping me to focus, to prioritise, to schedule and to plan – all seemingly mundane activities that deliver powerful results. Some people find religion; I found productivity.

Reducing the chaos

One of the most noticeable benefits of becoming productive is being able to say goodbye to chaos. When I began to implement productivity systems in my life, I began to feel in control. For the first time in my life, I had the steering wheel and I understood how to drive. Years of sitting in the back seat and allowing life to take me wherever had taken its toll. I was ready to take charge, and productivity was my means to make that happen. In the following sections, I list the process of gaining that control.

Getting organised

Getting organised was my first step to reducing the chaos. I decluttered my life, rid my surroundings of the unnecessary mess and took back control of my environment. The physical organisation had a positive impact on my mental state, and with some simple productivity systems, I mastered my disorganisation.

Taking the lead

If you want to take the lead and be in control, you have to take responsibility for your life and your actions. 'Someone made me do it' won't cut the mustard. If your life feels out of control, the first step to taming it is to admit that change is within your control and that the quality of your life depends on the actions and decisions that you take each day.

Eliminating stress

Getting organised and taking responsibility for your life will both contribute to a reduction in stress. Stress can have a negative impact on your physical health and well-being and the quality of your work. When you feel stressed, you can lose focus. The negative effects of stress can be felt in so many parts of your body. Stress always leads to a less effective immune system, meaning more sick days and fewer days getting things done. Getting organised and taking control sends a rude signal to your stress, saying, 'Get lost; I'm in control. I no longer need you hanging around'.

One great way to manage stress is to take better care of yourself. Exercise, nutrition and sleep are the main positive influencers of a happy and healthy life. Combined with a reduction in the not-so-healthy habits of alcohol, nicotine and excessive Netflix watching, you should be well on your way to a balanced, joyful life.

Calling the cavalry

There will be times in life where you simply need a helping hand. This is nothing to be ashamed or embarrassed about; it's more a sign of strength than weakness to recognise when you need help. Sometimes you need physical help (for example, when minding the kids or fixing something in the house). Other times, you may just need a friendly listener to talk through some of your issues with.

Improving work-life balance

The quest for work-life balance is a modern phenomenon. In recent years, people have become more aware of creating a life that makes them happy, one where work and personal life live side by side in harmony. But focusing too much on trying to get a perfect balanace can be a bad idea. Life doesn't work that way. When people try to improve work-life balance, they often find themselves overstretched trying to fit everything in. Although every part of who you are should get attention and perhaps balance, this should happen in an organic way. Focusing on the things that help you to live your best life will inevitably create a happier and more fulfilled life. Getting organised, planning what needs to be done and understanding your values are a good start.

Discovering your values

Understanding your core beliefs and values can assist greatly in helping you create a life that makes you happy. Knowing who you are and how you want to live your life each day can equip you with the toolkit required to create the life that you want. Your values are what help you to figure out your priorities, and understanding your priorities is crucial to be able to live your best life. Take the time to work out what your true values are. You can find a list of values on the web. Mindtools has an exercise you can do to help you figure it out: `www.mindtools.com/pages/article/newTED_85.htm`. This exercise will create clarity around how you should live your life by understanding what is important to you. If achievement is one of your core values, then it's okay to work a ten-hour day. If family also scores high, then you need to reassess the time spent working.

Understanding what is important will help you feel at peace with the decisions you make. Work-life balance isn't a set agenda; it involves creating a life that works for you. Understanding your values and living a life that is true to them will contribute to your personal confidence and your success.

Take your time figuring out what your values are, and don't allow anyone to tell you what they should be. This is an important exercise that must come from within.

Making time for what matters

When you understand your values, prioritising is easier. You'll be clearer about the things that matter and that merit your attention. Scheduling your time around the things that matter helps improve your work-life balance. Many people think that work-life balance means doing it all and having the lion's share – a great job, happy family life, hobbies, travel and much more. When you get organised and clearer about the things that matter, you realise that trade-offs always exist and that it isn't possible to do everything all the time. Trying to fit it all in causes stress and strain, not only on you but on your family, too. The solution is to pay attention to what matters and put aside the rest. Fitting things in can be a challenge, but when faced with a challenge, you must come up with creative ways to do the things that need to be done. Sometimes it involves dropping one thing to allow time for another; other times it requires some lateral thinking.

Making time for exercise

Exercise is usually the first thing people complain about not having time for. My reply is that there is always time for exercise – you just have to prioritise and think creatively about how you're going to fit it in. Here are some suggestions:

- Get an exercise bike and exercise while watching TV.
- Get up an hour earlier to go for a run or walk in the morning.
- Do a dance class or fitness class at lunch time.
- Rearrange your commute to include at least 30 minutes of walking or running.

You can exercise in many different ways and find plenty of hours in the week to fit it in. You just need to want to do it and be creative enough to find a way to.

If you work and have small children, you probably find it difficult to fit exercise into your busy schedule. Here are a few ideas to help fit exercise into your daily routine.

- Go to a park after work with a ball, and run for 30 minutes around your children while kicking the ball at intervals.
- Put on music, and dance like a lunatic for 30 minutes.
- Put an exercise bike in your living room, and cycle while reading your children a story.
- Put a child's seat on the back of a bicycle, and bring the child along.
- Do a parent and child fitness class (or start one up).
- Put your children on their bikes while you run alongside.
- Run around the playground while your children swing and slide.

Making time for relationships

When time is short, your relationships usually suffer. Children demand attention and usually get it, but this unfortunately means that little time is left over for your partner. If you feel you're not giving your partner the attention he or she deserves, think about what the ideal would be. Would you like to go on a date once a week or simply have a quiet night together at home? Decide what would work by discussing it with your partner; your needs will probably be different from his or hers. If you both want different things, try to compromise by taking turns doing what the other enjoys, or try to find something that you both like.

Don't wait until your life is happier, more organised or you're making more money to make an effort with your relationship. Sadly, many people leave it too late.

Doing epic stuff

Working more productively frees up time and gives you the head space to focus on the things you never had time for before. Have you ever wanted to start a business, a blog or even a book club? If you create systems in your life that will help you to work more quickly and efficiently, you'll free up time daily that can be used for doing epic stuff. Whether you want to learn a language, learn how to salsa or write code, a couple of hours a week can sort that out. Spend some time thinking about what you want, once you are clear about what you want to do. This will give you the motivation to make any changes required.

Embracing Business Benefits

Most people in business are well aware of the multitude of business benefits to be gained from having more productive employees as well as from more efficient production lines. Productivity benefits are obvious and widely felt when implemented in a business environment.

Increasing profitability

Companies experience an increase in profitability when it becomes less expensive to produce their goods and services. When workers become more efficient, less labour is required to produce the same amount of goods. The company could choose to reduce the number of employees to produce the same output, but if it chooses to maintain the same amount of labour, it will benefit from an increase in output.

Lowering operational costs

Companies can reduce operational costs through a number of initiatives. If individual workers improve their personal workflow, they will either produce more in less time or reduce the amount of hours they need to work to achieve the same output. Operational costs can often be reduced through an investment in technology, and over time improved processes can lead to a reduction in labour costs. The introduction of flexitime and three-day weeks can see productivity increase when people feel more valued and engaged and suffer less from stress as a result of less commuting. Often people can achieve the same amount of work in three flexi days as they might previously have done in a week.

Optimising resources

Often companies don't use their resources to the best potential. Employees are busy some of the time and looking for work to do at other times. Better human resource management offers a great opportunity to reduce costs and increase productivity. Better role distribution and more effective staffing can make a massive difference – the difference between profit and loss. Optimal workforce utilisation should be on the agenda for change. Improved workflow systems will identify places that roles are overlapping. Companies can rectify situations where employees aren't being used to their maximum potential, and they can start to use their resources efficiently.

Improving customer service

Improvements in productivity are usually felt all over an organisation. One of the external benefits comes when customers are given more time and attention. Systems run better, and the customer feels the benefit. Of course, when the customer is benefiting, the company benefits because happy customers lead to happy managers and happy shareholders.

Seizing the opportunity for growth

An increase in productivity is always an opportunity for growth. How this increase is used is up to management. If the productivity increase results in more time for employees, it's important to control how this time is spent. Far too easily, this time can get used up by mundane tasks and time-wasting activities that pose as valid tasks. Don't be deceived: a time suck is always a time suck, and if it wasn't important enough to take up your time before your productivity enhancements, it certainly doesn't merit your time now.

Reducing waste and environmental impact

The environment suffers when people aren't efficient. If you're not organised and take ten hours to do work that could be done in six, you use four hours of extra electricity that doesn't need to be used. When you don't look closely at the way you're doing things, you waste time, money, and resources. Heating can be optimised and not wasted. When you do this, you create a more pleasant and healthier working environment, which results in higher productivity and focus amongst employees. Good building design that maximises natural light leads to a reduction in lighting costs as well as an increase in workers' productivity and well-being due to good levels of daylight in the building. Lighting levels can have a significant impact on productivity and the mood of the people who work in the office.

Improving competitiveness

Anything you can do faster, more efficiently or better than your competitors gives you an edge. Increased productivity leads to increased competitiveness. If you can produce your products at a lower cost than your competitor, you can charge less. If you can deliver your service more quickly than your competitor, you can serve more clients or you can increase time spent on customer service, increasing your value add to the customer.

Harnessing Employee Benefits

Everyone is aware of the multitude of benefits that organisations gain from productivity increases, but the benefits for employees may not be as widely known as those noticed by the accountants and financial people.

Reducing employee burnout

When people have too much to do and not enough time to do it, it can result in stress, exhaustion or total burnout. Working more efficiently – whether a reduction in time spent on daily processes or a reallocation of roles and responsibilities – results in people being able to cope better with their workload and complete their responsibilities in the time allocated to them. This is a positive consequence for both employer and employee. Better time management leads to more organised, relaxed and efficient employees who can focus on their daily tasks rather than worry about all the things they're not getting to.

Enhancing well-being

Another benefit of improved productivity is personal well-being. Well-being can be described as a state where you're healthy, comfortable and happy. When you're more in control of your workload, you can be more in control of your life, having time to include exercise, to cook healthy food and rest when you need to relax. With less stress, you can listen to your body and give it more of what it needs. All the good things in life are within your reach. All it takes is a few little changes, and you'll see them all add up to stunning results.

Improving morale

When companies help employees become more organised and productive, they're investing in the well-being of the employee. Many workers see productivity as a way to squeeze more work out of the worker. This vision has to change. Increased productivity is a positive outcome for all involved. When employees understand what improving their efficiency can mean to them – reduced stress and increased control, well-being and focus – they can then embrace the process and accept the benefits that can be gained. When employees reap the benefits of increased efficiencies, it usually improves their morale and commitment toward the company.

Increasing engagement

More productive workers are usually more engaged in their work. Engagement is a result of a number of factors, which are often linked to the quality of leadership, the amount of autonomy an individual feels and the degree to which they feel in control of their work and workload. When the effort your put into your work makes a difference and your aren't just treading water, you'll be more focused and engaged. When employees take control to get their work lives organised, it usually leads to increased focus, commitment and engagement, or they will move on to another job role that they feel is more suitable for them.

Reaping Business Benefits

You can get business benefits from increasing productivity, and throughout this book I share many tips and techniques for mastering personal productivity. These techniques will also have a positive effect on organisational productivity because people are the lifeblood of any organisation. Investment in training in management and leadership programmes is essential and, more times than not, gives a positive return on investment, but what other approaches can a company make?

Investments in information and communications technology (ICT)

You can use ICT to increase productivity in your company in many ways. They include creating new business models, developing new applications and enhancing current business processes. Investments in hardware can help by reducing the time spent on outdated equipment; new software can be used in accounting, human resources (HR) or sales.

New applications

Many companies have designed and created their own bespoke software to suit their own business processes. When software is designed with the exact business process in mind, it can be very fruitful.

New business models

In 1997, Netflix started an online DVD sales and rental company, allowing people to rent and buy movies from the comfort of their own sofa. Over the years, it changed to a subscription-based model, allowing customers to rent a number of DVDs each month. Netflix had employed machinery to allow it to process so many orders and receive returns. The machine accepted returned envelopes, sliced open the envelope, identified the DVD inside and checked that it worked. It would then reinsert the DVD into the original sleeve. That disc could then be shipped out to another customer who had requested it. This machinery could work a lot faster than the original Netflix employee, allowing the company to keep up with the massive demand on its titles.

In 2010, Netflix changed its business model to an online streaming service. Recognising the changes afoot, it reacted quickly and shifted its model. To stream high volumes of data, Netflix had to make a massive investment in servers. Netflix revisits its hardware design yearly to ensure that it has the best technology to deliver its service. So to innovate and keep your organisation current and competitive, investments in ICT are often required. These investments almost always lead to things being done faster, more efficiently and better.

Investments in hardware

Outdated hardware wastes time. Old computers, printers and scanners that frustrate employees and need to be tweaked, poked or prodded to get things done are time wasters and should be recycled and replaced. Old machinery usually costs a company more in the long run. Newer machinery tends to work faster, produce more and cost less in maintenance and repairs.

Investments in software

Traditionally, before the advent of computers, companies carried out their business manually. They then progressed to use programmes, such as Microsoft Word and Excel, to manage data and information. Over the years, many advances have been made in the fields of accounting, HR and sales software along with many other areas. Most companies, regardless of size, see a massive increase in efficiency when they invest in accounting software. Combine this with a contact management system or sales software, and the potential for growth increases substantially. Investments in software have a significant impact on an organisation's productivity and increase the capacity for growth.

Get advice from other people in business before you invest in new software. You want to get the right software for your company and ensure that it works for the type of organisation you run.

Don't let a great sales person convince you to buy. Take your time over the decision, get advice and look at reviews online. Investment in software is a big decision, and you should not be pushed into it.

Lean programmes

Lean is about creating value for the customer while consuming the fewest resources. It focuses on effectiveness and efficiency in all areas of business. Lean was defined when describing Toyota's production system. Toyota's philosophy was to eliminate all waste and constantly pursue the most efficient methods of production.

Lean is not just for manufacturing companies. Many other companies and industries of all types have benefited from Lean improvements. Lean is about improving performance and being the best and most efficient you possibly can be in whatever you do.

People often misjudge Lean thinking by believing it's all about cost cutting and reducing labour to gain savings. In fact, Lean is a people-based approach, where teamwork and leadership are essential for overall success. It's about continuous improvement, problem solving, standardization and identifying better processes for every organisation. Benefits of Lean include

- **Improved quality:** Most companies see an increase in quality through all parts of the business. The output – whether a product or service – improves through improved processes and more attention to detail.
- **Reduction in expenses:** Lean helps to identify areas of waste, finding examples of unnecessary expenditure as well as suggesting more efficient processes. Areas that are often improved are resource allocation – that is, better usage of employees – inventory management, less money tied up in stock and less money being spent on unused software or other subscriptions.
- **Faster delivery times:** By mapping current processes, companies improve their processes, identifying areas that currently may be duplicated or that can be improved. When internal processes become more efficient, time is saved and customers benefit from faster turnaround times.
- **Improved customer service:** As well as faster turnaround times, more efficient processes alleviate busy customer service departments and help to allow the customer service agents to have more time to spend with each customer.
- **Increases in sales:** With an improvement in processes, faster delivery times and enhanced customer service, companies who engage in Lean programmes usually report an increase in sales.

Benchmarking

Benchmarking is a process whereby a company compares its performance with other similar companies. Traditionally, companies compared only their performances with their own past results. Nowadays, you need to improve your business by comparing it with others. There are different types of benchmarking, the most popular being financial benchmarking and non-financial benchmarking:

- **Financial benchmarking:** Financial benchmarking involves doing a financial analysis and comparison to look at overall financial performance and competitiveness. It compares things such as expenditure, cost of labour, equipment and energy. You can also compare things like cash flow, revenue collection methods and even budgets to see whether there's a better way to do things. Benchmarking will help your company to become more competitive and productive.
- **Non-financial benchmarking:** Non-financial benchmarking involves an assessment and comparison of other areas of performance, such as absenteeism, staff turnover and complaints. The benchmarking process is part of focusing on excellence and embracing change. For a lot of companies, change is a negative experience, but change is part of daily life and should be embraced more openly in the business environment.

Nurturing Productivity with Happiness and Positivity

Focusing on the positive is essential for a happy life, and a workplace that fosters positivity is going to be a lot more productive than one that is negative.

Having a workplace that respects its workers and creates an environment that is a joy to work in contributes to enhanced levels of performance and productivity. When people are happy and work in a state of flow, they're engaged, focused and motivated to get the job done.

Happiness is the new productivity

Vishen Lakhiani, the founder of Mind Valley, gave a TED talk titled 'Happiness Is the New Productivity' in which he spoke about creating a company of people who love what they do and work in an environment where they're valued and cherished. Lakhiani says that we need to be both happy in the now as well as have big dreams for the future.

The habit of gratitude

One of the daily practises Lakhiani has in his company is the habit of gratitude. The simple act of gratitude can raise levels of happiness. Mind Valley has a gratitude log that everybody contributes to daily. The practise of gratitude is widely becoming recognised as a powerful process in the search for happiness. Positive psychology has accepted the potential of a daily gratitude session. When you focus on what you have rather than on what you don't have, it's difficult to feel depressed or sorry for yourself. Gratitude is feeling thankful and appreciating what you have, regardless of what you don't have.

Make a list and write down all the things you're grateful for – for example, your health, your sight, your hearing, your home, your family and anything else that comes to mind. Put this list in a prominent place where you can see it daily.

Flexibility for workers

Successful leaders realise that their talents are what makes or breaks their organisation. Looking after their workers, giving them a happy, positive environment to work in, in which they're respected and their needs catered for, will have a positive impact on every part of the organisation. Flexibility has many benefits, including the following:

- **Work-life balance:** A flexible workplace allows your employees to have a say in how and when they work. This has a direct impact on their life balance. Having a choice to work from home enables individuals to work on their own terms and also gives them more time to relax and renew.
- **Extended team base:** When your workers don't have to come to the office, they don't have to live in the same city. This means you can work from a larger talent base and get the best person for the job as opposed to the best person living locally for the job. Having a more extended team base should result in a more diverse team. Different cultures, as well as a more gender-diverse team, should make for a more effective team.
- **Reduction in costs:** When more people work from home, there's a lesser need for office space and for heating, lighting and so forth. This will save money for the employer as well as for the employee with less commuting costs.
- **Increased morale and engagement:** More autonomy and control leads to happier, more engaged employees. Workers who are given the choice and can work the hours in which they feel most productive will positively impact morale and engagement. Flexibility is music to everybody's ears.
- **Increased productivity:** All these lovely benefits combined will lead to an increase in productivity as well as the fact there are fewer distractions than at the office. People who work from home report better focus and fewer interruptions from meetings and work colleagues, leading to a further increase in productivity and efficiency.

Part II

Getting Organised for Action

Five Ways to Prepare Yourself for a Productive Life

- The best way to get started is to get clutter-free. Declutter your home and office to help you to feel more in control of all areas of your life.
- Regular exercise will not only keep you healthy, fit and happy, but it will also give you extra energy and help you to focus on the right things at the right time.
- Healthy foods and plenty of water will keep your energy levels at an optimum level for productivity and performance. You are what you eat!
- The habit of rising early can help you to fit in all the things you currently don't have time for. Consider getting up an hour earlier, but make sure you go to bed an hour earlier to get sufficient sleep.
- Taking regular breaks is not only good for health but also for your efficiency. Add breaks into you daily schedule to get more done.

Head to www.dummies.com/extras/productivity for a handy article that discusses five steps for organizing your workspace.

In this part . . .

- Discover how to get organised to increase your productivity.
- Focus on creating and maintaining a healthy work-life balance, which will in turn help you remain productive.
- Find out how to manage stress for greater performance.

Chapter 4

Getting Organised

In This Chapter

- Understanding the basics of getting organised
- Improving your personal surroundings
- Making your office space productive

For years, a sentence went around in my head: 'If only I could get organised'. It was something I never consciously knew I desired, but instinctively I knew it was the solution to my problems. The day I said it aloud, something happened. I experienced a conscious understanding of what was required. An admission of the change that was inevitable was the beginning of a transformation that has brought only positive results. This chapter helps you move toward that.

Clearing the Way

I am naturally a disorganised person. I leave things lying around, not realising I am doing it. I step over mess, my mind miles away. Since getting organised, my life has changed. My natural tendencies haven't, and the mess still happens regularly, but what has changed is the way I manage myself effectively within the constraints of my personality. I have created systems that help me stay organised and keep the clutter at bay. I have solutions for storing and holding the things that I need. When I pick something up, I know where it goes or what needs to be done with it. This is what being organised is about, and being organised has radically changed my life for the better.

Believing in another way

Before you get started, you must believe that you can. If you have always lived in clutter, you may feel like there is no other way for you. Believe me when I say that if I can do it, you can, too. Getting organised and clearing the clutter from your life can be an amazing experience. Clearing your life of the things you no longer need brings about an almost spiritual uplift. Many others have done it before you and now bask in the peace and calm of a clutter-free environment. You can do it, too; you just need to believe.

Detoxing your mind

Your mind determines how productive you'll be. First, it controls how willing you are to make changes to your current system. It decides whether to believe you can do it or not. It decides on the attitude you'll adopt while making the changes, and it governs when and how fast you'll take action. Ensuring that your mind is in the right state is important, so taking the time to detox and clear the mind is time well spent. Here are a couple of ways to detox your mind.

Clearing your mind with a download

Clearing your mind is a habit that will help you stay organised, calm and stress-free. I recommend a weekly *mind download* to get everything off your mind and onto paper so that you can then process it and organise it into your workflow system.

The objective of the mind download is to gather all the 'unfinished business' that you have in your mind right now. These are the things that need processing and constantly nag or remind you that they need your attention. Get a pen and paper, and write down everything you need to do or would like to do. Include both work and personal.

When you start to write, follow these guidelines:

- Go for quantity.
- Go for speed.
- Don't judge.
- Keep writing.

When you've finished with your download, you can look at your list and decide what needs to be done with each item. If an item requires some time for you to work on it, plan time in your calendar. If the task is part of a bigger job, you may want to create a project category in a task management system to list all the things to do for the job. You can find more on task management in Chapter 13 and calendar management in Chapter 14.

Relaxing your mind by unplugging

Imagine going a full day without your phone or computer. Think what it would be like if you couldn't check Facebook or see what your friends had been tweeting all day. Suppose that the Internet was disconnected and you had no source of news for the day. How would that make you feel? Our minds are constantly connected. Information overload is part of every waking hour. People consume more information than ever before, and this constant connectivity has become the status quo. To clear the mind and prepare it for a state of calm productivity, unplugging from the information hub could be a welcome move. Try a day without the Internet. Commit to not checking your social media accounts and avoid taking any calls or checking emails. See how you feel after a day of peace and quiet.

Living in an Organised Home

Being organised at work is fantastic, but often people who are totally in control at work come home to chaos and disorder. If you're one of those people who is too tired or overwhelmed to get things in order at home, here are some simple ways to bring good habits back to your household.

Finding the source of the clutter

A disorganised home usually comes down to bad habits that you've cultivated over the years. These bad habits can be created by tiredness or laziness, or perhaps you are not getting any help at home. The big question is: How do you counteract these causes of chaos? Read on to find out more.

Overcoming sloth

One of the chief reasons for letting things go at home is tiredness. You may be too tired when you come home from work to keep things in order. When you get home from work, you probably like to relax and have some time to yourself. But don't you think this relaxation time would be a lot more relaxing if you weren't surrounded by mess and clutter? The first step is to schedule time to do a big declutter; call in friends and family to help you clear the house. After you free your environment of the clutter, you'll find it easier to maintain. You need to create declutter rituals (see the later section) to minimise the clutter creep and keep everything looking neat and tidy.

Taking responsibility

When sharing a home with a spouse, partner or friend, you may feel like you're the only one concerned with keeping it in order. You may try sharing the load, checklists, chore lists and other forms of treat and bribery, but you're the one ultimately left with the mop in hand. The way I see it, you have three options:

- You continue to fight for equality and justice.
- You stop cleaning and live in clutter, dirt and chaos.
- You get help in the form of a cleaner or housekeeper.

Assuming that you don't want to live in clutter, dirt and chaos, you're down to two options. If trying to do it all yourself is causing you stress and discomfort, you may want to find a professional to make your life easier. What you don't want to do is waste any more of your life, blaming others or your circumstances for your clutter. It's time to take control and responsibility for creating the environment you want to live in.

When you don't take full responsibility for your circumstances, you're the one who suffers most. When you hold yourself accountable for the quality of your life, your life will start to improve and take on a different momentum. Life becomes easier because decisions and actions are all within your control.

Starting the spring clean

The traditional spring clean is a great way to clear the house of cobwebs and other unnecessary stuff. Most people have too much stuff, even those who work on it regularly. Modern living is fraught with consumerism. People are enticed into the belief that they need loads of stuff to be happy. One pair of trainers is no longer enough: people think they need a different pair for each activity. They believe the marketers who say they need a coffee machine that wakes them up in the morning or a microwave oven that makes toasted sandwiches. Removing unnecessary stuff from your life is a good place to start. Clearing out the cupboards and the wardrobes of the stuff you think you might use in the future – but never quite get round to using – is a liberating task. Following are a few places in the house that collect the most clutter.

Junk drawers

It sounds odd to say it, but most people have a junk drawer. Should junk not be in the bin? My junk drawer consists of old batteries, bits of birthday candles, menus for take-away restaurants, half bags of seeds that are probably past their useful date, and anything else that doesn't have a home or a purpose. Clear out the junk drawer, and give things a place. Get a box or a bag for the batteries, and find out where you can recycle them locally. Get rid of the junk, and make more space.

Wardrobes

Everyone knows the rules when it comes to wardrobes: only keep the clothes you wear. That's easier said than done when you're looking at that leather jacket you spent good money on 20 years ago. Try to take a pragmatic approach when it comes to old clothes. If you haven't worn an item in over a year, donate or recycle it. You can sell old clothes that have value on eBay or similar sites. I have been aggressively decluttering my wardrobe for almost ten years, and I have never regretted donating a single item. I recently bought a book by Marie Kondo, *The Life-Changing Magic of Tidying Up*. She asks her readers to ask themselves the question 'Does this spark joy?' If not, thank the item and say goodbye.

Bookshelves

The bookshelves are a bit trickier, because I love my books. I have a Kindle, but nothing beats a paper book. Over the years, I have come up with different tactics for books. Building bookshelves and then pulling them down because they take up too much space. Since reading Marie Kondo's book, I have donated over 100 books and I've come to an agreement with my husband: when I buy one item, I must let one go. Easier said than done, but then again there is always the Kindle.

Designating the space

To get organised, you must have a designated space to put things in. If you're unsure where something goes, it will lie around until you make a decision. Identify the areas in your house that tend to attract clutter. There's usually a simple solution to every piece of clutter. In our house, hats and scarves were always lying about until we got a designated hat box. Find the points of clutter and provide a solution. Following are a few suggestions to get you started:

- **Shelving:** If you have too many books, you may want to consider installing sufficient shelving. But never rush into buying more shelving or furniture. Ideally, you should trim the fat to meet the space available, but if you genuinely don't have the space, you may need to put more in to accommodate your collection of books.
- **Cupboards:** Just like the shelving, you need to have sufficient cupboards to store your belongings, but the first step is always to try and make things work with what you have. The more cupboards you have, the more stuff you'll fill them with. You may need to buy boxes or baskets to fit into the cupboards and store different items.

  - **Boxes:** You could try putting fabric boxes in your cupboards for sports clothing or underwear. Shoe boxes are amazing – if you ever thought you didn't need them, think again. I have a large box that holds my boots all together, but for my shoes, I have an individual box for each pair. It keeps them in better condition and helps me to find what I'm looking for quickly.
  - **Baskets:** Small baskets can also be useful, especially for toiletries and makeup. Keeping all these items separated helps you find things and keeps your bedroom and bathroom neat and clean.

    Baskets can also be useful downstairs. If everyone has a basket, in the evening each person can take his basket and collect all his belongings throughout the house. This helps to keep the house in order and gives everyone a way to make tidying more pain-free.
- **Filing solutions:** To avoid paper clutter, make a space for a small filing cabinet or filing box where you can neatly file away all paperwork. Have a space for files in action as well as reference files to help things stay organised and structured.

Creating declutter rituals

When you create good habits, cleaning, decluttering and organising become a natural part of your life. Keeping the house in order no longer feels like a chore. If you can create these rituals that work for you, you'll be surprised at how they catch on for everyone in your household.

Visualising success

Before you begin any project, visualise your success. Be sure you understand what your ideal final outcome is to help move you toward that point. Seeing the perfect picture will excite and motivate you to keep working toward it.

Eliminating extras

Once a year, you should do a big declutter job where you eliminate all the extra stuff in your life – clothes, books, toys and even kitchen utensils – that you no longer use or need. This helps to keep things manageable and ensure that you have enough cupboard space for all your remaining belongings.

Cleaning as you go

After you've dumped the unnecessary, you should then create the 'Clean as you go' ritual. When you're cooking, wash the pots as you finish with them. Put vegetable peels in the compost bin, and put ingredients back in the cupboard after you've used them. For some people, this is the natural state of play; they don't even realise that they do it because it is second nature to them. If this is not something you currently do, put a sign in the kitchen to remind you of it. The bedroom is also a place where this can work. As you take something out of the wardrobe to try on, always put it back.

Swapping new for old

When you buy something new, it should replace something old. You can dump or recycle the older item. This ritual is great for ensuring that the amount of stuff in your house doesn't get out of hand. It also makes you a more mindful shopper because if you have to give up something you already have to be able to purchase a new item, you may be less likely to part with your money.

If you haven't used an item of clothing in the past year, you're unlikely to use it in the future. The space and peace that comes from a decluttered home far outweighs the joy you might get from wearing an item once or twice.

Introducing the clean sweep

One ritual that has worked well in my house is to do the nightly clean sweep. Before bed, everyone walks through the house and collects her belongings on her way to bed. This is a very simple task that maintains order and makes it a lot more pleasant to get up in the morning to a tidy house. Try to introduce this ritual in your home regardless of who lives there. Young or old can easily help out with this one. Provide a basket for younger children to put their toys and clothes into.

Establishing daily routines

Establishing other daily routines can help keep the bedrooms and play areas tidy. Create the habit of making beds in the morning or the habit of putting all clothes into the cupboards before bed. Smaller children can be encouraged to tidy away all their toys before bedtime. If you persist with helping children create these habits, you'll reap the benefits for many years. It's also a wonderful gift to give your children. If you're a disorganised adult, you know the stress and unhappiness that chaos can cause. If you can help your children become more organised now, you're giving them a greater chance at a happy, clutter-free life in the future.

Getting Organised at the Office

An organised office is a happy space to work in, and an organised environment minimises distractions and fosters focus. If your office environment isn't currently a den of Zen, you may want to consider doing an office purge to get you started.

Doing an office purge

A good office clear-out can have many benefits for you and your colleagues. A clean office creates a positive working environment and allows you to better focus. It will also give a better impression to customers that you mean business. Read on to see how you could benefit.

- **Finding things:** When people clear out their offices, they often have great finds, big and small. Items that were forgotten about or lost are found, and items that could be possibly useful in the future are given a new purpose. A clean office also ensures that things don't get lost again. Avoiding time spent looking for stuff benefits the company in the long and short term.
- **Finishing things:** After clearing the decks and uncovering forgotten files and objects, you may be inspired to finish something you had previously started. People often forget about projects, and work that they started gets left aside when something more urgent comes their way. When you clean up your act, you'll uncover all the half-finished jobs that need to be completed.
- **Dumping things:** A clear-out gives you the opportunity to dump all the things that you no longer need. I'm sure you'll find old office stationery, cables for computers that have long since passed away, and files that stopped being relevant when man first ventured into space. Dumping all the unnecessary stuff feels good and provides you with more space for important things.
- **Feeling good:** A clean, organised office helps everyone feel good and more inspired to keep things organised. A clean, productive environment positively impacts morale and employee motivation.
- **Looking good:** A clean, organised office not only looks good to the people who work there but also gives a positive impression to suppliers or clients who visit the office. When an organisation is clean and organised, it promotes more confidence in the abilities of the people who work there.

Organising paper files

If you haven't embraced the paperless world yet, you need to spend some time on paperwork. Paper lying around the office not only looks untidy but also makes it difficult to find what you're looking for when the time comes. The following are some ideas for keeping tabs on paperwork:

- **Reference filing cabinets:** Filing cabinets are essential for storing paperwork. Whether you have a small home office or work in a large corporation, you should have a filing cabinet to suit your environment. You can buy filing boxes for home use or small business purposes. Always return files to the filing cabinet after use to ensure that files don't get lost or misplaced.
- **Hanging files:** Inside filing cabinets, you should find hanging files. Leave these files inside the filing cabinet at all times; removing them may cause the wire hanger to get damaged and disturb your filing cabinet. Inside your hanging folders, you can place manila folders.
- **Manila folders:** Using manila folders to hold your documents is a great way to keep order. You can take these folders out of the hanging files if you need to work on them and then replace them after use.
- **Label makers:** Manila files should be labelled clearly with a label maker and added to hanging folders inside the filing cabinets. Labels make files easy to find and reduce the time you need to spend looking for the file you need.
- **Action filing system:** Keep your active files on hand for immediate reference. Invest in a desk file stand where you can place your files that contain work in progress. Action files are useful for things like bills to be paid, open projects, expenses and any ongoing work that you need to handle daily.

Introducing a paperless office

If you want to save space, the environment and time spent searching for files, consider going paperless. Scanning documents that can be archived and stored electronically not only saves you time and money, but it also creates a great impression for your clients and suppliers. There are many benefits in going paperless, including

- **Protecting the environment:** You don't have to be a tree hugger to understand the implications of deforestation. Protecting the environment should be high on everyone's agenda. Less paper has to be a good thing. Choose to eliminate paper files from your everyday workflow, and reap the many other benefits.
- **Sharing files:** File sharing becomes a lot less stressful and time-consuming. Having only electronic files stored centrally ensures that everyone has access to the information he requires.
- **Ensuring data security:** Having files stored on a server is a lot more secure than files stored in a filing cabinet. Customers and clients may have concerns about the security of their data if you don't have a robust data security system.

- **Maintaining backups:** If you accidentally lose or recycle a file, it's gone forever; delete an electronic file, and you should have a backup somewhere. Electronic files are a lot easier to duplicate and back up. Disaster recovery also becomes a lot simpler and efficient when you have to copy only electronic files and keep them off-site.
- **Saving money:** Of course, you'll save money from not buying paper, ink and other accessories for a paper-filled office, which is always an added bonus. Taking action to move toward a paperless office is a smart move. It doesn't have to happen all at once, and you should probably draw a line in the sand as to how many historic files you're going to scan into the system, but moving forward is a wise move and one you can only benefit from.

Keeping desks clear

Very often, organisations introduce a clean desk policy to minimise security risks. If documents need to be put away after a day's work, there's less likelihood of a sensitive file being left lying around. When desks are clean and all areas of the office are free from paper and clutter, your office looks appealing, professional and efficient. Employees feel more in control in a well-organised environment, and your customers will have a good impression of your company when they come to visit. If you want to get started with a clean-desk policy, here are a few suggestions for how to proceed:

- **Communicate the intention.** If you want to implement a clean-desk policy in your office, you need to start by letting everyone know. Communicating the intention and the benefits in advance will hopefully get people on board.
- **Provide lockable storage.** For people to be able to implement the policy, they must have the right tools at their fingertips. One such tool is a lockable storage for the files that need to be secured. Each person should have his own local storage for the files that he's working on. If you have a central area and it's necessary to walk a distance to follow the policy, you can be assured people will begin to cut corners and take chances.
- **Keep staff on track.** There are other potential benefits to this type of policy but only if workers are willing to get organised in advance. Keeping a clear desk while your cupboards are hiding a mess won't benefit your productivity too much, but keeping a clean desk because everything is in its place and organised is of great value to the individual and the organisation. Advise workers of the best way to use the new storage and ensure that it will be an asset to their personal organisation and not a hindrance.

Organising your email

Email is one of the biggest time wasters in the modern office. Scanning through spam and other unwanted email as well as using the email inbox as a to-do list wastes multiple hours each week. Email saps your time and energy, disturbs your focus and screws up your priorities. (But I do think it's a wonderful method of communication.) Managing email becomes a lot easier when you break it down into simple steps. The main steps are to process and then to plan the work that comes in the emails.

Processing

The first step to managing your email is to process the email that comes your way. This does not mean that you keep your email open all day and do the tasks that are inside in an orderly manner as they come in, neither does it mean you do them on an ad hoc random basis. Processing email should be done in batches if your job role allows for it. Choose four times during the day to process your email. When processing, you decide what it is and what needs to be done with it – does it need filed, deleted or acted upon? If an email needs to be acted on, the planning phase kicks in.

Planning

Plan what needs to be done and when. Deciding the priority of the email happens naturally when you decide when you want to do the task and how much time you need to complete it. One by one, go through your emails, process them and plan the work. Following this method gives you the opportunity to decide whether the work in your inbox is more important than the work that you're currently doing or the projects that you need to get done.

Doing

Any email that takes less than two minutes to reply to, do it straightaway. This will help reduce the number of emails that need processing and planning. Remember to delete the emails that you don't need to keep, always trying to reduce the number of emails in your inbox. You can read more on managing your email in Chapter 15.

Sorting your electronic files

Electronic filing is often forgotten about, and people place files at random locations locally and centrally. Files get duplicated, lost and overwritten as a lack of system prevents companies from gaining the benefits of centralised storage.

Creating a plan

To create an effective storage system for electronic files, put a plan in place to determine how and where files should be stored. If some planning is done in advance and you and your employees know how and where to store files, you can eliminate a lot of disorder. The best plan is to mirror your paper filing system. Use folders and subfolders and stick to a simple A to Z filing system.

Naming files

You may have existing naming conventions in your organisation, but if not, a simple way to name files is to use the name of the document and the date. If several people are working on the same document or if you have different versions of a document in existence at the same time, you can add the initials of the person who last edited the document or add version numbers.

Purging files regularly

Create a ritual once or twice a year to go through electronic files and purge the ones you no longer need. If you can get into the habit of this, your electronic filing system will stay organised and efficient. When your filing system has too many files and folders that are no longer used, it creates disorder and confusion. Less is always more.

Backing up files

To maintain an effective filing system, it goes without saying that you should back it up regularly. Cloud storage solutions are a great way to keep your files secure, but if you use hard drives and servers, you also need to back these up to ensure that you don't lose your data.

Avoiding the desktop

Saving to the desktop is a bad habit, one that often causes files to be duplicated and different versions to be created. Avoid using the desktop, and keep your files in the correct location.

Chapter 5

Embracing a Holistic Approach

In This Chapter

- Making exercise a habit that works for you
- Discovering your inner calm
- Giving your body the fuel it needs
- Working with your energy levels
- Getting up earlier to get more done

The first instinct of someone who wants to get organised is to look externally. People usually start by clearing up the clutter that surrounds them and then begin to look for apps or software to solve all their problems. Although this approach can work, it often leaves out a large part of getting organised.

Becoming more productive involves a lot more than improving your systems and technology; it requires a more holistic approach. You can't possibly function at your best if your body and mind aren't on board.

Holistic means looking at the whole picture. The holistic approach to productivity involves looking inward as much as looking outward. It encourages you to look at your habits and identify places where changes can improve your performance. It focuses on your health, your exercise habits, your eating habits and the way in which you approach your work. This chapter isn't an exhaustive guide to a holistic approach; you can make positive changes in many more ways. Here, I simply cover the ways that I am personally most familiar with – the changes that have worked for me and for my clients – and they include getting adequate exercise, practising mindfulness and meditation, eating well and taking time to rest and recharge.

If you commit to taking on more positive habits, your life will change for the better. Be prepared for more calm control, more health, more happiness and more success.

Richard Branson's #1 productivity tip

I have read a story about Richard Branson which says that on one occasion on Necker Island, Branson was asked the following question. 'Mr. Branson, what is your number-one productivity tip?' Branson sat back in his chair and answered with two words, 'Working out'. He later explained that he believes that working out gives him an extra four hours of productivity a day. If you look at the lives of many highly successful people, you will see that a daily workout is part of their routine.

Increasing Productivity with Exercise

The benefits of exercise are numerous, and you likely know all about them. You know about the extra energy, the improved well-being and the health benefits, but maybe you continue to skirt around the edges, doing a little this week and skipping next week. The following list serves to remind you of the benefits of exercise.

- **Having a healthy heart:** The heart foundation of any country will tell you the same thing: moderate exercise at least five days a week is necessary for a healthy heart. Regular physical activity reduces your risk of high blood pressure, heart attack and stroke as well as many other diseases.
- **Enjoying extra energy:** Exercise gives you energy. That old excuse 'I'm too tired to exercise' is no longer valid. Going out for a walk increases your energy levels and helps you to focus. When you exercise, your body creates extra energy to meet your needs, thus creating more energy for you to enjoy. If you do an intense workout, you'll come away feeling tired. Moderate exercise gives you a feeling of immediate energy. Of course, the amount of energy you feel depends on your current levels of fitness, but any exercise you do benefits you in the long run. Exercise is never a wasted activity.
- **Increasing happiness:** Many studies link physical activity with reduced depression and an increase in happiness. The general consensus is that exercise releases endorphins, which make people happier. Most people have felt the effect themselves from regular exercise. You probably don't notice that you're happier, but the days you don't exercise are the ones where you feel less energy and maybe even a bit blue.
- **Reducing stress:** Another benefit of exercise is stress reduction. Regular exercise can help to manage stress and release tension from the body. A good workout clears your head and equips you with the endorphins that help make life a little sweeter.

If you want to make exercise part of your life, the best thing to do is to create a habit. A habit will make whatever you do easier in the long run. When you create habits, you're setting up a ritual that you repeat daily until it becomes a natural part of everyday life.

Make exercise a habit by following my habit method, outlined in the sections that follow.

Starting with a plan

To make a habit, first you have to decide what you're going to do and when you're going to do it. Setting fixed days and times for exercise helps you avoid 'I'll do it tomorrow' procrastination. If you're forming a new habit, it's better to do a little daily rather than a lot twice or three times a week. Regular practise helps form the habit more quickly, and when you start reaping the benefits of regular exercise, you'll crave the extra energy and feelgood factor daily. If a daily practise really isn't realistic for you, see if you can manage three times a week. That will be great, too, as long as you stick to the plan: the plan is what will help you make it work this time.

The clearer you are about what you're going to do when and where, the better. Choose a type of exercise you like and be honest with yourself. Just because your work offers subsidised gym membership doesn't mean you have to become a gym bunny. Do a form of exercise that suits you and your lifestyle. Whether it's walking to and from work, doing a dance video, running or cycling – whatever you do, make the decision in advance and stick with it.

Starting small with ten minutes a day

Start small. Finding ten minutes a day for a new habit is a lot easier than trying to do something for an hour. Gradually increase the amount of time you spend on your exercise. If you want to start running, run for ten minutes, and after a couple of days it will become easier. Then increase the time. It is important to challenge yourself, but it's equally important not to do so much that it gives you an excuse or a reason to give up. If you commit to a minimum of ten minutes, you won't be able to use the excuse 'I'm too busy' or 'I'm too tired'.

Having clear intentions

When and where you do your exercise is important, but more important still is *why* you do it. Understanding your motivation, the 'why', behind your new habit will be of great value when trying to form it. Try to think

- How your life will be better when you've formed the habit
- Are you confident in your ability to create the habit
- How it will help you to become more aligned with your personal values

Understanding your intentions and connecting with them every day reinforces your desire and commitment to succeed. The *why* is essential for positive accomplishment.

Committing to 21 days

It is often said that it takes 21 days to create a habit. The research isn't consistent. The actual time it takes depends on the individual, the habit to be formed and probably many other factors. So if it isn't possible to say how long it will take to form a new habit and make it part of your life, why are we constantly told to commit to 21 days or similar figures?

Repetitive action is what enables a new habit to form. If you can commit to taking it on fully for 21 days, it won't seem like such a mammoth task. Twenty-one days is short enough to make the task appear achievable and long enough to create some sort of momentum. The trick is not to overwhelm yourself when starting out. If you have the tendency to avoid hard work or can't easily commit to anything that takes longer than five minutes, you have to coax yourself gently into forming a new habit. Think big, act small and you will make progress every day.

Doing one thing at a time

Many people who decide to change their habits want to do it all at once. Making a plan to start running, give up sugar, get up earlier and be a nicer person all in the one day isn't going to work. If you want to adopt a new habit, it's best to focus on one at a time. After you've mastered one habit and made it part of your day to day, you can think about creating another positive habit.

Using triggers to encourage the new habit

A *trigger* is something that you do every day that you can associate with a new habit to encourage you to behave in accordance with it. Linking your habit to a trigger helps you to remember to carry out your daily routine. A trigger can be an existing habit, like getting up in the morning or making your daily coffee, or it can be a time of the day, such as when you get home from work. If you decide to start the new habit of exercise in the morning, preparing your clothes the night before can be your trigger. After you've set the trigger in motion, you're less likely to avoid it.

Tracking your way to success

Keeping a record of what you're doing is a powerful way to encourage you to keep up the momentum. Apps exist that are designed to encourage you to check in every day when you've completed your habit. Apps such as #Coach.me or MyFitnessPal.com can be very helpful. Both are available in the App or Play store. You could also use a simple method like Jerry Seinfeld's 'Don't Break the Chain', where you simply use a wall calendar to mark off each day you've completed your habit with a big red X.

Finding an accountability buddy

You have a higher likelihood of success when you use a buddy to help you stick to your goals. A buddy will encourage you to go out and exercise when you don't feel like it. A buddy will motivate you when you're feeling like giving up. The best type of accountability buddy is someone you know but not too well – a friend of a friend or a work colleague. When you know someone too well, you're more likely to turn that person down, believing she understands you and will forgive you.

Steering clear of the pitfalls

If your attempts at habit change haven't worked before, here I show you how you can make it work this time. If certain people stand in your way, avoid them. If late movies prevent you from getting up to exercise, stop watching them. Take responsibility for the attainment of your goals. Don't be the one who is preventing your own success.

Overcoming the voice

Many people have a voice in their heads that makes excuses for them. You may have it, too. It gives you a way out by creating excuses so good that you actually believe them. The sort of things you may hear include

- I can't exercise because I stayed up too late last night.
- I forgot my running shoes so I can't go for a run.

- Life is too short; let's just go out and enjoy tonight.
- I'm on holiday, I'm sick, or I'm too busy.
- I can't go until my room is clean.
- I will just skip today and do it tomorrow.

People come up with a million excuses – all very believable – that generally allow them to convince themselves that they're not doing anything wrong. The problem is, these silly reasons are what are holding you back from being successful. The more you sabotage your chances with these excuses, the further you take yourself from living the life you want.

Write down the typical excuses you give yourself not to exercise. When you become aware of the loopholes you give yourself, it's easier to overcome them.

Adopting Meditation and Mindfulness

Meditation and mindfulness have become more popular in recent years. Both activities help reduce stress and improve focus and concentration, calming your mind and helping you live in a place of peace.

Reaping the benefits of meditation

No longer a practise just for monks, meditation has become a highly recognised daily practise for many successful people. Sports people, businesspeople and politicians reap the benefits of calming and centring their mind daily. The benefits include

- **Reduced stress:** Meditation is said to lower blood pressure and decrease any tension in the body. Tension can cause headaches, insomnia and many other physical ailments.
- **Increased happiness:** Stress is said to disturb the natural functioning of the brain and reduce the happy hormone serotonin. Meditation activates the body's one healing function and restores balance to the brain.
- **A feeling of peace:** Meditation reduces feelings of anxiety and brings more focus and clarity, helping you be more in control and at peace.

People who meditate are reported to be happier, more emotionally stable and more creative. There are numerous benefits, but the overriding factor is that meditation appears to be a real solution to the problems of modern society. If you tend to focus on the things that don't bring happiness and put your body under strain to do things you don't need to do to achieve more than you need, adopting the habit of meditation will help you to become happier and more in control of your life.

Learning to be mindful

Most people live their lives thinking about what they need to do next, the responsibilities they need to take care of and the things they're looking forward to absorb their waking hours. Sometimes their mind wanders back to the past, and they relive good memories or rehash regrets. Too little time is spent in the current moment, in the here and now of life. Life passes by, and they are rarely fully experiencing it.

Understanding your current time perspective can help you know where your tendency lies and how you can have a more balanced perspective on life.

Future focus

Most people have the tendency to have a *future time perspective*. This means that they're always thinking about what's going to happen next. A person with a future focus is rarely present in the now and is often stressed. When you have a future time perspective, you tend to worry about the possibilities of the future. Getting stressed about things that haven't happened and may never happen won't serve you or put you more in control of your life.

People with a future time perspective can also be dreamers, people who think big and have a grand vision for the future. This can be positive but not when it works to the detriment of your present-day happiness.

Past focus

If you have the tendency to focus on the past – whether on past happy memories or past regrets – you're likely missing out on the experiences of the present. People who focus on the past are often unhappy, thinking about times when life was better than it is now or regretting things that did or didn't happen. They fail to realise that they're letting opportunities for a happy life pass by daily.

Present focus

Although focusing on the present appears to be the ideal state, it isn't ideal if this is your sole focus. If you're thinking only about the here and now, you may not plan enough for the future and you may tend not to learn from past mistakes. If you're present-focused, you enjoy life's moments as they come, but, like anything in life, there needs to be balance.

Living with balance

It is important to shift your focus to the present moment sufficiently in order to experience the joys of daily living. In the present, you can feel gratitude, love, joy and peace. The future brings hope and excitement, the past, experience and satisfaction. Balancing your time perspectives will help you to live life in a balanced way.

Practising mindful living

Mindful living is a state in which you're conscious and aware of all that you do daily. Have you tried to cook dinner while helping kids do homework or tried to write an email while talking to a work colleague? When you try to split your focus, you're not living mindfully and the moments pass you by.

Mindfulness involves bringing your attention back to the present moment, regardless of what you're doing. You may be just sitting in a park watching the birds peck for worms, or you could be cooking, eating or playing. Whatever you're busy with, be where you are. When you train your mind back to the now, you'll begin to experience more peace in your life.

For more on living mindfully, see *Mindfulness For Dummies,* by Shamash Alidina (Wiley).

Engaging in mindful eating

Mindful eating is a great way to practise mindfulness. Focusing on the food on your plate and as it goes into your mouth not only brings more peace into your day, but it also brings peace to your mealtimes, which aids your digestion and can improve your overall health. Taking a moment at lunchtime or anytime you drink a cup of tea to really experience the moment, the taste, the smells and the sensations will contribute to a more peaceful life.

Focusing with mindfulness

When you learn to live in the moment, you train your brain to be more aware of every daily activity. You learn to avoid distractions and manage interruptions more effectively. By doing this, you benefit from an enhanced focus and concentration, giving you the ability to focus on the right thing at the right time. The peace that mindfulness brings contributes to a calm control, allowing you to think more clearly and prioritise correctly. Mindfulness is a healthy way to increase productivity and have a happier life.

Nourishing Your Body

Everyone's heard the phrase, 'You are what you eat', but people continue to fill their bodies with food and drink that doesn't nourish them. Energy levels, focus and performance are all dependent on the fuel that you feed your body. Eating regular healthy meals, avoiding too much sugar, alcohol and caffeine and ensuring you drink sufficient water will all contribute to a healthy productive body.

Eating foods that keep you productive

Almost all people know what foods are supposed to be healthy. A balance of protein, carbohydrates and fats should keep you on the straight and narrow, but you may need to think more carefully about your diet to stay focused, energised and in control.

Here are some helpful suggestions for what to eat when to keep you productive and focused throughout the day:

- Start the day with a smoothie. A smoothie rich in protein and fruit will give you plenty of energy to get you to lunch.
- Stick to protein and vegetables at lunch. Avoid the carbs that make you sluggish in the afternoon.
- Try eating more omega-3 fatty acids found in fish. It's a powerful brain food that has a direct effect on your mental state.
- Exchange some of the meat you eat for protein-rich legumes like lentils, chickpeas or beans. All supply long-lasting energy and fibre, keeping you satisfied without slowing you down. There are lots of great websites that can guide you to eat more healthily and gain from the goodness of fresh and wholesome produce.

Avoiding foods that zap your energy

There are certain foods that have a negative reaction in the body and can make you feel more tired than nourished. These should be avoided if you want to be productive. They include

- **Starchy foods:** White bread, pasta and cereals can cause your blood sugar to soar followed by a crash. Avoiding foods like this at lunch will do great things for your afternoon productivity.

- **Fatty foods:** Fatty processed foods are a no-go zone, as your digestive system has to work hard to process the fats, leaving you feeling like the hammock is your only possible move for the afternoon.
- **Sugary foods:** When you eat a lot of sugar, the carbohydrates get used up quickly, blood sugar rises and then your brain stops producing the chemicals that keep you alert. Sugar slump!

Plan your work lunches in advance. Shop on the weekend so you have the food at hand in the house. Having healthy options easily available will help you avoid making the wrong choices when you're hungry at work.

Staying hydrated to focus

The human body is made up of somewhere between 55 to 75 per cent water. If you let the level of water drop, every cell in your body is affected, even the ones in your brain. Dehydration makes you feel less energetic and affects your ability to focus. You have to stay hydrated to be able to do your best work.

To start your day in the right way, drink a glass of water as soon as you get up in the morning. Try it with fresh lemon juice to add flavour and continue to drink water throughout the day.

Dehydration can often be mistaken for hunger, so if you stay hydrated, you can keep hunger at bay, keep your energy levels up and focus like a Jedi.

Working with Your Energy Flow

To work at your best, you must have physical energy. And to have physical energy, you must nourish your body, exercise it and get adequate rest. Introducing these healthy habits into your life will increase your energy and help you to achieve your goals.

Sleep

Lack of sleep is not a state anyone aspires to, unless you're a student on your first holiday to Ibiza. For the rest of the human race, sleep is essential, and lack of sleep can cause many negative outcomes and even illness. Lack of sleep affects your focus, concentration and problem-solving abilities. In other words, you become a little dumber. Not getting enough sleep over time can affect your blood pressure and increase your risk of many other serious conditions, like stroke and heart problems. Don't accept lack of sleep as the status quo. Get help from your doctor and try to get to the root of the problem before you start to suffer.

If you wake at night with things on your mind, try doing a mind download (see Chapter 4) to help capture what is on your mind and free your mind to relax.

Renewal

Relaxation is an important step on the path to productivity. It may sound counterintuitive, but rest, relaxation and renewal will help increase your performance and productivity. The more you push your body to perform, the less likely the output will be optimum. All athletes know there must be a balance between work and effort and rest and renewal.

Your natural cycles of energy during the day require times for rest. Taking a break to get more oxygen into your blood will be more beneficial than trudging through the workload to get more done. More and more research is being done on how naps, breaks and even holidays can improve your performance and productivity.

Meditation

Meditation is a great way to relax both body and mind. Taking time out to breathe and be still is a healing process. Regular practise will help to regulate your energy flow and balance your emotions. For more on meditation, see earlier in this chapter.

Avoiding doing too much

The best way to maintain your energy is not to do too much from the outset. If you have a tendency to take on too much, you might want to get into the habit of using your calendar to schedule all the work that you do. For more information on managing your calendar, go to Chapter 14. This will give you a visual guide as to how much time you do have available and where you can fit in new commitments or responsibilities. Learning to say no is difficult for some people, but you must realise that when you say yes to one thing, you're always saying no to another. Your time is finite, so when you take something on, you need to let something else go. Letting something else go may mean you decide it's not a priority or you delegate or outsource it to someone else.

Finding the balance

Finding the balance is probably the secret to life's happiness. The balance between work and rest can sometimes be difficult to find, but over time, most people find the sweet spot. Ensuring that meditation and mindfulness are part of your every day will help you find that place of calm control.

Rising Early to Succeed

Time is a limited resource, but there is a way to increase the number of hours in the day: simply get up earlier. I'm not suggesting sleeping less than the recommended seven hours but rather shifting when you sleep. If you currently sleep nine hours each night, you could get up an hour earlier and gain 365 hours a year. That translates to 15 extra days a year to do stuff.

Morning hours are more productive for most people because they're often quiet, undisturbed time you can use to focus on your priorities. Many successful people are early risers, some by nature, others by working hard to create the habit. All have benefited from their early morning habit.

Fitting it all in

Early mornings help to fit everything in. If you use the early mornings to exercise, meditate or write, your evenings can be used for family time, socialising or hobbies. Morning hours are a great way to make time for the things you never seem to have time for. When you stay up late at night, like most people, you may use that time watching TV or browsing the Internet. Wouldn't it be better to reduce these time wasteful activities and rise an hour earlier to do the things you long to do?

Deciding what to do

If you decide to rise early, you need to have a strong motivation to do it. I started to get up early to do yoga and meditate in the mornings. Later, I realised if I did my daily workout in the mornings, I had more energy throughout the day. I rarely get tired, and I feel more positive and in control. Decide why you want to do it. Be clear about your motivation and connect with the feeling of success when you achieve it. It may seem obvious, but often people do things just because they sound like a good idea. Often they have no real motivation to follow through.

Focus on creating a new habit of rising early; try it out for a month, and record the benefits from doing it.

Creating the habit of mornings

It's difficult to start rising early if you've never done it before. If I can do it, believe me, anyone can. Like any new habit, it takes time. The time you get up depends on what time you need to leave for work and how much time you need in the morning to do what you want to do. You could try a 5 a.m. rise if you're brave, but remember that you need to go to bed early enough to give yourself at least seven hours of sleep. Sleep deprivation is a bad thing.

Gradually change the time

When you commit to rising early and you decide on the time you want to get up, you may want to gradually adjust the time. If your normal wakeup time is 8 a.m., start by getting up an hour earlier, and little by little you'll adjust your body clock to a 5 or 6 a.m. start.

Don't watch TV or movies before bed

You'll likely have to make sacrifices for your new habit. You can't keep doing things the way you've always done them and expect to get up early without a glitch. But if you want to get up early, you need a good night's sleep.

Take some time to relax and unwind before bed. Meditation is a great way to calm the mind before bedtime, or even listening to some relaxing music. Avoid the blood, guts and action movies if you want to dream about fairies and butterflies.

Go to bed earlier

Your body needs at least seven hours of sleep, so if you intend to get up at 6 a.m. every morning, you need to be asleep by 11 p.m. Prepare your body for the change, and give it the rest it needs.

Don't eat dinner before bed

If you won't sleep well after watching an action movie, you have even less chance if you watch *Too Fast, Too Furiou*s with a pizza and beer right before bed. If you're trying to digest a meal while sleeping, your body isn't fully relaxed. You are more likely to get a good sleep if you eat your dinner a couple of hours before bed.

Track your progress

Keep track of your progress. Note how many days in a row you have managed to get up early. Tracking progress helps you see whether you're as good at something as you assumed you were. Maybe you'll find out that you're doing a lot better than you thought. Tracking your progress is a great motivation to keep up the good work.

Prepare your tools the night before

Being prepared in advance will increase your chances of getting out of bed when you said you would. If you try to wake up to go for a run but as you lie in bed you start to wonder where your running gear is, you may just turn over and give it a miss. If, on the other hand, you wake and see your running gear sitting on your chair waiting for you to put it on, you're more likely to follow through on your commitment. Or if you want to write in the morning, have your desk cleared and ready to go. If you want to meditate, make sure you have made the decision as to how and where you'll do it. This advance preparation will help you hit the ground running.

Chapter 6

Stress Management

In This Chapter

- Recognising when you're stressed
- Figuring out what's causing your stress
- Finding ways to manage stress
- Avoiding stress at work

Stress has so much to answer for. It's responsible for marriage breakdowns, work failures and major illnesses. It's a natural part of your life, yet if not managed it can take control of it. Regardless of the source of stress, all types of stress affect your performance, your ability to focus and your ability to get your work done. This chapter shows you how to identify, manage and defeat stress.

Recognising the Signs of Stress

Often, the signs of stress aren't so obvious. Neck tension, headaches or irritability can all be seen as normal symptoms of everyday working life. However, these signs could be warning signals that something is wrong. Getting headaches daily or even weekly is a sign that something isn't right in your body. Ignoring it or popping a pill will only push it back for so long. More serious symptoms such as depression, anxiety or insomnia should never be ignored; get expert advice if you experience any of these symptoms. Getting to the root of why any of these symptoms are appearing is the only logical thing to do. Improving performance is one thing, but improving life expectancy is a lot more pressing.

Experiencing muscle tension and headaches

A sore back, neck or shoulders is a common complaint that most people have suffered at some stage. Too much computer time, too much gadget use or simply too much time sitting badly in your chair can cause your muscles to tense and set in motion a series of aches and pains that take longer to do away with than it took to acquire them.

Muscle tension can be simply physical, from bad posture or from extended time in one position, but it can also be a sign of stress. You tense your muscles without realising because your body is in a state of anxiety and strain. Tension headaches also result from stress and anxiety. A build-up of stress can cause the muscles at the back of the neck to tense, which can initiate a tension headache.

When your muscles feel tight, stop what you're doing, stand up and stretch to touch your toes. Try to let your shoulders relax and allow the upper half of your body to drop down. Take some deep breaths each time, relaxing a little more into the stretch. This is a great way to release the tension in your upper back and shoulders.

Dealing with anxiety

Feelings of anxiety are an obvious sign that your body is under stress. Stress can be caused by many factors – problems at home, financial worries or conflict at work for example. Because these are common issues that many people experience throughout their life, people begin to accept them as the norm and often don't seek to get to the bottom of the issue.

When your life is out of your control or when you don't feel like the master of your fate, this can cause a feeling of helplessness. If you regularly feel anxious, it's important to get to the source of the stress. Feelings of anxiety can lead to panic attacks where excessive adrenalin causes palpitations and lightheadedness. Panic attacks can be unsettling and lead to other problems, such as not wanting to go out or be in crowds of people.

Suffering from depression

Stress over time can lead to withdrawal, helplessness and depression. When you don't feel in control of your daily life and this feeling is continuous, it can lead to depression. If you're having trouble coping with a part of your life, this stress can wear you down. It can affect your relationships, your concentration and your sleep. If you begin to experience many of the symptoms of stress and depression, you may begin to have trouble with your daily routine, and going to work may feel like it's too much to bear.

If you begin to feel symptoms of depression, seek professional help. Your doctor can help you by talking through your options with you.

Feeling tired all the time

Constant tiredness is often a sign of stress. If you wake up in the morning feeling tired and don't often feel like running or jumping during the day, you might be feeling the effects of stress. This type of tiredness is usually referred to as *fatigue.* If tiredness is impacting your study or work or preventing you from exercising, it will have a negative effect on your life and relationships.

This excessive tiredness can be caused by an overstimulation of adrenal hormones, which are being produced by the body in a state of stress but not being used in the modern office working day. One way to reduce these hormones in the body is to exercise, but most people avoid exercise when they're feeling exhausted, thinking that they don't have the energy even to walk to the shop. The reality is that a walk is probably the best thing you can do. Fresh air and exercise can help shift the tiredness rut.

Exercise is a proven strategy for fighting stress, anxiety or depression. Exercise increases the happy hormones in your brain as well as helps shift your mood and perspective on your current life. You may have more issues to sort out than a walk can solve, but a walk is the first step to making positive changes that can have encouraging effect on your life.

Getting insufficient sleep

Being excessively tired can often be accompanied by another ailment that only results in compounding the effect of the tiredness: lack of sleep. Lack of sleep can also have negative effects on the body.

Insomnia, the inability to sleep, is another common symptom of stress. If you can't fall asleep when you're tired and you wake up in the night, you may very well be stressed. People who are stressed have overactive minds that don't allow them to relax sufficiently to fall asleep. Some people may fall asleep easily but wake regularly or aren't able to get back to sleep if they wake during the night. Sleep is a vital part of human health, and lack of sleep can worsen the symptoms of any existing ailments you may have. If insomnia or poor sleeping habits are affecting the quality of your life, you need to look at the root of your stress to be able to handle it.

If you regularly get less than seven hours of sleep, you could be suffering from sleep deprivation. Not to sound overdramatic, but lack of sleep over time can lead to many physical ailments and illnesses as well as emotional issues.

Being unable to focus

An inability to focus can often be a sign of stress. Stress can cause a fuzziness and inability to concentrate; stress can cause an increase in the production of adrenalin and cortisol, causing your brain to become more hyperactive. The more active your brain becomes, the more difficult it is to focus on just one thing. When your brain is overworked, it can lead to mental exhaustion, and it's definitely not the time to make important decisions or do your best work. Meditation is a great way to calm the mind and help you to focus.

Becoming irritable and angry

Maybe you're feeling more irritable than usual. Is this irritability leading to anger outbursts? Stress is often guilty for increased levels of irritability and anger. Stress is often guilty for a 'short fuse' or more impatience than normal. When people become argumentative and defensive and sometimes even aggressive, these negative unwanted emotions are often a sign of stress.

Identifying Possible Sources of Stress

Many sources of stress exist, most of which people experience at some stage in their life. In this section, I cover some of the most common sources and what you can do to reduce their impact.

Workplace stress

Stress in the workplace is common and can be caused by a number of reasons. If your job is having a negative impact on your life, it's important to look at your options and see whether you can alleviate the stress. If the stress is ongoing and you've tried to do your best to tackle the issues, you may have to consider looking for alternative employment.

In the following sections, I discuss some common triggers for workplace stress and what you can do about them.

Poor management

When managers fail to manage, they leave behind a trail of unhappy employees. A manager's role is to enable employees to do their jobs. If you have a micro manager who prevents anything from getting done or a detached manager who gives little or no guidance, this will make it more difficult for you to do your job. If you find yourself in this situation, you could try to speak to someone higher than your manager or to the Human Resource department.

If you don't get positive results from these actions and your job continues to cause you stress, you may be better looking for another job.

- **Unclear objectives:** One of the fallouts of poor management is a team that doesn't know what its goals are. Lack of vision and leadership leads to employees wasting time on the wrong things because they don't have clarity about what the organisation or even their team is trying to achieve. If you are unclear about your team or your personal objectives it is your responsibility to go find out. Speak to you colleagues or your manager and make sure you know exactly what is expected of you.
- **Unclear responsibilities:** Unclear roles and responsibilities lead to unnecessary stress as employees struggle to get work done not knowing whether it really is their responsibility or not. Often work doesn't get done because the task has no owner and nobody knows who should be doing it. To avoid this scenario, always ensure there is clear division of labour and ask management to clarify this on paper if necessary.

Team conflict

Positive team conflict is a good thing, as people with differing viewpoints thrash out their opinions. However, excessive conflict or conflict that can be upsetting or undermining to certain individuals can cause large amounts of stress. Conflict of any sort needs to be handled correctly, but the nasty type should be handled promptly for damage control. Bring the team together and facilitate an agreement for the good of the team.

Following are some of the causes of team conflict and what you can do about them.

- **Lack of communication:** Lack of communication or misunderstandings can often be the root of team conflict and can lead to many other issues in a work environment. Communication is key to any working relationship and must be fostered at all costs. Communicate with your manager or boss when the workload is too much or if you have problems doing your job. Most stress points can be solved with timely communication. Whether you are the boss or the employee, make sure you communicate regularly and effectively to the people you work with. This will save lots of conflict and challenges in the future.
- **Excessive workload:** If you simply have too much to do, you're likely to feel stress in your attempt to get it all done. The first thing to do is to acknowledge you have only a finite number of hours in the day. The second thing to do is to decide how many of those hours you're willing to work. Work expands to fill the time you have, so if you work until you drop, you still won't get all the work done.

  Prioritise your workload by clarifying your goals and objectives. If all your tasks are related to your goals and priorities, you'll have to make decisions about what work needs to be done now and what can wait until a later date. Check out the Eisenhower matrix in Chapter 9 to help you prioritise your workload.

Parenting stress

Parenting is a tough job. Whether you have a 2-year-old who won't sleep or a 15-year-old who won't get out of bed, each phase has its challenges. When a child is sick or a crisis happens, you can get off course. With the day-to-day stresses, you're expected to deal with them. Day-to-day parenting can have a steady progressive deteriorating effect on your health and well-being. Does that sound exaggerated? It's important for you to recognise that if your kids are stressing you out, you need to do something about it. Nobody else will notice, and most people will tell you to get on with it, but for your health and for your well-being as well as your kids', the sooner you tackle your stress the better. Take a look at Chapter 17 for tips on becoming more productive as a parent.

Relationship stress

All relationships have ups and downs, and relationships suffer when you're suffering from stress in general. You may have to make allowances at times because your partner is going through a stressful event, but ideally your relationship should be a source of comfort and support. If this isn't the case and your relationship is the main source of your stress, it may be wise to talk to a professional. If your relationship problems are having a direct effect on your work and your quality of life, it's time to question its value in your life.

Moving house stress

Moving house should be a happy occasion, but it's considered one of the most stressful life events that you can experience. Whether you're moving into a new, perfectly furnished house or an old croc in need of renovation, you can expect a degree of stress to be involved in the process. Buying a house can be treated like a project in itself. Negotiating, organising, buying and selling all have to be done in the right order of play. Accept the body of work, make sure everyone that can help out does, and try your best to plan for the move when you're not in your busiest period in work.

Wedding stress

According to the Holmes & Rahe Stress Scale, getting married ranks number 7 on the list, higher than getting fired or getting pregnant. A wedding is another massive project to organise. If you can afford it, get a wedding planner; if you can't, consider getting a friend to help you plan. Whatever way you do it, make sure you plan far in advance of the day. Find a wedding app that will prompt you to remember all the things that need to get done. Get as much help as possible from the wedding party. If anyone offers to do something, accept. Life is too short to stress over what's supposed to be the happiest day of your life, and in reality nobody will notice the detail except you.

Life events stress

Bereavements and other trauma cause stress in your life. When these types of events occur in your life, you may be able to take them in your stride. But if you're finding it difficult to cope and your work and relationships are suffering, you'll benefit from seeking out professional help. The first port of call should be your doctor; she can advise you of the different types of help available in your area for the cause of your stress.

Reducing Stress

Knowing the signs of stress is important, but more important is knowing how to combat stress. Numerous techniques and tactics exist for coping with stress, many of which you're probably familiar with. Managing stress is about taking control and making the decision to do what it takes to remove harmful stress from your life starting today. In this section, I provide my top tips for reducing stress.

Acknowledge the source of stress

An important first step in any change process is self-awareness. You need to understand where you are now. There is no point in tackling your stress without knowing first what the source is. Often, people blame the source of their stress on the wrong things or the wrong people. Stress at work manifests itself as anger toward your children's mischievousness, which can lead to an overreaction and excessive discipline. Often, people accept their current state by justifying it with some belief to help them process the fact that they haven't been as successful or they aren't as wealthy as they thought they'd be. Getting to the root of your stress will help you find the right solutions for you to be able to manage and hopefully eliminate any future stress from your life.

Take some time to think about the source of your stress. Write a list of the things that you think create stress in your life. Score each one a number between 1 and 10. When you are more aware of what is causing your stress, look at the solutions for ideas how to tackle it.

Stay active

Staying active is one of the single best ways to manage stress. The negative effects of stress on the body can be neutralised with a regular exercise habit. Regular moderate exercise will help keep both body and mind healthy and give you the energy you need to manage a busy life. But remember that you need to tackle the root of your stress. Exercise will help you to manage the stress, but the ideal scenario is to eliminate the source of the stress entirely. If work is the cause of the stress, speak to a friend or colleague and look at your options. If financial stress is affecting your life, get expert advice from a money advice service that will help you to budget and manage your money better.

Eat right

Did you ever notice that when you're really busy, bordering on overwhelmed, you eat rubbish? The very time your body is being pushed to its limits, overworked, and not getting either enough sleep or exercise is the very time a pizza and beer sounds like the perfect meal. When you're busy, you tend not to have time to shop and cook and therefore reach for the convenience food. More often than not, convenience means unhealthy. There are other options, of course, but a tired body will crave the carbohydrates that will give it the energy it longs for.

When you're feeling stressed, you need to eat a healthy, balanced diet and avoid the immediate sugar and caffeine hits that your body tells you it needs. Planning your weekly meals in advance can be a great way to combat the 'too busy to cook' feeling. You could take a small amount of time out of your weekend to shop and cook for the week ahead. Freezing meals in advance can take so much stress out of your day. Knowing that dinner is taken care of, whether that dinner is for one or for eight, having it prepared in advance will help you to feel more in control of your week.

Two vitamins that are important to include in your diet and that may be negatively affected by stress are vitamin B6 and vitamin C. Lack of vitamin B6 can cause both physical and mental tiredness, so adding vitamin B6 to your diet should help for stress and tiredness. You find vitamin B6 in fish, a lot of fresh vegetables, dairy products, and whole grain cereals.

A lack of vitamin C can be caused by stress itself. High levels of stress suppress the body's production of vitamin C, and lack of vitamin C can lead to a damaged immune system, lethargy, and scurvy. Alcohol and smoking are also said to reduce levels of vitamin C, so you may want to pop a vitamin C pill with your next pint. You can get vitamin C naturally through fresh fruit and vegetables.

Reduce alcohol intake

For many people, the glass of wine with dinner or the beer they crack open when they get in from work seems like a harmless way to melt away the stresses of the day. One drink shouldn't do you any harm, but a couple of drinks later and you feel worse than you did before, you sleep badly and you feel exhausted the next day. Alcohol isn't a good solution for stress. It makes some people feel blue, adding to the problems of stress. Avoiding or at least reducing alcohol consumption will help you to manage stress better and help you clearly steer out of the issues that are causing you stress.

Limit caffeine

Caffeine is a powerful stimulant, so powerful it can increase your blood pressure, stimulate your heart and switch on your mind to become awake and alert at a moment's notice. Too much caffeine can have a negative effect, with lethargy, headaches and poor concentration among the long list of side effects. Reducing your intake of caffeine is a wise move when you're stressed. Remember that caffeine is in tea and cola drinks as well as some of the energy drinks on the market. Avoid energy drinks at all costs because the amount of caffeine in a lot of these drinks is dangerous for the body. Try naturally caffeine-free alternatives like chai or rooibos. These teas have a pleasant flavour and are much better for your health.

Regulate sleeping habits

Sleep is a great tonic. It rests, re-energises and rejuvenates the body. It also rests your mind, helping it sort out and process what has happened during the day. You need to get sufficient sleep in order to manage stressful episodes in your life. People who are sleep-deficient have trouble managing their emotions, making decisions and solving problems. How you feel during the day is directly dependent on how much sleep you get at night.

To ensure that you're getting enough sleep and that your sleep habits are not contributing to your stress levels, you need to create good evening habits to help you wind down before bed. Start by eating your dinner at a reasonable time, with plenty of time for digestion before bed. Create a wind-down routine for bedtime. Avoid watching stimulating TV or movies, which make your brain active before bed. Take a bath or listen to soothing music before bed to relax you enough to fall asleep easily. Try to sleep only when you're tired, and avoid taking naps during the day.

Plan your budget

Everyone has financial worries from time to time, but if financial worries are an ongoing state, it can lead to anxiety.

Getting your finances organised is an important step to reduce stress. If you have a budget that can withstand the ups and downs of life, you'll feel more in control and you don't have to worry about how the next bill is getting paid.

Start by creating a spreadsheet to track your income and expenditure. Microsoft Excel can be used for this or any other spreadsheet software. Identify all your sources of income (what comes in each month), and track your expenditure (everything you spend each day).

Budgeting is often one of those activities that make you feel like you're missing out on life. Reducing your spending may feel like you have to do without. To counter this, think of budgeting as a way to put you in control, to help you make choices about the way you spend your money. If your budget shows you that you're spending over a thousand (pounds/euro) on your daily latte, you're now in the position to *choose* to spend that money on a family holiday or to continue buying your latte. Now you know what you're giving up in order to drink your daily latte! Budgeting empowers you to be in control of your finances and your life. The more in control you are of your money and the more you understand what you spend, the less likely money is to be the source of your stress in life.

The sooner you make a budget, the more money you could be saving to pay for the things you need or really want.

Eat the elephant

There is a joke that asks, 'what is the best way to eat an elephant?' The answer is 'bite by bite'. The same applies in life. Biting off only as much as you can chew is a wise tactic. When you have a lot to do, the best way to manage a project is to tackle it task by task. Organising a wedding can be a stressful event because there is so much to plan and arrange and not let it disturb the day job. Planning for Christmas is another event that has a lot of different tasks involved in it. Both of these tasks can be classed as elephants. The way to handle them is bit by bit or bite by bite. Keep track of all tasks in an app like Evernote or in a spreadsheet. Mark off the tasks as you complete them and celebrate your progress regularly.

Say no

Stress often comes when you do too much: for example, agreeing to do work or help all those around you and sacrificing your own relaxation time to make other people's lives easier. Whether it's work or personal stuff, you need to learn how to say no. When you say yes to someone, you're saying no to something else. There is always a trade-off.

Be aware of what you're saying no to. If you agree to work late, you might be late for dinner or for the bedtime story. Be mindful of what you're missing. When you're clear about what you need to get done and when you know your values and your priorities, it's easier to say no to people. Saying no doesn't mean you're selfish; it means you're self-aware and conscious of your priorities in life. Learning to say no can reduce your commitments and help you to focus on the more important things.

Find time out

Being a busy person can sometimes mean that you get little time to yourself. Time out is crucial for a happy balanced life. Time to unwind, detach, unplug – whatever way you see it, you definitely need it. When you have downtime, your body and mind get to unwind and prepare for another busy day ahead.

Hobbies are a great way to relax and help you focus on something other than your problems and stresses. Fishing, gardening and painting are great ways to chill out and let life slow down for a little while. If you have small children, this can be more difficult to do, but remind yourself how important it is for both you and your children to have a relaxed and stress-free parent.

Identify one thing that you will do to take time out this week.

Learn to meditate

Meditation may just be the key to your lifelong happiness. There are so many benefits to daily practise, and stress reduction is one that can be life changing. Meditation is easier than you may think, and a daily practise of 10 to 15 minutes can bring noticeable results. If you want to begin to meditate, you could try out an app like Headspace, buy a CD by an expert such as Deepak Chopra or Wayne Dyer, or do a simple breath meditation where you follow your breath and focus on your breathing for 10 to 15 minutes.

You don't need to force your thoughts out of your head, but allow them to drift in and out, not holding onto them but watching them as they flow out as easily as they came into your mind. You can't stop your thoughts, but gradually you'll be able to focus your mind in a way that the thoughts reduce and stillness replaces them.

Practise relaxation techniques

Like meditation, relaxation techniques can help to calm your stress and ease your woes. Often people forget to breathe. When you're stressed, your breathing becomes more shallow and rapid. This type of breathing deprives your body of oxygen and energy. It makes your muscles tense and can have a negative effect on your blood pressure. Relaxation and relaxed breathing can therefore be a natural antidote for stress.

Practise relaxation by following these steps:

1. **Find a comfortable spot where you won't be disturbed.**
2. **Sit comfortably in a chair or lie down on your bed or the floor.**
3. **If you're sitting, place your hands on your knees with the palms open. If you're lying down, relax your arms beside you with the palms facing upward toward the ceiling.**
4. **Close your eyes and start to relax each part of your body.**

   Relax your feet and toes. Relax your ankles and your calves. Relax your thighs and knees. Relax your hips and your back, letting your back be supported by the floor or the chair. Relax your neck and shoulders. Relax your face and your head.
5. **Take a deep breath in and let it out.**

   Breathe in and out deeply and slowly. Visualise the breath reaching your diaphragm and flowing outward as you breathe out.
6. **Continue, and with each breath, relax a little more, breathing in and out.**

   Whenever you mind wanders, bring it back to your breathing and focus your mind on your breath.
7. **When you're ready to finish, take your time and gently open your eyes.**

   In your own time, you can stand up and continue your day.

Get a massage

Massage is one of my favourite techniques for stress relief. Not only does it relax your muscles and give you a feelgood factor that can't be denied, but it can also lower your heart rate and blood pressure. Many workplaces have introduced massage as a perk for their employees, as they see the positive effects that a short massage can give. The reduction in stress-related tensions, a little time out and a free perk from the boss are all positive reasons for employees to feel good after a massage.

Regular massage can help to reduce the effects of stress and anxiety and help you to feel happier about your life. Try to include massage in your life weekly. If you aren't lucky enough to have a boss who subsidises the weekly massage, maybe you have a partner that will oblige. A weekly massage is the ideal scenario, but if that isn't possible, treat yourself to a monthly massage to work those tired muscles. Your body will thank you for it.

Get organised

Poor time management can contribute to things feeling out of control. If you're not on top of your to-do list and you can't see when or how you're going to get it all done, you'll feel stressed and overwhelmed. Getting organised by adopting a task management system and committing to use your calendar to plan your week will help get your life under control. Identifying your priorities with the Eisenhower matrix (see Chapter 9) and the Pareto Principle (see Chapter 7) will help you gain some perspective. It will help you to eliminate the things that are taking your time that don't need to be done at all and help you to identify the things that need your focus and attention. Getting organised will go a long way to reducing stress and getting your life in order.

Managing Work Stress

Getting organised is the starting point for handling a heavy workload, and many chapters of this book are dedicated to helping you get organised and learn how to manage your work with ease and sophistication. In this section, I explore some of the main ways to take charge of your work responsibilities so that stress doesn't become part of your day.

Clarifying the big picture

Start by clarifying the big picture. What is it you're trying to achieve? Understanding the goal helps you to recognise the priorities and know what you need to work on first. Too often workplaces fall into disarray and chaos because workers are focusing their attention on the wrong things. Whether through lack of communication or lack of comprehension, the cost of not understanding the big picture is too great. If you're in a situation where you're unsure of what you're working toward, don't go another day without clarifying what needs to happen. When you know what the goals are and what the vision for the future is, only then can you spend your day productively working toward achieving these goals.

Creating milestones

You can't simply deal with work stress in one hit. When you look at the big-picture goals without breaking them down, they can be overwhelming. The way to achieve a big goal is by creating milestones or smaller goals that can help you visualise each success. When you move step by step through a project, the goals and milestones are more fathomable, realistic and achievable. If you are writing a technical manual for a product your company produces, breaking down the manual into chapters gives you obvious milestones. Each chapter completed is a cause for a mini celebration.

Taking breaks

One of the best ways to manage stress and reduce the likelihood of stress-related symptoms is to take regular breaks. Regular planned breaks give you time to stretch, breathe, drink water and do all the things that help you be a temple of Zen. The Pomodoro Technique (see Chapter 11) advises bursts of work for 25 minutes with a 5-minute break. I often take five minutes to do a yoga pose or to simply stretch and touch my toes. I find this helps to release the tension in my neck and helps me avoid the tension headaches I often get if I sit and write for too long.

Communicating the problem

Stress in the workplace can be caused by different sources. It can be caused by conflict and misunderstandings between teammates, or a boss who doesn't understand your needs or clients who ask for too much. Whatever the source of the stress, it is vital that you communicate the problem with whoever is involved.

If you've had a misunderstanding with a work colleague, take the time to work things out. Make a time to discuss your issue, clear the air and move on. Holding on to your problems and not communicating them will lead to further stress. Communicate where possible, and seek out help when you can.

If your boss is asking for unrealistic targets, you need to speak to him about it. If doing all that he asks in a working day isn't possible, track everything you do in your calendar and show him how you're spending your time. Explain how long things take and tell him that you're willing to learn a better way if he reckons there is a quicker way to do things.

If your clients are causing you stress, calling you all hours of the day and asking for unrealistic requests, it may be necessary to push back on your client communications to have time to actually do your job. If constant emails and phone calls are disturbing your flow of work, you need to tell the people responsible. Tell them that you will reply to emails within 24 hours because if you have to reply to all emails they send, you won't have time to do the work you need to do for them. Communicate what you think they need and let them explain what is most important to them, but take control of the relationship before it controls and consumes you.

Reducing Employee Stress

Stress causes muscle tension and headaches. It also causes reduced immune function, which can lead to minor and sometimes major illnesses. It therefore correlates that stress causes large amounts of absenteeism, costing organisations greatly each year. If you're a manager or are responsible for people in any way, this section will help you to understand and deal with the problem of stress in your workplace.

Observe and react

The first thing organisations can do is to be on the alert for stress. When it comes to employees, it may be a little more difficult to recognise the signs of stress, but they will be there. Poor performance, irritability and aggression toward teammates may be more obvious signs to pick up, but tiredness, headaches and anxiety may be hidden from sight. It's important to uncover the stress and openly come up with solutions to try to nip it in the bud. Even if the source of the stress is personal and not related to work, you should still help solve the issue, if not for humanitarian reasons then for the simple fact that you'll benefit from a more relaxed, stress-free employee.

Work flexibly

One of the major advances in modern working environments is the ability to work the hours that suit you in a location that suits you. Working from home has become more acceptable and even appreciated by employers. It has been recognised that not only does working from home reduce stress and improve work-life balance for employees, but it can also contribute to increases in productivity.

Working away from the office gives a person focused time to get her work done. Office environments are fraught with interruptions and distractions, never-ending meetings and work colleagues, managers and clients disturbing you every hour. Flexible working cuts down on the dreaded commute, giving an employee back a couple of hours of her day, which allows her to use this time to exercise or pursue hobbies that will contribute to her overall health and well-being.

Flexible working can also contribute to reduced costs for an employer. If large numbers of workers work from home, for example, heating and lighting bills are reduced.

Encourage daily exercise

The number-one solution for tackling stress is exercise. Too many employees don't have time to exercise. They work long hours trying to get ahead and stand out in their organisation only to find themselves exhausted, unfit and stressed. Bring exercise into the workplace. Provide lunchtime classes or subsidise gym membership.

Some organisations make fitness part of their employees' performance review. Employees need to set fitness goals along with their yearly performance goals. This is a clever tactic to show the importance of exercise to both the individual and the organisation. Regardless of the route an organisation takes to help promote healthier employees, it's important that a culture is set where exercise is rewarded and encouraged.

Create a fun culture

Fun can be a great stress buster, a good belly laugh. Do people laugh at your workplace? It's important that people have fun at work. Not being too serious all the time helps promote a more relaxed environment where people feel free to be themselves. When employees are more relaxed and humour is part of their day to day, stress levels fall and productivity rises. One way to create a culture of fun is to have a breakout area in your office. Some companies have pool tables, table tennis tables or other games to help their employees switch off and unwind. Another great way to foster friendship, trust and ultimately happiness and fun is to share time together outside the workplace. Arrange staff nights out or team challenge days to enable employees to get to know each other better.

Create a comfortable, bright work environment, a place where people want to spend their day. Gone is the trend of clinical professional office places where there is no character. People spend many hours each day at the office; make it a place that's nice to be.

Include healthy treats

Offering massage, yoga or meditation classes each day can do wonders for employee stress levels, and they can also boost staff morale when employees recognise that their health and well-being are important to the company. A lot of companies offer these benefits but have a poor take up on them because employees are too busy with a heavy workload. If you're going to offer these benefits, you have to create a culture in the organisation that recognises the personal benefits of taking part. It's no good making them available but not respecting people for taking the time out to go have a massage. Encourage breaks for renewal; everyone will benefit from them.

Walk the talk

As a manager or employer, you need to display the behaviours that you're trying to promote. If you want people to be relaxed, stress-free and in control of their working day, management should walk around looking relaxed, in control and stress-free. 'Do as I say, not as I do' doesn't wash anymore. If you want to develop a particular culture, management needs to walk the talk.

Offering yoga, massage and other perks won't catch on unless they're seen as acceptable by the upper echelons of the organisation. Culture is an accumulation of all the behaviours in an organisation. If management doesn't do it, it won't catch on. If you want to reduce stress in your organisation, start with your senior team. Encourage them to exercise daily, take time off for meditation and close their door when they need to focus. Everything that is good for the boss will be good for the masses.

Water the plants

Yes, I mean literally. Having plants in the workplace creates a more relaxed, pleasant environment to work in. Giving employees their own plant to look after can also create a sense of belonging and ownership. Not only do plants make a more pleasant office environment, but they also reduce air pollutants and create a healthier office. Choose plants that don't need too much care and that don't grow too big. The last thing you want is to lose people to the foliage around them.

Foster great management

One of the chief reasons employees leave their jobs is due to their direct line manager. Not-so-perfect relationships have many causes, but often they come down to a manager's lack of training in emotional intelligence. Listening, communicating and empathising are all skills that many managers lack. If a manager lacks basic management skills, he'll struggle to manage people effectively. His own lack of self-awareness will often lead to team members being unhappy, dissatisfied and disengaged.

Poor management leads to stress and anxiety. It's vital for people in a management position to have all the skills necessary to lead a team. Organisational health depends on it. People's lives depend on it.

Create collaborative environments

Creating a culture of collaboration and trust will make for a happy, productive workplace. Human beings crave interaction, even those who seem not to need human connection and interaction. Create environments that foster collaboration and sharing, but create them in such a way that it's also acceptable to work alone and in a focused way. Creating a workplace where people understand the need for collaboration as well as the necessity to get work done quietly allows people to work comfortably and in the space they need to get things done.

Listen to feedback

Feedback is an important part of any working environment. Employees receive feedback on their performance and advice on how to improve their strengths and weaknesses, and employers receive feedback on how the employees feel about their jobs and the way they're being managed. Feedback is a mechanism for growth and improvement. Lots of employers think feedback is a one-way technique, not realising that they, too, can benefit by becoming better leaders and running better organisations.

Part III

Applying Productivity Techniques

	URGENT	LESS URGENT
IMPORTANT	Do first/Today tasks	Schedule this work
LESS IMPORTANT	Tasks to be delegated	Does it need to be done at all?

Have trouble focusing? Turning on some music may help. Find out how in a free article at `www.dummies.com/extras/productivity`.

In this part . . .

- Discover how to focus and how to determine what merits your focus.
- Gain tips for avoiding procrastination.
- Find out how to better manage and track your time.
- Understand how to use the Getting Things Done (GTD) methodology.
- Become familiar with additional productivity techniques.

Chapter 7

Learning to Focus

In This Chapter

- Learning to focus on the right things
- Discovering what disturbs your focus
- Realising what it takes to stay focused

The ability to focus on the right thing at the right time is a skill too few people have conquered. Master this skill and you'll achieve more than you ever thought possible. Removing the mass of distractions of everyday life is challenging, but it is achievable. In this chapter, you discover what stands in your way and find out how you can minimise the distractions of life and get more done.

Identifying Your Focus

So little time, so much to do. How do you decide what to focus your attention on? What merits your attention, and what deserves to be dropped? Understanding priorities is a challenge for a lot of folks. Distinguishing what you like to do from what you ought to do can be a test in itself before the work has even begun.

Clarifying your goals

Your big-picture goals should be your beacon of light. Chapter 2 outlines why goals are so important and how and why to set them. If you need help identifying your focus, look at your goals. Your goals guide your daily focus. They help you recognise whether the tasks you're busy with are your priorities. If a task has no connection to your end goal, you have to ask yourself whether it needs to be done at all.

The Pareto Principle

In the early 1900s, an Italian economist by the name of Alfredo Pareto observed that 20 per cent of Italy's population held 80 per cent of the wealth. Intrigued by this discovery, he took a look at other economies and found similar distributions of wealth.

In the 1960s, a quality expert by the name of Juran took this principal and applied it to his area of expertise. He observed that 20 per cent of products caused 80 per cent of defects. It was he who coined the principle after Pareto.

The Pareto Principle is widely used in business and sales. Sales experts have observed that 80 per cent of revenue often comes from 20 per cent of clients and that 20 per cent of product ranges tend to give 80 per cent of profits.

A simple exercise that helps you identify your core daily tasks and encourages you to spend more time on the right ones is based on the Pareto Principle.

Pareto productivity

When it comes to the world of productivity, often 20 per cent of what you do gives you 80 per cent of your results. Before Juran coined the phenomenon the 'Pareto Principle', he first called it 'The Law of the Vital Few and the Unimportant Many' (check out the nearby sidebar 'The Pareto Principle'). When you analyse what you do each day, you'll find that a lot of what you do is trivial. You likely spend hours each day replying to emails, sitting in meetings, trawling through social media sites in case you missed a cute baby picture or a cat opening a fridge. You still need to do a certain percentage of the unimportant tasks, but if you can focus your attention even 10 per cent more on the vital few, think of the impact that could have on your work and life.

Ask yourself this question regularly: Is the work that I am doing right now adding value?

Fill in Table 7-1 to help you figure out where your focus currently is and where you want it to be.

Having filled in Table 7-1, answer the following questions:

- What two tasks currently take up most of my time?
- What two tasks should take up most of my time?

Table 7-1 How to Prioritise with Pareto

Daily Tasks	% of Time Spent Actual	% of Time Spent Ideal
1. Emails	20	10
2. Meetings	40	20
3. New Project	0	50
4.		
5.		
6.		
7.		
8.		
9.		
10.		

Focussing Like a Monk

Confucius said, 'He who chases two rabbits catches none'. That's all well and good if you're a monk living in the mountains, but for most people, the challenge is not a pair of bouncing bunnies but rather a multitude, so many that you can't even begin to count them. They dart about, jumping from one task to the next, never completing always starting, and they multiply – we all know how quickly they can multiply.

I spent 30 years of my life chasing rabbits, always attracted by the movement and the lure of something new, something different, but never quite catching any. Implementing a few simple strategies changed my world and allowed me to focus long enough to achieve great things. But it wasn't only the big things that made a difference; it was the little things, the day-to-day tasks, the tasks that if not completed can affect the quality of my thoughts, my emotions and my life.

Using your calendar

I often ask an audience, 'How many of you use your calendar?' Usually about 70 per cent of the room put their hand up. When I ask the succeeding question, 'How many of you use your calendar for more than meetings or appointments?' most of the hands disappear.

Using a calendar to track your meetings and appointments is great, but if you can start to use your calendar to schedule and plan all the work you have to do, you'll become 100 per cent more effective, productive and focused. Using a calendar had the biggest impact on my personal productivity. I began by scheduling time for writing; I found that making the decision in advance increased my chances of actually doing the task by about 80 per cent. Such a simple act helped to focus my brain and helped me to commit to actually doing a task.

Scheduling time wisely

Think about all the things you need to get done. Are there enough hours in the day to get them done? Scheduling time for tasks is a great way to determine whether you do have enough hours for everything on your to-do list. It also compels you to make upfront decisions about when you're going to tackle a task, and it encourages you to decide how long a task should take.

Scheduling time for the tasks you need to do, rather than simply listing them, helps you naturally start to prioritise each task. When you take those tasks and schedule them into your calendar, the picture starts to sharpen, and you begin to see things more clearly. This also allows you to plan work according to your energy levels. For example, just after lunch isn't the best time to tackle a complicated task.

When you schedule your tasks into your calendar, you naturally block out all other tasks and distractions. It becomes easier to focus because you've specified a time period to get the work done.

Schedule your most important tasks and project work for the morning. Afternoons are good for meetings, emails and other administrative tasks that don't need as much focus and attention. People are generally more alert two to four hours after waking, so if possible tackle your big tasks first.

Allocating a time box

Time boxing is a term used in both time management and project management. It refers to allocating a time box or fixed period to a task or planned activity. Somewhat like using your calendar, it allows you to plan the amount of time you're going to spend on each activity and what time is available to you.

The added advantage of time boxing is that visual view of how many hours are in a day. People often complain about not having time to do the things they want to do. For example, do you want to write a book or take up art, music or fencing? Figure out how much time you need to practise these activities per week. If you want to write a novel of 90,000 words and you spend three hours a week writing, you could have the book written in eight months, assuming you write approximately 1,000 words in an hour.

Or say you want to start exercising, but you never seem to be able to find the time. The Heart Foundation says that 30 minutes of activity a day leads to a healthy heart. This could even be a brisk walk to and from the train station on your way to work, so it doesn't have to be a planned aerobic workout or a run every day.

If you think you never have enough hours in the day, take a look Figure 7-1.

	Mon	Tue	Wed	Thurs	Fri	Sat	Sun
00:00							
01:00							
02:00							
03:00							
04:00							
05:00							
06:00							
07:00	Exercise		Exercise		Exercise		
08:00							
09:00							Write
10:00						Walk	Write
11:00							
12:00							
13:00		Yoga		Yoga			
14:00						Write	
15:00						Write	Guitar
16:00						Write	
17:00							
18:00							
19:00		Guitar		Guitar			
20:00							
21:00							
22:00							
23:00							

Figure 7-1: Time boxing put to work.

© John Wiley & Sons, Inc.

There are 168 hours in a week. The average adult sleeps seven hours a night during the week and nine hours on the weekend. People work, on average, eight hours a day with three hours for commuting. This leaves 60 hours a week to do whatever you want. Now for most people, this time is taken up looking after children or aging parents, helping out in the community, cleaning, cooking and so on. But the reality is you should have a couple of extra hours you can carve out for yourself. And when you do – that is, when you allocate a couple of hours each week to pursue a hobby or a task that you need to do – the time box helps you to focus and get it done.

Open up a spreadsheet (or draw on a large sheet of paper) and create a table with 8 columns and 24 rows. Start by entering the hours you sleep, and then add in your typical work hours and all your other responsibilities. Take a look at the number of hours of free time you have. Decide what new hobby you want to make time for and allocate at least three hours a week for it.

Becoming more assertive

Being more assertive and giving your own priorities preference is a skill a lot of people need to learn. How often is your focus disturbed by someone looking for your help? How many times a day are you interrupted for your input? Interruptions are a major concern in most working environments, especially in the modern phenomena of the open-plan office. How can you ever be expected to get work done if your focus is constantly being disturbed by your colleagues and teammates?

Becoming more assertive is definitely part of the solution. Striking a balance between being a cooperative and collaborative team member and actually getting your own work done can take some practise, but understanding that it's sometimes necessary to say no is a positive start.

The following question may help you decide whether to say no: If I say yes to helping out my colleague, what am I saying no to? For example,

- If I say yes to staying late to help write this report, I am saying no to reading a bedtime story.
- If I say yes to delivering this presentation, I am saying no to helping out at the diversity event.

Understanding what you're saying no to will empower you to make the right decision at the right time.

Knowing your goals and priorities can help you determine whether you have time to help someone else out. And being more organised and in control of your own workload frees you up to be available to others.

If you're having trouble focusing because of distractions or if you need to get some important work done for a deadline, remove yourself from your usual environment. Go to a meeting room, or work from home. It's up to you to take control of the situation, and if an environment isn't working for you, do something about it.

If you allow others' priorities to take preference over your own, not only will your work suffer but also your personal life and relationships may suffer from your anxiety and stress. If you don't give your own work the attention it deserves, you may become overwhelmed by all the tasks you never seem to get done.

Batching your work

Batch processing your work can also be a good way to focus on the right things; it avoids the trap of multitasking and task switching. If you batch all project work or similar types of tasks together, you'll work more efficiently through your tasks when the time comes. Batching your work allows you to focus on one project at a time and not worry about your other projects. Batch processing your email is another great way to save time and avoid distractions. Keep your email closed during the day, and open it only when you have allocated time to process it. (You may read more on taking control of your inbox in Chapter 15.)

Blocking out the noise

'Noise' comes in many forms. It could be the physical noise from the people around you. It can be the surrounding environmental noise from equipment or electronics, or it can be simply the noise in your head telling you that you need to be somewhere else or doing something else. A number of tactics may help get you started blocking out the noise so you can focus, as I discuss in the following paragraphs.

Make your own noise

If there is too much noise in the environment, consider listening to music. I listen to soft classical music while writing, which allows me to block out the sounds around me and helps ensure that I don't get drawn into conversations or disputes happening close by.

Remove yourself

If the noise is too much or you don't have earphones at hand, remove yourself from the area. Find a quiet room, a coffee shop or a park bench in summer. There is no reason to sit and complain if you can stand up and walk away.

Ask others to be quiet

If the distraction is coming from people chatting who should be working or from overzealous coworkers speaking on the phone, you could always ask them to keep it down. As long as you are polite and to the point, it may be all that is needed to return the area to a Zen haven of diligence and productivity.

Breathe and refocus

And if it is all getting too much, stand up and breathe. Take a couple of moments to focus on what you want to get done. Reassess how much time you think it should take and if you have the time available. Ask yourself whether the task needs to be done today – that is, is it your number-one priority?

At times, it's difficult to focus because you're not working on the right thing. If you find this happening, look at your priorities and readjust them. Your subconscious can be a powerful tool that needs more attention. If something is niggling at you, perhaps it's your subconscious giving you a heads-up that your priorities have shifted.

Refocussing: What You Need to Stop Doing

It's often easier to think about what you need to do as opposed to what you need to stop doing. But to be able to focus intensely on something, you may first need to turn your attention on what you need to eliminate from your daily life.

Creating a stop-doing list

When feeling overwhelmed, you may find it useful to make a stop-doing list. If you work for yourself, you understand that your time costs money. Each hour you spend on administrative tasks or supportive tasks is an hour you aren't earning. Your specialised skill or talent is what you get paid for, so you should be outsourcing a lot of your administrative tasks, freeing you up to focus on the real money-earning work.

For those of you who work in an organisation, maybe you're doing more than you need to be doing. Take a look at the leadership pipeline and ensure that everybody is doing the tasks he's getting paid for. Should you be delegating more? Should some people take on more responsibility and others less? When people are clear about their responsibilities, work flows more efficiently and you can get a lot more done. Take a look at the nearby sidebar 'The Leadership Pipeline' for ideas on progressions across your career.

In your personal life, what can you offload to someone else? Do you have a cleaner, a housekeeper or a gardener? If you can afford them and would rather write a book than mow the lawn, go hire some people.

And then there are the tasks that don't need to be done at all. Eliminate those from your to-do list.

Time to take action! Get out a pen and paper, and write down all the things in your personal and professional life that you need to stop doing. Don't try to sneak in cleaning out the fridge – hire a cleaner – you aren't going to get out of that one so easily!

The Leadership Pipeline

The Leadership Pipeline is a model developed by Ram Charan, Stephen Drotter and James Noel and appears in their book *The Leadership Pipeline* (Jossey-Bass, 2000). The model highlights six progressions that managers can go through as they develop their careers. The six levels are

- Managing self to managing others
- Managing others to managing managers
- Managing managers to functional manager
- Functional manager to business manager
- Business manager to group manager
- Group manager to enterprise manager

Understanding where you are in the pipeline and what your responsibilities are will help you to delegate effectively. Knowing the requirements of the next level of leadership is also useful so that you're ready for your next promotion.

Disconnecting

Our world has never been so connected. We receive information from the other side of the world more quickly than news of our neighbours. Although this can have a multitude of benefits for business and society, it also has its disadvantages. Our world is always 'on'. From smartphones to tablets and smart TVs, nowhere are we disconnected from the information hub.

In this section, I discuss how disconnecting can really help you focus. Can you imagine spending a week without your gadgets? What about a day? Would you survive it? If you're tough enough, also be sure to check out the sidebar 'Feeling brave?'

Suffering from information overload

The modern phenomenon 'information overload' has negative consequences for our society. We consume information at the speed of light. We feel compelled to keep up with the excess of news coming our way 24 hours a day. Many parts of our lives suffer when we allow too much information and connectivity into our lives, including the following:

- **Personal relationships:** Seeing a family out for dinner, children with their faces down in an electronic game of some sort or parents with phones perched on the table for fear of missing out on some life-changing update, is an all-too-common sight. What happened to the chatting, the joking and the laughing? It may be time to pay more attention to the real world and the people who are right in front of you.

- **Work relationships:** Work relationships suffer as people are compelled to bring their phones into meetings, not fully present or engaged on the topic being discussed, always scanning emails and receiving updates on the latest, newest, coolest next big thing. If you're paying more attention to your virtual communications than your physical ones, don't expect to get attention and respect in return.
- **Standard of work:** If you're allowing yourself to be disturbed regularly by the online world, you can't possibly deliver the standard of work you're capable of. Every time your focus is disturbed, it takes at least 15 minutes to regain it. Think about how many times you let your attention shift to other things. If these attention disturbers were eliminated from your day, would your standard of work increase?

Overcoming information overload

To be able to focus and get anything done, you need to disconnect. You need a period of peace and calm each day where you can renew yourself and get ready for a new day of data download. If you're constantly being bombarded with new information, when can you assimilate or focus on the old data? Here are a few things that you can do to regain your focus and get the world of information into perspective:

- **Switch off your phone.** Agghh! I know it sounds a bit scary, but you can do it. Get into the habit of switching off your phone when you get home from work, especially if you have kids. If the only time you see your kids during the week is that period between the time you get home from work and bedtime, they deserve your undivided attention for that short period each day.
- **Listen to music or read a novel.** We all have a tendency to reach for our phones when we're waiting. Whether we're waiting for a bus, waiting in a queue or waiting in the doctor's office, out comes the phone. Why not bring a book with you and use those times to increase your knowledge or simply find out 'Whodunnit?'
- **Leave the phones outside the bedroom.** Use an old-fashioned alarm clock, and read a book before bedtime. You'll sleep better and have a much higher chance of getting lucky than if your head is stuck looking at your screen.
- **Turn off all notifications.** Turn off email notifications and any social media notifications on your computer, phone and tablet. Take back the control, and go to your email or to your social media sites only when you have scheduled time for them, not when you're beckoned there by an enticing picture of a cat.

Feeling brave?

Here are two really challenging ways to disconnect. Go on, you're braver than you might imagine . . . give them a go!

- **Don't access Facebook and Twitter for one week.** Take control of your social media accounts, and take a break for a week. Watch how productive you are and probably happier, too. If you want to make it much easier on yourself, delete the apps from your phone. If you use them for work, schedule some posts in advance and ask someone to monitor your account for you.
- **Don't read newspapers, online news or any other form of world news for one week.** Take a break from the media and the bad news. Fill your days with positivity and motivating material. Avoid the negativity and bad news at least for a little while.

Stopping the multitasking

Multitasking has its advocates; most parents can cook, clean and soothe a crying child all at the same time. Tell them to focus on one thing at a time, and they will tell you to take a hike. Multitasking is in the job description. All experienced drivers are able to drive and hold a conversation at the same time, maybe even learn French while they commute back and forth to work.

So why all the negative press about multitasking? Is it something we should all be getting better at in our world of overload and overwhelmed? As Seneca once said, 'To be everywhere is to be nowhere'. I explain further in the following sections.

Task switching

There is no such thing as multitasking. Our brain is simply not capable of doing it. What we're actually doing is task switching.

The frontal part of the brain called *Broadman's Area 10* is responsible for the brain switching from task to task, and whereas we may think we are multitasking, we are simply getting good at switching from task to task.

But what about the juggling clown on the unicycle? Multitasking becomes possible only when at least one of the tasks becomes automated. Driving, cycling and walking are all examples of habits we have formed. Our brain has automated the tasks, and it doesn't take any cognitive load to complete the task. This frees up the brain to focus on the juggling while the cycling happens without thought.

Multitasking and focus

Although sometimes multitasking can be useful, like listening to audio books while you go for a walk or cook dinner, the truth is that multitasking won't help your productivity levels, and it definitely won't help you focus. Focus is about eliminating the distraction so that your brain can concentrate on the work you want to get done. You know that feeling when you're in the zone, when nothing but the right task is occupying your thoughts. This is what you should aim for. This is the fierce focus that will allow you to achieve great heights. This is the full attention that your goals deserve and is the true path to your success.

The fewer distractions you allow, the stronger your focus will be.

Making New Habits for Focussing

Learning to focus is like learning a new habit. The habit consists of three parts.

- Identifying what merits your focus
- Adopting the traits that will contribute to your success
- Eliminating the distractions and barriers to focus

If you can master the habit of identifying what to focus on and create the correct environment, you can conquer the power of focus.

Automating the habitual

By making decisions in advance for habitual tasks, you eliminate the need to make daily decisions. If you do your expenses every Friday at 2 p.m., you don't have to waste time thinking about doing it at any other time during the week. If you create a food menu for the week and shop accordingly, no time will be lost deciding what to eat and when to buy it.

Automating the habitual is an act that not only benefits your focus but also helps you make progress in all areas of your life. If you can make upfront decisions about what you're going to eat, the exercise you'll do and the budget you'll commit to, you'll see powerful results.

Here are some tasks that you can schedule and develop into a habit:

- Exercise
- Meal plans
- Meditation

- Budgeting
- Bill payments
- Savings
- Hobbies, such as writing, journaling or painting

Another great way to automate tasks and remove thinking time is to create checklists. Create a holiday checklist so that each time you pack for holidays you know what you need to bring. I created some checklists for my kids, one for getting ready for school and another for bedtime. The morning checklist eliminated a lot of stress and tension from having to tell my kids repeatedly what they needed to do next. The checklist did away with the need to shout, scream or nag and empowered them to complete their morning tasks more quickly and efficiently.

By planning tasks in advance, you remove the worry and stress associated with trying to fit it all in. When you come to do the task, you know how much time you have allocated to spend on it, eliminating a lot of wasted time pondering the logistics.

Use your calendar to schedule the tasks you need to get done. Plan time each week to look at your goals and ensure that you are focusing on the right things.

Choosing supportive habits

Automating tasks is a habit that helps you focus. Other powerful habits have a positive effect on how well you can eliminate the disruptions.

Exercising regularly

The power of exercise should never be underestimated. It can improve your health, well-being and some say even your wealth. Exercise is a habit most successful people have mastered. If your life is not going the way you want, take a look at your exercise habits. Exercise should be part of your daily life, not something you do twice a week. Working out daily will give you more energy during the day. It will help you to be more focused and productive. It will also give you a lot of those feel-good chemicals for free and enhance your happiness levels. How could you ever say no?

Being mindful

Mindfulness is the practise of living in the present moment. Most people spend their days thinking about what has past or contemplating the future. Too little time is spent in the here and now. People let magic moments pass by unnoticed because they allow their thoughts to drift elsewhere. A clever monk called Lao Tzu once said, 'If you are depressed, you are living in the past. If you are anxious, you are living in the future. If you are at peace, you are living in the present'.

Practise mindfulness by noticing what is going on around you. If you're holding a physical book, notice the feeling of paper in your hands and feel the weight of the book in your arms or on your lap. Listen to the sounds around you. Observe how you feel. Is your body relaxed? Can you feel the chair beneath you? Or perhaps you are lucky enough to feel the sand between your toes. Wherever you are, take some time to be mindful and live in the now.

Practising meditation

Although similar to mindfulness, meditation is more about helping you to understand your mind and the world around you. Basic mediation techniques are similar to mindfulness, teaching you to focus on your breath, walking or eating.

Making meditation a habit can help you to take control of your mind and any negative thoughts that you may have. It will also help you to focus and feel calm. Start small and try ten minutes of meditation a day. Do it at the same time each day to help you form a habit more quickly.

Rising early

Mastering the habit of rising early can be a difficult one – believe me, it's taken me years to conquer – but the benefits are countless. I'm not a morning person, but the sad part is I'm not an evening person, either. I'm just a sleeper. But when I realized how much of my life I was wasting asleep, I quickly changed. Getting up early is a great way to fit in all the things you don't have time for during the day.

Take a look at these examples:

> Too tired to exercise when you get home from work? Get up early.
>
> Would love to write a book but don't have the time? Get up early.
>
> Want to try meditation but your mind is too busy to get started? Get up early.

All these examples will benefit from rising early. It's a great time of the day to get work done undisturbed, an ideal time to write interrupted or a perfect time to exercise or practise meditation – the habits that will extend your energy and focus throughout the day.

Taking breaks

Regular breaks improve your focus and concentration. Our primitive brains allow us to focus only for a short time without wandering. If you need to focus on important work, you must take regular breaks. It may sound counterintuitive, but it will boost your efficiency and effectiveness.

Drinking water

A dehydrated brain is not pretty and neither is the work you produce when you're lacking water. Drink plenty of water during the day if you want to stay alert. A hydrated brain is not exactly beautiful but can create work of great beauty.

Eating healthily

You would never feed a Porsche low-grade fuel, so don't even think about feeding your body with processed food. They even knew it back in ancient Rome: *corpo sano, mente sana* means healthy body, healthy mind. Give your body what it deserves, and it will reward you with quality work that you deserve.

Sleeping soundly

With a healthy body and a healthy mind, all that is missing is time for renewal. Lack of sleep impairs memory and learning ability. People who suffer from insomnia or who get inadequate levels of sleep tend to show high levels of cortisol, the stress hormone. Sleep, while important for focus and productivity, is vital for health and well-being.

Chapter 8

Avoiding Procrastination

In This Chapter

- Understanding what procrastination is
- Finding out why you procrastinate and how to overcome it
- Discovering why procrastination isn't always a bad thing

Are you a procrastinator? Do you put off 'til tomorrow what should be done today? Fear not: procrastination is something all human beings do at different times in their lives; sometimes it's useful, but many times it's not. This chapter helps you understand why you procrastinate (and it's not always because you're lazy!). It also outlines times when procrastination can negatively affect you and how it can sometimes contribute to your personal success.

Understanding Procrastination

People procrastinate for many reasons, and there are many types of procrastinators. There are those who put off doing their homework until the last minute, and those who avoid going to the doctor when they have an infection. The consequences of both activities are different. Some procrastination does no harm and can sometimes even be beneficial, but certain types of procrastination can have damaging effects on your job, your relationships and even your health. Understanding the why will empower you to make the necessary changes to stop procrastinating and start getting more of the right things done.

Lacking clarity

A major reason for procrastination can be the lack of understanding what exactly is involved in completing a task. The task appears too large; the thought of tackling it can be overwhelming. Tasks such as submitting taxes or cleaning under the bed often seem like overwhelming tasks. If you envision monsters at every crossroad, taking time to evaluate what a task involves can take the Freddy Kruger out of the task. Sometimes, people refer to large tasks as elephants, and everyone knows the answer to the question, 'How do you eat an elephant?' is 'One bite at a time'.

But how do you get started? You first have to get clear about what your final outcome should be. What is the ideal result from completing the task? Getting clear on the result helps direct the course you take.

Take the example of submitting your taxes. Anyone who is self-employed understands what a mammoth that can be. Write down your ideal result: 'Submit completed taxes on time' (preferably without owing too much!). When you're clear about the final goal, you can work toward intermediate milestones. Tackle the tasks month by month. If a month contains too much work, break it down again into income and expenditure per month. Writing each step down and planning each step will give you focus and provide you with the opportunity to tick off each sub task as you complete it. Ticking boxes or putting a line through completed tasks puts you in a success frame of mind, assisting with motivation and overall success.

Lacking focus

Not having clarity about what you want to achieve leads to a lack of focus and a tendency to procrastinate on certain tasks. Many individuals don't understand their priorities, leading them to spend inappropriate amounts of time on inappropriate tasks. This phenomenon can sometimes create 'the busy fool' – the hardworking employee who keeps her head down and works her butt off only to find that the company priorities remain undone.

Get clear about your priorities. Don't spend your time working only on stuff that you enjoy; focusing on the priorities will get you much better results.

Here are some ways you can avoid falling in to the lack-of-focus trap:

- **Set goals.** Setting goals gives you a clear focus. Understanding what you want to achieve keeps you focused day to day. As the late Stephen Covey said, 'Begin with the end in mind'. If you're clear about your goals and why you want to achieve them, you'll no longer suffer from a lack of focus. If you work in an organisation and you're unsure about your goals, make it your business to go find out. Speak to you manager or boss about the organisational goals and the part you play in achieving them. The clearer you are about the end goal, the more focused you'll be each day.

- **Understand priorities.** In a work environment, too many people don't understand their priorities; they find it difficult to judge what task to do when. Priorities are strongly linked to your goals. Ask yourself, 'Is what I'm working on getting me closer to my organisational goals?' If you're unsure, ask or discuss with your team. Effective communication can assist clarity and focus. (Refer to Chapter 9 for more on prioritising.) Getting organised will also help you get a clear vision of the big picture. The more organised you are, the easier it will be to see your priorities.
- **Avoid distractions.** We live in the age of distraction. Constant connectivity and information overload are part of our day-to-day lives. Staying focused is a real challenge for most people. But when you're clear about your goals and priorities and understand why you want to achieve them, you're less likely to get distracted.

  Turn off notifications of emails, tweets and posts, and go to them only when you schedule time for them. Yes, you need to schedule time to check your social media accounts and your email. If you allot time for these tasks, you'll be less likely to flick in and out of them while you're trying to get work done. Switch off gadgets when you need to focus, or remove yourself from any environment that disturbs your focus. Don't sit around complaining that you can't focus – get up, and do something about it.

Lacking vision

Many procrastinators lack vision. They don't have a vision for the future that inspires them to move from the sofa. If you lack vision, ask yourself the following questions.

- Where do you want to be in ten years' time?
- What do you want your life to look like?
- How do you want to feel each day when you get up?

In a work scenario, too many managers get caught up in the day-to-day activities that they forget to plan for a sweet future. They allow themselves to become reactive, spending their day firefighting – that is, responding to all fires in a timely manner like a good firefighter. But they forget that their job shouldn't be to fight fires but to effectively plan for a successful future. Their responsibility is to figure out why the fires keep happening and plan for avoiding them.

Lacking energy

Modern life is tiring, all that racing around to complete tasks and fulfil responsibilities. Feeling tired all the time is a genuine reason for procrastinating. You work hard all day, get home to children or other responsibilities and by the time you do all the daily chores, you're too exhausted to do anything else. Lacking energy is real and can be a challenge. So what can you do about it?

If you lack energy, you need to look at your life and see what you can do to change your circumstances. Very often, people don't exercise because they don't have enough energy. Exercise creates energy and will give you that extra boost to get more done. Richard Branson's super levels of productivity are often attributed to his daily workout. All high achievers use exercise to enable their industrious activities.

A lack of energy can also be caused by a poor diet or lack of sleep. Consider the following factors, and ask yourself what you can do about it.

- **Exercise:** Are you exercising enough? How can you incorporate exercise into your life and make it fun? *Remember:* exercise doesn't have to be a chore; you can dance, swim or be involved in a team sport as your form of exercise.
- **Diet:** Are you eating a healthy, balanced diet? Consider reducing your alcohol or sugar. Spend time planning your weekly meals. Do the shopping on the weekend. If you have healthy food on hand, you're more likely to stick to a healthy diet. Don't buy processed foods, and leave the chocolates and cookies on the shelf in the supermarket.
- **Sleep:** Are you getting enough sleep? Do you have a set time to wind down before bed with no electronics? Do you go to bed at the same time every night? Consider your sleep patterns, and think about what you can do to improve them. Never watch TV in bed, and leave your gadgets outside the bedroom if you're serious about getting better sleep.
- **Doing too much:** Have you bitten off more than you can chew? Sometimes life throws you more than you can handle. Looking after family and aging or sick parents while holding down a job can be a typical period in most working adults' lives. If you simply have too much on your plate, call in the cavalry. Pay for help if you can afford it; if not, ask your family and friends to help with the everyday chores. Tuck your pride away, and ask for help.

Spend some time taking an objective view on your life. Observe your current habits and if you aren't currently doing regular exercise, start by introducting a little bit into each week. If you know your diet needs attention, buy a healthy cookbook and go food shopping. When you find the source of your low energy, you'll be able to make the changes needed to boost your energy and help you power through all the work that needs to get done.

Lacking patience

No one likes to suffer. If the choice is watching a good movie or doing a report that is due next week, I know which one I'm more likely to do. We often lack the patience required to delay the tasks that will give us joy right now and postpone the tasks we dislike. Most human beings will opt for immediate rewards over delayed benefits . . . or will they? If you have a tendency to delay gratification, what does this say about you?

Many studies have been done over the years on the subject of delayed benefits. One of these studies took place in the late 1960s at Stanford University. Walter Mischel, then a professor of Stanford University, conducted a series of experiments on pre-schoolers between the ages of 4 and 6. The studies focused on delayed gratification. The children were shown a plate of marshmallows and offered one marshmallow now or two marshmallows if they could wait a short period. The studies found that the children who could delay gratification tended to be the adults who had better life outcomes, educational scores, lower body mass index, and other measures.

Each time you check your mail or open up Facebook, you're searching for a little hit of dopamine to ease the boredom. There's nothing wrong with this as long as you're moving through your to-do list and getting real work done. This behaviour becomes a problem when you aren't getting any work done at all. It's important to be able to delay instant gratification, to have the patience to delay your reward until after you get the real work done.

Rewarding yourself every time you accomplish a big task can help toward motivation. Plan some time to complete a task that you have been avoiding and decide on the reward. It may be 20-guilt free minutes online, or it could be a massage or hot bath.

Beating Procrastination

Is your life negatively affected by your constant procrastination? Or are there things you need to get done and you just haven't been able to find the time to do them? If so, this section is for you. Here, I highlight some time-proven strategies that will have you ticking the boxes on your to-do list faster than Usain Bolt.

Using your calendar as a tool

The calendar is your number-one tool for beating procrastination. If you schedule the tasks that you want to get done, you're halfway to completing them. Time and time again, people have a truckload of things to do, but they never seem to get around to doing them. Most of these people allow the day to day to take over. Don't panic if you're one of these people; you aren't a freak of nature. In fact, you're probably the norm. If you allow the emails and the interruptions to take over your day, they will kindly oblige. The sad thing is, they will do it today and every day until you stand up and say, 'No more! I am the captain of my fate. I am ready to take control and plan my priorities. I am ready to get things done'.

Start to use your calendar to plan everything you need to get done. Your calendar is not just for storing meetings and appointments. Your calendar is a planning tool to help you figure out when you will get all your priorities done. Don't put things in your calendar that aren't priorities; doing so will minimise the impact of your calendar. If you look at something that doesn't really need to be done, you'll likely skip over it and not actually do it. If you start skipping over tasks and only do the things you like, you're back to the original problem and the calendar won't work for you.

You can also use time chunks that fit in with the Pomodoro Technique. The Pomodoro Technique is a way to manage your work in time chunks of 30 minutes. So you work for 25 minutes, and then you take a 5-minute break before you start again. (Read more on the Pomodoro Technique in Chapter 11.)

Your calendar is the best way to work on your priorities. Your inbox is the best way to work on other people's priorities. Which one will you choose?

Scheduling 'next actions'

At times, you may feel that a task is too big to put in your calendar. You're stuck because you don't know where to start. Enter 'next actions' – coined by David Allen in his book *Getting Things Done* (you can read more about this book in Chapter 10).

Allen describes the next action as 'the next physical, visible activity that needs to be engaged in in order to move the current reality toward completion'. And now translated into English: the *next action* is the very next thing you need to do to complete a task or make progress with a project.

Assigning next actions helps break down a project into manageable steps, removing the sense of being overwhelmed that people feel when facing a large project. When you schedule your next action, it's easier to hit the ground running when you sit down to work. You don't need to spend time figuring out what you should work on; you're ready to roll.

When you sit down to plan your work, always ask the question, 'What next action will help me move closer to getting this job done?'

Identifying your MIT

Your MIT, or most important task, is the thing that really needs to be done or the thing you really want to get done today. Test yourself by deciding to do an alternative task, and you'll feel the unrest rise up inside you. Take a couple of minutes to ask yourself what really needs to be done. Then schedule the next action to help you make a start and take action. Sometimes you just need to get started, and after you do, the rest is not as bad as you thought. After you get started, momentum usually whisks you away.

Start each day by identifying your top three MITs. Write them down, and schedule them into your calendar. If you can start knocking MITs off your list, you'll feel a whole lot better.

Practising the two-minute rule

Another concept from David Allen's book *Getting Things Done* is the two-minute rule. If a task will take less than two minutes, do it straightaway. Don't postpone it for a later time. The two-minute rule is designed to help you take action and remove a number of small tasks from your task list. This habit delights you with the satisfaction of completion, entices you with the temptation of further cheap thrills and seduces you with its ease and speed.

Here are some suggestions for things you can do in two minutes:

- Reply to an email.
- Make a phone call.
- Wash your cup and plate after lunch.
- Clear your desk after work.
- Put out the trash bins.
- Stick the laundry in the washing machine.
- File a document.

Start practising the two-minute rule and you'll feel a greater sense of achievement; you'll stop putting off the simple things and create the momentum to keep moving.

Trying the ten-minute rule

Many years ago, I was feeling frustrated and underachieved. There was so much I wanted to do, create and be, but all of it seemed so far from my reach. A great friend of mine gave me some sound advice, which I have used many times since, 'Ten minutes a day will get it done'. I took her advice, and from it I wrote my first book *Chaos to Control.*

My ten-minute rule has helped me to start the habit of exercise, the habit of meditation and the habit of writing.

Procrastinators often suffer from inertia – the inability to move or to act. Isaac Newton said that an object in motion will tend to stay in motion, so if you can take action with the ten-minute rule, you can create the momentum to keep things going. Making a start is always the most difficult part; after that, the wind will carry you home.

Saying no to perfectionism

Are you a perfectionist? If you're like me, most definitely not, you can skip over this bit. If you are, read on. Do you like to do things properly? Like really well? Do you loathe moving on to a new task when the first one hasn't been completed to your satisfaction?

I'm not a perfectionist, but I live with one. In my world, it doesn't take five hours to clean a car or three hours to clean a kitchen. In my world, these tasks take minutes. But living with a perfectionist, I see the pitfalls daily. If you spend a lot of time completing a task to the highest standard, unfortunately there won't be too much time left over to get things done. A further downside of taking more time than the average Joe is that you see a task as being much bigger or taking more time than the rest of us. You are, therefore, more likely to procrastinate, feeling the magnitude of the work to be done. Some perfectionists wait for the ideal moment to complete a task by putting it off sometimes for irrational amounts of time.

But enough about the problem; what you want to know is what you can you do about it, right? The next few sections suggest ways to kick procrastination where it hurts and bounce into action.

Keeping sight of the big picture

Be clear about your end objective or your desired outcome of a task, and ask yourself if the level of detail you're pursuing is necessary. Do you need to add the extra layer of wax or clean those cupboards once again?

In a work environment, get clear on the standards required. So often, extra work goes unrecognised and unappreciated. Make sure what you're working on is contributing to the overall goals.

Staying clear about priorities

Understanding your goals and then your daily and weekly priorities will help you judge how much time you can afford to spend on any one task. Spend time working on a goal plan, and outline your monthly priorities. Each week, take an hour to review your week. In this time, you can think about the priorities for the week ahead.

Using your calendar to stay on track

In your weekly review time, schedule your week in advance and create time for these priorities in your calendar. By taking some time in advance to think about how long a task should take, you're more likely to try to stick to the time allocated and not spend too much time on the detail.

Allowing yourself to fail

It may take some time to get used to doing things differently, but you won't improve unless you try. Trying and failing is much better than never having tried. Permit yourself to fail, and expect it. If you try to lower your standards, you may drop them too much to start, but you'll find the balance eventually.

Understanding the trade-off

There is always a trade-off. When you spend more time on one thing, you're neglecting something else. If you stay at work late to finish some work, does your child go to bed without a bedtime story? If you put the cherry on top of your monthly report, does your other work suffer? Don't bury your head in the sand. If you are being a perfectionist, something or someone else is doing without.

Parkinson's Law

The term *Parkinson's Law* first appeared in 1955 when historian and author C Northcote Parkinson wrote an article for *The Economist* in which he described the phenomena of Parkinson's Law: 'Work expands to fill the time available for its completion'. He later put his theories into a book titled *Parkinson's Law 1957,* which opens with the proverb: 'It's the busiest man who has time to spare'.

Using Parkinson's Law to your advantage

Have you ever heard of Parkinson's Law? It essentially says, 'Work expands to fill the time available for its completion'. That means that if you have a day to do a job, it will take a day; if you have a week, the same job will take a week. If, as a perfectionist, you take one hour to complete a task, next time you do it, give yourself half an hour. Working against the clock may be the ideal way to get you to drop some of the perfecting work. Each time you schedule a task, give yourself half the time you normally do and bring Parkinson's Law into play.

Discovering Good Procrastination

Ready to sound smart? Okay, here goes . . .

The word *procrastination* comes from the Latin word *prōcrāstinus* – *prō* is 'in favor of', *crāstinus* is 'of or belonging to tomorrow'.

People's understanding of procrastination is usually negative. It's the postponing of tasks and responsibilities mostly to an irrational level, negatively affecting the normal flow of life and work. People usually assume that the delay will have a negative impact on their lives and the lives of others.

Procrastination doesn't have to be something negative. Putting things off until tomorrow can sometimes be the right decision, allowing you the time to think clearly and rationally. It can also sometimes help you work more efficiently by bulking tasks together or taking time out for more creativity. The trick is to delay or procrastinate for the right reasons and not use the delay as an excuse to be a sloth.

Processing batches for efficiency

An efficient way to manage tasks is to batch them – that is, to collect similar tasks together because they're in the same location or because they're of the same type. For example, although it may sound like a good idea to make all the beds in your house at the same time, it probably makes more sense to tidy each bedroom while you're making the beds to minimise the time you spend relocating from room to room.

Sounds like a no brainer, but you'd be surprised by how many people task switch every day, wasting time changing to the new task and refocusing on what needs to be done. Using your inbox as a to-do list or working from a traditional to-do list are classic examples of task switching. Doing the next task on the list regardless of how long it will take and what input it entails is not the most efficient way to work.

On the other hand, batching similar tasks together cuts down on the time and loss of focus involved in task switching. Postponing tasks relating to a particular project until you aim to work on that project is an efficient use of your time.

Adam Smith discussed the division of labour in manufacturing in his book *The Wealth of Nations,* published in 1776. Division of labour or specialisation leads to increased levels of production due to specialisation and avoids waste of time and effort caused by changing from one task to another. They knew it back then, but people still choose to do things their way, negating the benefit and time saving, either because of lack of planning or for the instant gratification of a tick in a box.

Each time you switch from one task to the next, it's estimated that it takes up to 15 minutes to refocus. Think about how many times you switch between your email, the project you're working on and Facebook? How much focused work do you actually get done in a day?

If you want to benefit from batching work, start by creating separate project lists in your task management tool. Don't respond to emails in the order they come in to your inbox; instead, batch similar work to be done at the same time. It makes a lot of sense, doesn't it?

Slowing down big decisions

Another example of when procrastinating is wise is when you have to make a big decision. Sometimes you need to think quickly, and sometimes you need to think slowly. Big decisions usually benefit from the latter.

Problems can arise in life if you can't make a decision about something important that will affect your future. You second-guess yourself and worry about all the possible outcomes. What if you do it and regret it? What if it's the wrong decision? You may recall a similar situation where a friend or perhaps a family member told you to 'go with your gut' and that your first instinct is the right one. Truth is, that's not always the case. Perhaps your first reaction is one of prejudice, prone to bias and preconceptions about a person or a subject. Would it then be wise to go with your gut?

Taking time to think about things is the best strategy when it comes to big decisions. But don't let it fester in your head. Write it out. The old-fashioned list with pros and cons is a great way to work through a decision. Make sure you plan to put time and attention into your problem, use your full brain power to focus on the issue and assess all the advantages and disadvantages.

Another great piece of advice is to sleep on it. Always give yourself a night to mull over your decisions. Your brain never sleeps, so sleeping on a problem allows your subconscious mind to figure things out overnight.

When it comes to problem solving, procrastination is the sensible thing to do. Taking time out to think things through is generally the wiser approach.

Make sure you set yourself a deadline. Taking time to consider all options is a good idea, but when a decision has to be made and you pass the deadline, you're more likely to make the wrong decision when you're clouded by the stress and anxiety of unmade decisions.

Taking time for creativity

Creative people can often be excellent procrastinators. They wait and wait for the inspiration to take hold and carry them to a promised land. They can lose days and weeks and years waiting – waiting for the right moment, the right idea, or the right time to share their gifts with the world.

Although it's difficult to be creative on demand, millions do it every day; illustrators, authors, designers and developers have to be creative every day, come what may. Would it be useful for these people to wait, to take time out to allow the creativity to flow?

You can allow yourself the luxury of waiting at times, but other times, you just have to show up. Even though your first idea, your first drawing, illustration or design may not be your best, the most creative, innovated and talented people all make a habit of showing up. Show up each day at your computer or your desk, and you're more likely to have that breakthrough idea. Wait for inspiration, and it may never come. Sometimes creativity comes from pure hard work, or as Thomas Edison said, 'To have a great idea, have a lot of them'.

In other words, schedule time each day to do some work. Your inspiration may not come immediately, but the more time you spend working, the more opportunities you give your ideas to come out.

Planning for procrastination

If you're going to procrastinate, what you need to know is how and when to do it. When will it benefit you, and when will it hinder your productivity? Here are some examples of times it may be useful to procrastinate:

- When you have a big decision to make
- When you have a lot of similar work to be done and can batch it together
- When you need time and space to be creative

These examples of procrastination aren't thoughtless and carefree but structured, weighed up and planned.

Choosing your priorities always comes with a trade-off because, in truth, you're always procrastinating. You choose one task to work on by postponing another. You make decisions daily without sometimes being conscious that that is what you are doing. For example, you make simple decisions like these every day:

- Will I finish this report now or answer my emails?
- Will I go for a run now or leave it until this evening?
- Will I make a cup of tea or finish this illustration?

Every minute of every day, you have decisions to make. Most days, these decisions don't cause you any problems because the outcomes aren't life-changing or threatening. You make them with ease, constantly readjusting and reprioritising as the day goes on. The trick is to realise that everything has a trade-off. Procrastination is okay when you've decided that your priority lies elsewhere. It's only when you fail to prioritise correctly, when you choose to procrastinate at the wrong time on the wrong thing, that procrastination becomes something negative.

If you're willing to get organised and to adapt a system to take control of your workload, this should cease to be a problem. The systems and techniques in this book will empower you to take action. They will show you how you can prioritise with ease and hopefully with grace.

Chapter 9

Good Time Management

In This Chapter

- Figuring out how to track your time
- Using prioritising methods to determine what's really important
- Finding ways to manage interruptions

Have you ever felt that there simply aren't enough hours in the day? Or that life is passing you by and there is still so much you want to achieve? Why is it that some people seem to achieve so much more with their time than others? Time management is the process of planning how much time you'll spend on tasks or activities during any given day. The purpose of which is to increase your effectiveness and productivity.

If you want to make more of your time, read on and see how you can become a high achiever by managing your time like a pro.

Keeping Track of It All

Time tracking is the process of noting what you do with your time. Like a lot of things in life, understanding your current position is a good place to start. Being aware of how things currently are will put you in a position to make better decisions about what needs to change. Very often, people are unaware of the real truth. They think they're working as hard as they can, but in fact they waste time on social media or chat a little bit too much with their co-workers. Until you're honest with yourself about what the true picture is, you won't make real progress.

Tracking your time

If you're not currently tracking your time, I recommend that you start today. The benefits of time tracking are numerous, and the effort required is minimal. Whether you're a freelancer, consultant or work for an organisation, time tracking is a tool that should be used by all.

Understanding the current status

When you start to track your time, you get a good overview of what you're currently doing with your time. You may or may not like what you see, but you'll get a bird's-eye view of how you spend your days. You'll be able to assess how much time you spend on any given activity each week. Often people misjudge the amount of time they spend working on a task if they don't write it down. For example, it may feel like I spent all day yesterday writing this book, when in fact I started at 11, took a two-hour lunch break at 12:30, and knocked off early at 4. From working all day to actually working only three hours is a big difference in time. Although you may think this example is extreme, when you start to track your time, you'll see that a lot of time is wasted each day in trivialities, distractions and interruptions.

Helping you to prioritise

After you're clear about how you're currently spending your time, you can measure this against what you should be spending your time on. What are the activities that add value to your day? What work will help you reach your goals? What are the tasks you need to focus on? Are these featuring enough in your daily logs?

Check out Chapter 7 for an exercise that uses the Pareto productivity method. It's designed to help you focus on your priorities. When you spend a little time looking at the real picture, you'll be able to readjust the current situation to get closer to the ideal situation.

Tracking billable hours

For a lot of freelancers, keeping track of hours worked for your client can be difficult. If you don't currently have a formal method of recording hours worked for each client, I can guarantee that you're losing money. If you don't write it down, you'll inevitably forget to bill for some of the work you've done, such as replying to emails, queries or phone calls, or even small tweaks you've made to a project. All these items should add to the total time worked for your client. Time tracking will help ensure that you're accounting for all your hours and being compensated for them, too.

Mapping available hours

Does your team have availability for a new client? How will you know unless you're effectively tracking how they use their time? If you want to ensure that your organisation doesn't sell over capacity or isn't underutilising resources, time tracking is the tool to help you plan your resource usage. You may have one team member working much harder than the rest. Get the true picture, and make clear, informed decisions.

Identifying your profitable clients

With time tracking, you can identify your profitable clients or, more importantly, the unprofitable ones. Which clients are taking up a lot of your time but not paying you enough for doing so? The Pareto Principle discussed in Chapter 7 says that 20 per cent of your clients give you 80 per cent of your revenue. So who are the 80 per cent? Are they worth holding onto as clients? Tracking the time you spend on each of your clients will help you make informed decisions about whether each client is truly profitable or costing too much to service. It's a good idea to regularly assess your clients in this way. If clients aren't profitable, unless they're trophy clients, it may be wiser to let them go, ever so gently.

Understanding work rhythms

You can fight the natural rhythms of life, or you can choose to work with them. Every person has a different work rhythm: some work best in the morning, and some are more productive in the evening. Most organisations have a natural rhythm based on the type of work, the industry expectations and the type of people employed. A young workforce may be slow to start in the morning, producing their best work in the afternoons and evenings, whereas a more middle-aged workforce will tend to be more productive in the morning. Time tracking will help you uncover the rhythm and plan work accordingly.

Tracking your energy

When you start to track your time, you'll build up a picture of how you work each day, what your preferences are for working and at what time of the day you're most productive. Clever people use this information to improve their lives and their circumstances.

If you never produce anything of value before midday, you may need to look at your bedtime routine. Understanding your natural energy and working with it will increase your productivity exponentially.

Moving with circadian rhythms

We all have an internal body clock that dictates when we should sleep and when we should be chirpy and alert. A circadian rhythm is a biological process that prescribes our energy levels throughout the day. Although this information has been available for years, people don't appear to be learning their lesson.

Christopher M. Barnes, an assistant professor of management at the University of Washington's Foster School of Business, explains that most work environments don't allow for natural energy rhythms. Deadlines are often set for the end of a day when workers have spent most of the morning answering emails and going to meetings. The afternoon for most people is a time of low energy, reaching its worst at about 3 p.m. Barnes says that not everyone has the same rhythm. You've probably heard of the early larks and the night owls, but the typical pattern is most common and determines most people's day.

Although most workers would like to work at maximum performance at all times of the day, this is not physically possible for humans. If organisations aren't willing to work with people's natural ebb and flow in productivity or aren't willing to bring in flexitime for one and all, we may have to look at bringing in Battlestar Galactica's Cylons to achieve afternoon productivity.

Learning from your logs

The reality is that everyone has to work through energy slumps and produce work when he's tired and sluggish. But why fight the system? Why not work with your energy and not against? Start by taking note of your most productive times during the day. Do you work best in the morning or evening? Do you have a tendency to waste time in the early part of the day and settle down to get stuff done in the afternoon. If this is your typical day, go with it, plan to do your most cognitive work in the afternoon and plan meetings and administrative work for the morning. If you are the type to focus better early in the morning, don't open your email until you have completed some valuable work. Plan the meetings and low energy work for the afternoon. If you take control of your own energy levels and plan your days according to your own energy levels, think how much more productive you could be.

Using time-tracking tools

Technology has brought a breath of fresh air to the world of time tracking. No longer is it necessary to take a pen and paper and think back on the week to what you were doing on Tuesday at 2 p.m. Although, of course, filling in your time chart on Friday isn't what management had in mind, the reality is that most employees fill in their charts quickly before going home, making the entries somewhat less than accurate. Thankfully, time-tracking software has saved the day.

Time-tracking sheets

If you're a sucker for the traditional and prefer paper timesheets, go for it. You'll still benefit from seeing what exactly you spent your time on throughout the week. To ensure maximum benefit, fill in the timesheet as you complete a job; don't wait until the end of the day and definitely not the end of the week to fill it in.

If you find it difficult to remember to fill in your timesheet, set a reminder or create a poster with the words 'Fill in timesheet' and put it in a prominent position near your desk. You can remove it once you've mastered the habit.

Time-tracking software

Five years ago, I struggled to find a piece of software to track my time; today, there are too many to choose from: Rescue time, Toggl, Harvest, Klok, Project Hamster – I even found one called Freckle, which appealed to my freckled head. There are so many new start-ups popping up each day, it's hard to keep track.

The beauty for the end user is that the time-tracking tools don't just track time, but they also offer invoicing, expense management, and some even offer task management. Most of these tools come at a price, but the time saved from using them will repay any minor cost involved. You'll also notice a natural increase in productivity from using a time-tracking tool. When you track your time, and become more aware of how you currently spend your time, you will become empowered to make the changes required for increased personal productivity.

Remembering that your time costs money

How much is your time worth? It's important to know how much your time is worth and what exactly you are getting paid to do. When you understand what your time is worth, you will be less likely to waste time or to spend your time on work that could be done by others. If you are employed for your expertise in selling, you shouldn't be using your time improving HR policies. Too many people waste too much time doing work that belongs to others or that they could be paying someone else to do. Get clear on how much your time is worth, and either outsource or delegate the work that you shouldn't be doing.

Take a look at your 'stop-doing list' (see Chapter 7), and make sure you're making the most of your time. If you find you don't have enough hours in the day, you can probably stop doing some things to free up time for more interesting achievements. Your time is precious and, as you well know, very limited. Don't waste your valuable time doing things that you don't need to do or, even more importantly, that shouldn't be done at all.

Prioritising

Prioritisation is to plan tasks that need to be attended to in order of their relative importance. Understanding what is priority in a world where everything is urgent and needs to be done yesterday is difficult for many people and is one of the biggest complaints I hear from busy teams in organisations. Figuring out what requires your attention is a skill and, once acquired, will stay with you for the rest of your life. In this section, I discuss a few models to help you prioritise. But before you choose a model, you need get the basics right.

First, get rid of the work that doesn't add value. Don't waste your time doing things that don't need to be done. The perfectionist is one who spends time double-checking and reworking to ensure precision, and although attention to detail is a positive trait, spending too much time on the finishing touches can be time misused. Often people spend too much time creating systems and procedures but no time on the actual work they are getting paid to do.

Simplify your life by doing only what you need to do. When you reduce the quantity of things you need to do, it will be easier to see the wood from the trees or the daisies from the weeds and focus on what truly needs done.

Next, you can't prioritise correctly if you're unclear of your goals or your company's goals. Your priority is to reach your goals. If you're working on stuff that doesn't help you get closer to your goals, guess what? You're wasting your time. Your priorities appear in the place where your daily tasks overlap your goals. Most people work in a way similar to that shown in Figure 9-1.

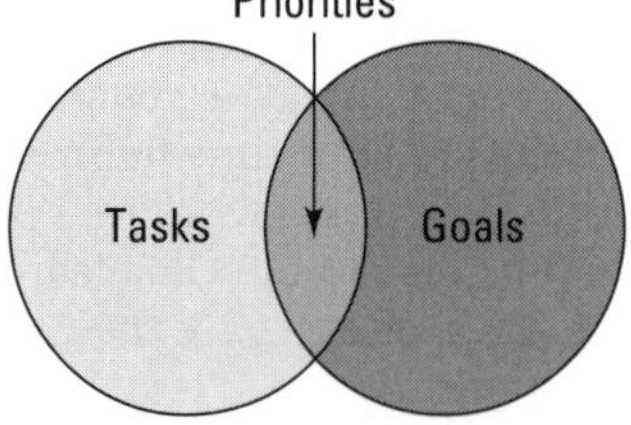

Figure 9-1: Daily tasks not aligned with goals.

In this example, only a small amount of daily tasks overlap the goals, which means that a minimal amount of priorities are being worked on daily. This isn't a good scenario because too many tasks are thankless tasks, tasks with no true value.

In Figure 9-2, you can see that the majority of tasks tackled each day are tasks that are aligned to the overall goals. In this scenario, priorities are being worked on as part of the day to day.

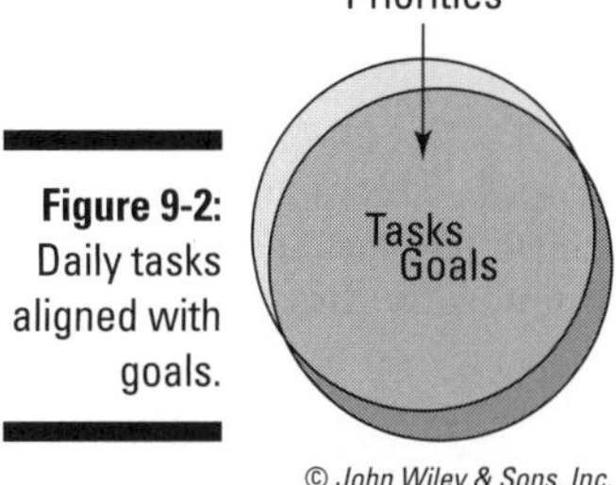

Figure 9-2: Daily tasks aligned with goals.

© John Wiley & Sons, Inc.

When goals are communicated through an organisation, employees are much clearer on priorities. If workers are unsure what the organisational vision is, you can be guaranteed they don't know which project takes precedence over the next. Spend time clarifying and communicating goals to ensure clarity for all workers. Keep goals visible and current so that priorities become apparent, and productivity and positivity rise.

If you're a manager, verify job goals and responsibilities. Make sure everyone on your team is clear about what is expected of him or her. When errors happen, check back to ensure that it wasn't due to uncertainty in this area. For yourself, make sure you're clear about what is expected of you. When you're unsure about whether something is your responsibility or not, clear it up with your own boss.

Winning with the Eisenhower matrix

Dwight D. Eisenhower, the 34th president of the United States of America, was a master of time management. He once said, 'What is important is seldom urgent, and what is urgent is seldom important'. People often misinterpret what is urgent and what is important. Making a clear distinction between the two can help you prioritise and make better decisions.

Urgent means something that should be done now, not later and definitely not tomorrow, but right now or else somebody's head will drop off. Urgent happens when you're in reactive mode, and it's usually in response to someone else's demands and goals, the urgency usually highlighted by another person.

Typical urgent tasks can come in the form of

- Incoming phone calls
- Emails from customers
- Most interruptions
- All bosses' requests

Important tasks can generally be connected to your longer-term goals. You understand and know it's importance and therefore plan for its inclusion in your day. Important tasks can become urgent, but generally they're not.

Typical important tasks include

- Scheduling
- Budgeting
- Exercising
- Attending strategy meetings

Unfortunately, the world of information overload has clouded people's understanding of what constitutes urgent or important, and people behave like everything urgent is important, and that isn't the case. You can use the Eisenhower matrix to take a step back and understand the differences between what's urgent and important; check it out in Figure 9-3.

	URGENT	LESS URGENT
IMPORTANT	Do first/Today tasks	Schedule this work
LESS IMPORTANT	Tasks to be delegated	Does it need to be done at all?

Figure 9-3: The Eisenhower matrix.

Write a list of all the things you need to do (if you don't already have it written down). Assign each task to a quadrant in the matrix:

- Important and Urgent
- Important and Less urgent
- Urgent and Less important
- Less urgent and Less important

When you identify where each task resides, you can decide what you need to do by reading the next sections.

Important and urgent

Important and urgent tasks need to be done straightaway, today if possible. It may be useful to use a timer to help you to focus and get the job done on time. Take a look at the Pomodoro Technique in Chapter 11. Moving forward, you may want to try to plan and schedule these tasks better so that they don't have to become urgent. If these are generally tasks delegated to you by your manager, discuss it with her and suggest that next time you're given more notice so that you can schedule your work better.

Important and less urgent

Important tasks are all the things that will help you get closer to your goals. This is the work that you know in advance needs to be done and should be scheduled in your calendar. In an ideal world, most of your important work should reside in this quadrant, but this isn't always the case. You'll often find your life goals in this quadrant. Important but never acted on. This is why the items that ended up in this zone should be scheduled and planned. No more procrastinating; time to make progress and get your goals.

Urgent and less important

This is the zone in which most people spend most of their day, reacting to emails, phone calls and interruptions. None of it is important, but all of it is urgent and generally other people's priorities. Spending more time planning and scheduling your important tasks will help you limit the amount of time and attention you give to these sorts of tasks. Your calendar will help you to prioritise your work and make better decisions around what you need to do with your time. These may also be tasks that you can delegate to others (if you're lucky enough to be in a position to delegate) or outsource to free you up for the important and urgent stuff.

Less urgent and less important

You mean people actually spend time doing these tasks? Yep, they sure do, not me, of course, but other people. These are the time-wasting tasks, the types of tasks you do to avoid the important and urgent tasks you don't feel like doing – surfing the net, trawling twitter, thinking you're engaging in digital marketing or 'networking' at the water cooler. These tasks should be saved for your downtime, your personal time after all your urgent and important tasks are done for the day.

Try out the Eisenhower app, go to `www.eisenhower.me/` and download the app, which can help you to prioritise your tasks each day. It also comes with a Pomodoro timer to help you to focus until the task is done. You can read more on the Pomodoro Technique in Chapter 11.

Using an action priority matrix

The *action priority matrix* is another matrix that you can use to decide which projects merit your time and attention and which should be dropped. The reality of life is that you have limited time; therefore, you have to make sacrifices.

The action priority matrix helps you make decisions about what to focus your attention on and what to throw in the ditch. This exercise is an antidote to the 'so little time, so much to do' crisis everyone suffers from. The tool hinges on impact and effort.

As you can see in Figure 9-4, four areas exist in the matrix:

- **Quick wins:** Quick wins are high impact, low effort. These are the projects you want more of. They give you a good return for relatively little effort. Focus on these when possible.
- **Major projects:** These are in the high-impact, high-effort category. They have big impact but unfortunately are usually long and take a lot of effort. Major projects often drown out possibilities of innovation or quick wins as everyone's total commitment and effort is invested in the major project.
- **Fill ins:** The fill ins are low impact and low effort. They're not worth putting time or attention into. If you have time to waste, you may choose to do a fill in; if not, drop it.
- **Hard slogs:** Nobody likes a hard slog, low impact with high effort. If you find yourself engaged in a hard slog, take some time out and go find a quick win or a major project. Your time is more precious than that.

Score your projects on the activity priority graph from 0 to 10, 0 being minimum impact and minimum effort and 10 being maximum impact and maximum effort. Using this matrix gives you a good overview of current projects in progress and helps you to figure out what is worth your time and effort and what is ready for the dump.

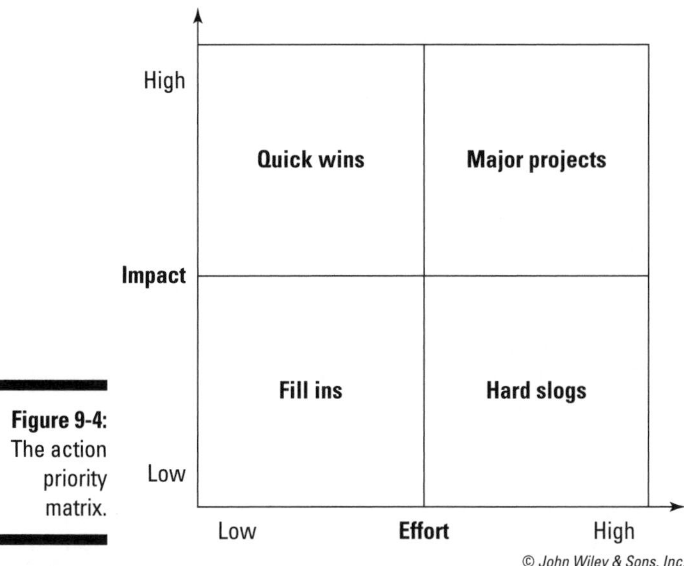

Figure 9-4: The action priority matrix.

Using these prioritisation tools is a great way to stop and reassess your current work and responsibilities. Taking time to look at the big picture every now and again ensures maximum productivity and efficiency. Too often when you're busy trying to get things done, you fail to look up and see things as they really are. Prioritising becomes a lot easier when you take the time to get organised.

A weekly planning session will improve your ability to reprioritise on the go during the week. Every day the priorities will change, and you'll need to reassess. When you do, you'll be surprised how easy prioritisation becomes once you have spent some time understanding your goals, roles and responsibilities.

Managing Interruptions

The biggest frustration of working life: interruptions. How can I focus like a monk with all the monkeys jumping from tree to tree? Trying to focus in an environment of interruptions is difficult. Whether you're interrupted and need to reprioritise what you're working on or interrupted and go back to the same task, your focus has been disturbed. Some studies show that it takes up to 15 minutes to regain your focus after being disturbed.

So how can you manage interruptions more effectively? Read on.

Interruptions from people

If you work in an open-plan office, chances are interruptions are part of your day to day. Knowing how to manage interruptions effectively should be high on your agenda (if you have an agenda). Here are a few things you can try to minimise the dreaded, 'Have you got a minute?'

Tell them not to disturb you

Don't knock it 'til you try it. Sometimes it's as simple as letting people know you don't want to be disturbed that does the job. Make a simple Do Not Disturb sign and stick it to the back of your computer screen. Make a bunch of funky signs and pin them all over your desk. Whatever way you tackle it, just let the people know you are out of touch.

Use earphones

Using earphones can be a more subtle way to tell the masses that you're busy concentrating on something more important than them. Stick your earphones in and escape the outside world. Even better are headphones, as they ensure even the hard of sight don't miss the fact that you're plugged in.

Let them know

Even more direct than the Do Not Disturb sign, just let them know. Let your co-workers know how much interruptions effect your workflow; chances are they all feel the same way. Speak to management. It's always better to address the subject than suffer in silence. Unless of course the problem is your manager; then suffer in silence.

Leave the area

If possible, move away from your desk, go to a meeting room or a coffee shop or work from home. In some work environments, there may be no break from the interruptions other than getting up and moving away. It's up to you to take control and change things if they aren't working for you.

Shut the door

If you're lucky enough to have four walls and a door, use the door. Even if you're a manager and want to give the impression of always being available, sometimes it's necessary to close the door. Let your team know when it's okay to disturb you. Remind them that you have work to get to also.

Plan for interruptions

If you have to accept interruptions as part of your job title, try to plan for them a bit better. Plan to do your important work early in the morning before the majority of people arrive in the office so that when they come knocking you feel a little more in control having got some work done.

Get a new job

When you've tried everything possible and things aren't getting any better, it may be time to consider saying adios. The choice is yours: you can sit in misery each day, not getting your work done, or you can move to pastures that are greener and hopefully a lot quieter.

Interruptions from technology

Technology can also be guilty (if it had emotions) of interrupting your focus and concentration. IMs, emails, phone calls, alerts, tweets and more interrupt people daily with urgent trivia. If you want to remove all the interruptions from your life, you must consider this side of the coin.

Switch off notifications

Block the interruptions from social media and email by turning off all notifications of messages, posts, tweets and so on. See Chapter 15 for more information on switching off notifications.

Batch process email

Don't leave your email open all day long. Schedule times during the day to batch process your email. Spend a half hour to an hour about four times a day to work through your email, replying to shorter emails and planning the work to be done in larger emails.

Don't 'reply all'

If you want to minimise your email, don't clutter up other people's inboxes. Don't reply all unless required. Reduce the number of times you cc multiple people and include only people in an email who really need to be part of it.

Making interruptions a thing of the past

Managing interruptions is about taking control. It's about making decisions to improve your work environment and making work work for you.

Take time to assess the source of the interruptions and have a think about what changes you can make to minimise these interruptions. Here are a few of my own possible solutions:

- **Task management:** There are many software tools that can improve communications by sharing tasks and minimising time spent discussing tasks and responsibilities.
- **Calendar sharing:** Share calendars for openness and transparency. If you populate your calendar and share it, you'll remove the necessity of questions around your movements or availability.
- **Document sharing:** An internal document management system will ensure that all company documentation is stored in an efficient way. This will reduce the possibility of interruptions looking for internal information.
- **Internal memos:** Work events, announcements, and information can be circulated with internal memos.

These are just a few examples of possible solutions for your interruptions. Don't take this lightly, and take the time to find the source of yours. Managing the route of your interruptions will have a major impact on your and your team's productivity.

Chapter 10

Getting Things Done (GTD)

In This Chapter

- Getting to grips with GTD
- Making GTD work for you
- Exploring some GTD tools

Getting Things Done (GTD) is a productivity method helping people manage all the things they have to do each day. Created by productivity guru David Allen, it was designed to give people a way to handle all their to-dos, tasks, responsibilities and ideas in an effective and productive manner.

Not for the faint-hearted, GTD is a detailed system with a structure for everything – it even has a place for your spare underpants. If you invest the time in implementing this system and learn its ways, the rewards will stay with you long after the spare pants do.

Introducing the GTD Workflow

The GTD method pivots around a workflow system to manage your daily tasks, responsibilities and projects so that they all get air time and ultimately get done.

The concept is based on five pillars, or steps, that you need to stay focused, productive and organised. The five steps are as follows:

- **Capture.** Start by collecting everything that needs to get done.
- **Clarify.** Decide what 'it' is and what needs to be done with it.
- **Organise.** Plan it for action.
- **Reflect.** Review frequently.
- **Engage.** Take action.

Understanding your 'stuff'

David Allen, author of *Getting Things Done* (Piatkus, 2002), defines stuff as 'Anything you have allowed into your psychological or physical world that doesn't belong where it is, but for which you haven't yet determined the desired outcome and the next action step'. Stuff relates to all the things floating around in your head: ideas, tasks and dreams. The Getting Things Done system helps you to get everything out of your head and into your system so that the stuff, as well as the work that you have to do, gets tackled and done.

Capturing

Capturing the work needing your attention is the first phase of an effective workflow. This may be the daily work that needs doing or a personal project that you want to undertake. Capturing your intention is the first step. To-dos, responsibilities and priorities sometimes wander around in your head, taking processing space from your brain. The aim is to get it out of your brain and into your system so that you can process it at the right time.

At this stage, how you capture the work isn't important, as long as you capture it. Your system for capturing your work to do should be so easy that you never shy away from it. If you have to boot up your computer and type in a password, open a program and add a task, chances are you won't do it. On the other hand, simply jotting down a note in a notebook or adding a task to an app on your phone has a much higher chance of success.

Capturing includes the paperwork, the emails and any other format work that comes at you.

Clarifying

If you don't clarify what needs to be done, you won't get very far. Writing down 'Plan project' doesn't tell you exactly what you need to do and how long it's going to take to do it. Instead, identify the next thing that has to happen for the project to move forward, such as 'Schedule meeting with all stakeholders re: project initiation'.

It's much easier to prepare for and complete tasks that have a clear outcome. This phase of the workflow is important for things to flow effectively and to avoid any blockages to moving things forward.

To avoid procrastination and overwhelming yourself, clarify the tasks you need to do. Unclarified tasks are ripe for procrastination.

Organising

If your tasks and responsibilities are clarified as shown previously, organising them for action becomes easier. This phase is about scheduling and planning the work that needs to be done. It's about prioritising and understanding what needs a reminder and what needs to be done straightaway.

This phase is where you try to find a place for everything, a holding bay, until it's time to surface and get the job done. You'll schedule some things in your calendar, planning for a time over the next week or two when you want to have the work complete. For some items, you'll assign a strict deadline and an allocated time to get them done. There may be other tasks that may need to be done as part of a project. These tasks can be added to a project list to be worked on at a later time.

It's a good idea to store all the similar to-dos together so that when you're ready to work on a particular project, you have all the items to be done together and ready to go. Create a separate tasks list for each project. If you are using Outlook tasks, create different categories. If using Google tasks, create different lists.

Reflecting

Things don't always go as planned. You create a wonderful schedule, but then some inconsiderate soul interrupts your plan! A customer calls or a manager beckons, and your perfect plan falls apart. To make GTD work, you need to regularly reflect on what you have planned.

Reprioritising is part of life. Reassess whether yesterday's priorities remain today's. Regularly look at the big picture and ensure that your priorities and goals remain the same.

Engaging

And now the work begins! Choose your next action and get going. This is the time the work actually gets done.

When starting out with GTD, or any new productivity system, keep engaging with the work; otherwise, you run the risk of spending too much time organising and categorising and not enough time actually doing any work. This is what productivity expert Mike Vardy refers to as 'doing productive' and not 'being productive'. This is a trap we all fall into when we search for apps and software to make us more productive. We tweak and organise to make it just right, and we spend far too little time engaging with the work that needs to be done.

Understanding the Capture Tools

Capturing all the work you need to do is your starting point. Some of your work is captured for you automatically, like emails in your inbox. Other work comes at you from your mind and more still from your boss (if you have one). You need to have a system for effectively capturing this work in a way that will keep you in control of all your to-dos.

Your email inbox

Your email inbox kindly captures all the work you need to do via email. It does this unselfishly and gives over so much space for the collection of your work – how kind!

Unfortunately, your email inbox isn't fussy; it allows spammers space in your inbox along with sales reps, charities, friends and family. But this is okay if you help them all move along. Because what you need to know is that your inbox is not a place for storing emails; it's a place for collecting them. After you've processed them and told them where to go (quite literally, in the case of the spammers), you can then focus more clearly on clarifying and organising the work to be done.

Get into the habit of looking at the emails that arrive just once. Make a decision about what needs to be done and remove the email from your inbox. You may need to plan some work in your calendar or add a new task to your tasks list. Keep making decisions and work toward a clutter-free inbox.

Read more on email management in Chapter 15.

The handy notebook

Old school! Capturing your work to be done on paper is probably the simplest and maybe the most effective.

Carrying a notebook or piece of paper with you allows you to capture any task, responsibility or idea when you think of it. It also ensures that you never forget about anything and that you're not reminded about things that you need to do at the most inappropriate times. Getting things out of your head is a core concept to Getting Things Done. Getting them out of your head and into an effective and efficient system is a massive step in the right direction.

Your in-tray

An in-tray is the place on your desk for unprocessed paper. What's unprocessed paper? It's the paper that you haven't decided what needs to be done with yet. It's stuff you need to do something with, but it may not be scheduled or planned.

Keep all your unprocessed paper in your in-tray. As you process this paper, you make a decision on what needs to be done with it. It may be actionable and have a task attached to it. In this case, you may need to file it in a current project folder on your desk. You may need to file it for reference, or it may just need to be shredded or recycled. Keep only two trays on your desk, one for 'Work In', the unprocessed stuff, and one for 'Filing'.

Find out more about filing in Chapter 12.

Voice mails

Work is sometimes captured on voice mail. People leave messages, sometimes asking you to do stuff but more often than not just asking you to call them back. Returning phone calls can be just as much a chore as any other tasks, and you'll need to be reminded to make these calls.

Capture voice mails by writing down all the calls you need to make so that you don't have to rely on your memory to call people back. Keeping a separate list for calls to make when you're in the position to make calls can be very useful. In Getting Things Done lingo, this is called *context* – tasks to do when you're in a particular place, at a particular time or at a particular level of energy. You can read more on context later in this chapter.

Voice notes

Voice notes are another way to capture thoughts or ideas. A voice recorder is a handy tool you can use to record your own voice, and it's often the quickest way to capture a thought, idea or task. Often, people forget to process voice notes. Allen suggests handling this by placing your voice recorder in your in-tray to remind you that you have voice notes to process.

If your voice notes are on your phone, make sure you add your voice notes into your normal system. Whether you use a journal or an electronic tasks programme, you want to make sure your notes find their way into your normal system and don't get forgotten about.

Knowing the Organising Tools

After you capture your work, you need to clarify and organise it. Organising your work is the difference between an effective and efficient system and chaos. Having a system you can trust is paramount for real personal productivity.

Your calendar

A calendar may seem like the most basic piece of kit but is actually a crucial part of your system. Scheduling and planning your work is how your work gets done.

Having an up-to-date calendar that you use not only for storing meetings and appointment but also for planning the work that you need to do will help you to overcome procrastination and enable you to get a lot more work done.

Use a calendar for stuff that needs to be done on or by a particular date or time. Entering it into your calendar and not a task management app enables you to get a visual picture of all the stuff you need to get done over the next couple of weeks. Having this visual view of your workload helps to plan and prioritise all that needs to get done.

The task management system

The second part of your organising system is your task management tool. There's plenty of choice, from Outlook Tasks, part of Outlook in the Microsoft Office Suite, to apps like Omnifocus and Evernote.

The most important thing to consider when choosing a task management system is whether you can use it with the GTD methodology. You want a system that is compatible with all your devices. Not all task management systems are PC- and Mac-compatible, with some only developed for iPhone and not Android. Consider all these factors before deciding on your task management system. Later in this chapter, you can find more information on some of the most popular systems used for GTD.

Checking Out the Core GTD Concepts

There are many powerful techniques that make up the GTD system but following are some of the core concepts. These are the most valued parts of the model that make the advocates of GTD longstanding and loyal followers. GTD has the power to transform lives and listed in this section are some of the simple techniques that allow that to happen.

Out of your head

In the book *Getting Things Done* (Piatkus, 2002), David Allen likens the human brain to overloaded computer RAM. He explains that people go around with their minds overloaded with things to do:

> The short term memory part of the mind – the part that tends to hold all of the incomplete, undecided and unorganised 'stuff' – functions like a RAM on a personal computer. As with the RAM, there's limited capacity. There is only so much stuff you can store in there and still have that part of your brain function at a high level.

Get things out of your head regularly with a mind dump. Take a pen and paper and start dumping everything you need to do. Put everything down, from small to-dos to the largest goals you want to achieve.

Don't try to format the items or separate them into personal tasks and work tasks, just allow them to pour out of your head as they come. Doing it in this manner allows a flow of unrestricted thoughts and tasks. It ensures that you don't forget about anything and that you capture everything. After you're done, you can then clarify and organise the items for action. (Go to Chapter 4 to find out how you can process your mind dump.)

The mind dump helps to prevent the stress and overwhelming feeling that comes from having too much on your mind. This ensures that you continue to get as much work done as you possibly can. You can later add the items from your mind dump to your calendar or task management programme. Getting them onto paper is only the first step to helping you free your mind from worry and stress.

Make the mind dump part of your weekly review session (read more on the weekly review later in this chapter). By doing it once a week, you'll keep things up-to-date and free your mind from the responsibility of remembering all that you need to do.

Do a mind dump right now: go fetch a piece of paper or notebook and a pen. Take some time on your own and write down all the tasks, responsibilities and stuff you want to do. *Remember:* don't try to format it at this stage – that comes later. Keep working until you feel you have exhausted all the ideas in your head. Each week that you do this download, you'll find less and less stuff to dump. Each week, you'll reduce the amount of things that you're storing in your mind, and you'll naturally move toward adding items to your calendar and tasks list as you think of them rather than leaving them ruminating in your mind.

Horizons of focus

Being productive and effective with your time on a day-to-day basis takes more than just organising your daily tasks and dealing with your email. What a lot of people fail to do is to shift their focus from today to the bigger picture.

This is what David Allen refers to as *horizons of focus*. Your daily focus is one thing, but if you're not clear about the higher purpose, your daily focus is likely to be blurred and unclear. Allen describes six horizons of focus in his book *Getting Things Done.* These horizons are agreements that you have with yourself; each has a different time horizon and impact on your life. Allen uses an airplane analogy to explain your life from ground level up. Check out the nearby sidebar 'Horizons of focus: Where to start' for help getting off to a flying start.

The runway

The runway is your ground level, akin to your day-to-day responsibilities and demands. The runway is often the area where people get bogged down because they have so much they have to deal with from the moment they wake up to the moment they go to bed. These are your next actions from the context of GTD. The problem is, the runway is often so cluttered with things to do and next actions that you may not get the chance to look up and rarely do you take flight to the next level.

The 10,000 feet level

The 10,000 feet level is your projects, all the projects that create your next actions. They're the tasks and daily to-dos that occupy your day. Projects in the GTD sense can be defined as anything that takes more than one action to complete. So this could include anything from organising a birthday party to installing a new customer relationship database in your organisation. Many people have many projects on the go that they haven't fully identified.

The 20,000 feet level

The 20,000 feet level consists of your areas of responsibilities. What are you responsible for in your job, family and community? Understanding these responsibilities ensures that you have a clear picture of all the projects that is your duty to begin or complete. This level usually consists of your 90-day goals. Ninety-day goals usually consist of short-term projects that need completion in each of your areas of focus.

The 30,000 feet level

At this next level are your areas of focus, or where your life is going. Everyone has areas of responsibility and things that he should do, but what about the things that you want to do, the future projects and goals that you want to achieve? What new projects would you like to be working on?

The 40,000 feet level

At 40,000 feet, the focus is on goals. What is the big picture? These are the goals that affect your job, your company or your future development. Where is your company headed? What do you want to achieve in the long term? In your personal world, what do you want your life to look like in five years? When you think at this level, you'll undoubtedly think of new projects you want to undertake and new actions to move toward achieving them.

The 50,000 feet level

This is the big one – your purpose. Why are you on this planet? What were you put here to do? Are you in the right job? Are you living in the right place? Are you working too hard and neglecting your family commitments? The answers to these questions shape your life for the future, so it's important to put some time into thinking about the 50,000 feet level.

Horizons of focus: Where to start?

Some people like to start with the 50,000 feet level, understanding why they were put on this planet and deciding on the big-picture plan according to their purpose. It makes sense. The problem with that is a lot of people are so cluttered with the day to day. A lot of runways are so overloaded with stuff that there is nowhere for the airplane to even taxi, never mind take off. For this reason, the best place to start is with clearing the clutter from your life – that is, the physical clutter that gets in the way of both your thinking and your action. After you get the physical mess a little tidier, you can then take a two-pronged approach. Working a little at runway level to keep things ticking over while going to 50,000 feet to figure out whether what you're busy with each day has purpose. Does the daily grind tie in with your higher raison d'etre?

After you've defined all your horizons of focus, review them at each weekly review. Very briefly cast your eye over them to ensure that everything you do for the coming week ties in with your objectives and goals. Once a month, you can spend more time on your review. At your monthly review, you can take some time to refocus, to be sure that you're still headed in the right direction.

Next actions

Actually getting work done involves doing the next action required in the project.

In David Allen's view, everything you do or need to do can be reduced down to the next action required to move toward getting it done:

> You can't do a project . . . you can only do an action related to it. Many actions require only a minute or two, in the appropriate context, to move a project forward.

For example, painting the guest room can't be done until you first decide on a colour. When you decide on the colour, you must then go shopping for the paint. A project like painting a room doesn't happen all at once; it happens with a series of next actions.

The beauty of the next action is that it discourages from procrastination. If you think of your projects in terms of next actions, you can focus on a smaller piece of the project each time, avoiding the overwhelming feeling or the inability to take on a larger project.

Think about a project in terms of, 'What is the very next action I need to do to get this project started?' If that next task is to make a phone call or to send an email, do that action. When you get started, it's easier to keep going, or, as Isaac Newton said many years ago, an object in motion is more likely to stay in motion. After you overcome the inertia of not getting started, you'll be on a roll.

The next-action part of GTD also helps you clarify what exactly you need to do with an item. You'll often find things on your to-do list that are fuzzy, such as, 'Do something about website'. If you think of items in terms of next actions, you can define the to-do more clearly and thus work through your lists more quickly and efficiently.

Begin defining next actions with physical verbs. Using physical verbs helps you gain more clarity about what your final outcome is. What exactly do you want to achieve from the next action? The following list gives you an insight into single action verbs and ensures that your clearly defined next actions get done.

- Buy
- Call
- Find
- Organise
- Print
- Review
- Take

When you start to use the next-action thinking in meetings, you'll begin to have better outcomes. Meetings are often unproductive and inefficient because people spend hours discussing and debating a subject only to leave the conversation unresolved until the next meeting. The degree of follow-up actions is generally poor in most organisations. Lots of money is wasted daily from inefficient meetings.

A way to avoid this waste of time and money is to close every agenda item with the question, 'What is the next action, and who is going to do it?' This forces clarity and accountability for every topic of conversation. Use this question at your meetings, and say goodbye to inefficient meetings You'll be ticking stuff off your to-do list like a roadrunner (although apparently coyotes are faster than roadrunners, so you'll actually be ticking stuff off your to-do list like a coyote).

Contexts

Rarely will you manage to do everything on your to-do list there and then. Maybe you don't have the correct tools that you need, or it could be because you aren't close to a person required to assist you with the task, or perhaps you simply don't have the right amount of energy. This opens the door for what David Allen describes as contexts. He suggests that if you put a context to all your tasks, you move through your work more efficiently and more rapidly.

Why worry about doing your taxes when you don't have all the receipts with you? What's the point in thinking about gardening when you're still at the office? What benefit is there in thinking about making phone calls when you're in a formal meeting? Many times you think or worry unnecessarily about work that can't be done because you don't have the appropriate context.

Productivity expert Mike Vardy defines contexts as 'add[ing] value to your tasks so that you can connect with them better. This allows you to use them to work on your tasks and projects through different lenses'.

Creating lists according to contexts can help make your task management much more efficient. Here are a few contexts to get you started:

- Calls
- Computer
- Errands
- Home
- Office
- Waiting for lists for projects

Other possible contexts could be based on time or energy:

- Low energy
- High energy
- After lunch
- Early morning
- 10-minute tasks

You can choose from a million possible contexts. When you find the ones that work for you, stick to less than a dozen; otherwise, you'll confuse yourself and lose the power of using contexts.

Projects

Projects can be defined as anything you need to get done in the next couple of weeks or months that requires more than one step to complete. David Allen reckons that people have at least 30 to 100 projects on the go at any one time. Defining a project and creating a project list ensures that the project continues to get forward motion. If you were to define only next actions, there's a chance you wouldn't schedule a follow-up action. Not having a natural place to look for your project's next action, you'd be at risk of delaying the project or, worse, forgetting about it altogether.

When you have a project list, you can add any tasks that you think of at any time. Any emails that come into your inbox that are associated with the project get immediately added to your project list and taken out of your inbox. When you add them to the project list, you no longer have to think about them. Then, when it's time to work on the project or to schedule a next action, you can check your project list and you have everything where you need it.

When defining projects, use physical verbs, such as the following:

- Design
- Finalise
- Handle
- Implement
- Resolve
- Submit

Reconnecting and Reflecting: The Weekly Review

The weekly review is the time you set aside each week to ensure that you stay organised and that nothing slips through the cracks. This is an essential part of the Getting Things Done methodology, a time when you work *on* your system rather than *in* your system. Your weekly review gives you an overview of where you are and where you're going.

The weekly review is your time to reconnect with your goals, your purpose and your projects. It's a time to refocus and to reassure yourself that all that you're working on is connecting you to your end goals. The review ensures that you're working on the right things and that you haven't forgotten about anything. It helps you to create a plan for what needs to get done in the week ahead.

Schedule a recurring appointment in your calendar to do a weekly review. The first couple of times you do your review, you may require an hour and a half or two hours to complete it. After you've done it for a couple of weeks and get into the swing of things, an hour should suffice.

Don't spend your review time actually doing work. You'll be tempted to complete some actions as you review your work, but if you fall into this trap, you won't complete a successful review and you won't be as organised as you can be for the coming week.

The review can be broken down into several parts, as outlined in the following sections.

Email

Process your email to stay on top of things; check out the following options for the best way to handle emails.

Delete

Delete as many emails as possible. If you've read it and don't need to keep the information, delete it. Don't keep emails for 'just in case'. Filing emails away takes them out of sight but doesn't take them out of mind; your subconscious mind always knows they're there until the day IT contacts you and says you're over capacity or you miss an email because your server rejected it.

Get friendly with the delete button. You'll find that you rarely need to look back at all the emails you've stored over the years.

File

File any emails that you really need to keep. For example, maybe you need to keep records of important conversations or crucial information for your organisation.

Keep as many folders as you need but as few as possible. Avoid subfolders, which make finding the folder you're looking for trickier and more time-consuming.

Implement the two-minute rule

When you're processing your email and you come across an email that you can deal with in less than two minutes, do it right then. The two-minute rule allows you to actually get some work done as you process your email. These are the only emails that you're allowed to tackle while you're doing your review, though. Refrain from answering any emails that will take you longer to craft a reply to.

Take action

Create an Action folder where you dump all actionable emails while you're processing your email. You must then sort through these emails and plan for action, either in your calendar or task management system.

Next-action lists

After you've completed processing your email (see previous section), take a look at your next-action list. Make sure all your tasks are up-to-date. Have you completed the tasks you need to do this week? If not, why not? Do you need to schedule time in your calendar to get things done? The review of the next-action list allows you to reassess the importance of the tasks you've assigned yourself and gives you the opportunity to review their priority.

Project lists

Review your project lists. Do you have any new projects to add? Are there any projects on your project list that are no longer relevant or that you really don't have the capacity to complete? Removing projects from the list is just as important as adding to it. Add any actions to be completed for that project onto that project list. Keeping all tasks associated with projects together gives you a better overall perspective of a project as well as helps you maintain your focus on the right thing at the right time.

Don't keep projects on your list that you're unlikely to undertake. Doing so creates a feeling of frustration. Only keep projects on your project list that are in progress or that you definitely, completely, 100 per cent plan to undertake in the near future.

Calendar

Review your calendar once a week. Check that everything you had scheduled for last week has been completed. If there is anything that hasn't been done, be sure to reallocate some time to complete it. If you find certain items on your calendar are rescheduled a number of times, ask yourself why. Be honest with yourself and decide whether the item really is a priority. Are you avoiding the task, or did you miss it because of an unfortunate interruption?

Don't put anything in your calendar that you don't intend to do. Your calendar is for tasks that you want to do on a particular day or at a particular time. You must commit to doing the work that is planned in your calendar; otherwise, your calendar will lose its efficiency and credibility. Only enter tasks that you will commit to doing.

Goals

Take some time each week to review your goals. Take a quick look at your short-term and long-term goals. Are you on track? Are the projects and actions you're working on daily getting you any closer to these goals? Keeping your goals in the forefront of your mind helps your productivity daily. You're less likely to waste time working on things that won't contribute to the big picture.

Getting Familiar with GTD Tools

You'll find many GTD-compatible tools, from paper to fancy software, helping you to manage your to-do list. Some people prefer to use an all-electronic approach, remaining completely paperless. Others attempt to use just paper.

I use a hybrid approach, using both electronic and paper methods. I keep all my notes and tasks in an electronic system, but I like to use paper to doodle, to sketch ideas or to capture day-to-day reminders.

The following sections list some of the tools that you may use to get started. The core tools consist of a journal, task management software and a calendar.

Journals

The most basic element of GTD is capturing the work you need to do as it comes your way. A basic notebook or journal of any sort will suffice. The trick is to have it with you always and always use the same one. If you start to bring a number of notebooks around with you, you risk losing one or not having the right one with you at the right time. Stick to one notebook for all notes, ideas and plans.

You can use both a paper and electronic approach. If you use paper to originally capture your idea, you can then process it and add it into a particular task list or add it into your calendar to schedule a time to complete the work. At the end of each week, review the notes you made in your journal and add any notes to project files or create notes for ideas, goals or dreams you want to remember. Then scratch out the page in your journal so you know that the page has been processed and that you don't need to read that page again.

GTD-compatible apps

The GTD methodology has its own software that has been designed and developed to work specifically with this method. Other existing software has been adapted and retrofitted to work with GTD. You may choose to invest in a piece of software like Omnifocus or decide to use an existing piece of software like Microsoft Outlook. The choice is yours; it's a matter of finding which one suits your way of working and your own personal requirements.

After you've read about the different options in this section, check them out online and then choose to work with one. Commit to it for at least three months. It's necessary to give the system a chance to work for you. If you can commit for at least three months, you'll really see the benefit, or alternatively, you'll be ready to make an informed decision that this software isn't the right one for you and you can try a different one.

Omnifocus

GTD is not the only way to use Omnifocus, but it is widely regarded as the GTD software. It prompts you to start with a *brain dump,* getting everything out of your head and into the Omnifocus inbox. From there, you can begin to process your 'stuff'. You can then add items to projects lists, action lists or larger work areas.

The software is designed to allow you to view your work from different perspectives. When you're planning, reviewing or doing, you'll want to look at your work in a different way.

Omnifocus also allows you to add contexts, such as a physical location or a physical item required to do the task. You may also have people as contexts, such as your boss or a work colleague.

All these features encourage you to focus on the right thing at the right time, reducing any overwhelming feeling from having too much to do, while keeping things in check and in control. Omnifocus is a popular task management tool for those who are keen to use the Getting Things Done methodology as part of their daily system.

Microsoft Outlook

Microsoft calls its office software a productivity suite of software. It designs its programmes to make lives easier. The truth is, Microsoft Outlook is a productivity suite in itself. It's powerful enough to run both your professional and personal life and keep you organised and in control. Millions of office workers spend their day between their email and calendar. A lot of folks don't do much else. You can very easily use Outlook as a GTD tool, scheduling your work in the Calendar, postponing tasks to be done with the task manager and taking notes with the Notes facility. It's easy to defer or delegate tasks, schedule a next action or file an email for reference later.

It takes a little bit of work to set things up to follow the methodology, but for the lazy, you can install add-ins to do the setup work for you. Using a GTD add-in for Outlook enables you to create next actions and automatically add items to projects and action lists. The Categories feature in Outlook Tasks is very useful for creating contexts or areas of focus.

Evernote

Evernote is a simple note-taking app that has many uses. It allows you to take notes, capture ideas, store research and write books. One of the great benefits of using Evernote is that it is a cross-platform, multi-device app, allowing you to sync your work across all your devices, accessible to you whenever you need it and wherever you are.

In recent years, Evernote has become a popular app for applying GTD. People use Evernote and GTD with two main methods. The first is called the 'The Secret Weapon', a method devised by Braintoniq to create one perfect system. It's one place to keep everything, to store your to-dos, goals and projects. The second is the David Allen's official guide to Evernote and GTD. While using the same concepts, they approach things slightly differently.

The Secret Weapon focuses on using Evernote's Tags for what Getting Things Done calls contexts. Organising your system by means of where you'll be when you do something – 'home', 'work' or 'town' – or when you intend on doing it – now, next or later – or who you'll be with when you do it – Amy, John or Sarah.

In David Allen's *Best Practices Guide for GTD & Evernote*, he focuses on using Notebooks and Notebook Stacks, another feature of Evernote. A lot of GTD enthusiasts would rather use the context or tagging approach as laid out by Braintoniq in The Secret Weapon. Personally, I prefer the Notebook approach, using Notebooks for different projects, but again, this is down to personal preference.

Things

Things is a simple task management system for Mac. It's a cloud-based system that allows you to have your to-dos on your iPhone, iPad and Mac. Its quick entry window allows you to do your mind dump directly into your task management system, enabling you to keep the process fast and streamlined.

Like other systems, Things allows you to add contexts and projects to your system. It also prompts a weekly review-type system ensuring that you keep everything up-to-date.

Tabbed folders

To stay organised, you need to get some folders. Separating filing from action will help you keep things under control. Make sure you get enough folders to organise your files, and use a simple A to Z filing system. Clearly label your reference folders by using the little tabs of your folders; you can then place these folders inside whatever system of hanging folders you have.

You should also have an actionable filing system on your desk for work in progress or projects in action. You can use a desk file stand and the same tabbed folders labelled clearly. You can use these folders for storing the paperwork from the work that you're currently working on. Only when you're finished with a project should you file the paperwork away in your filing cabinet.

Labeller

A label printer is one of man's best friends, a perfect partner for your tabbed folders. The labeller helps you clearly label each folder so it's easy to find when you need to look for a file.

You may think that you can recreate the same system by printing out labels or even by writing the labels in neat handwriting. Don't be fooled into thinking it's the same. The labeller helps you to create a file at a moment's notice and ensures that nothing ever gets left lying around.

This is not a place to save money. Your labeller will facilitate a clean, organised office space helping you to focus and get more done.

Calendar

The tool for the things that need to be done at a particular time or on a particular date, the calendar is the best anti-procrastination tool around – what gets scheduled usually gets done. Those who fight the calendar usually argue that life gets in the way or that whenever they schedule something, their boss or a client has a different use for their time. The advantage of the calendar is that if it didn't get done, it's very easy to reschedule the item. With an electronic calendar, all you have to do is drag the item into an available time the next day or whenever you have a spot open.

Life will always have different plans for your time, and something will always stand in the way of your perfect plan, but at least nothing will get forgotten about. And by scheduling your priorities in your calendar, you can get a visual picture of how long it will take you to complete a project or a series of tasks.

The tickler file

The tickler file is a collection of 43 folders. These 43 folders consist of a folder for every day of the month (31) and one for each month of the year (12). The tickler file allows you to store paperwork according to when you might need it or when you need to complete the work. For example, you may want to put tickets for a concert into the day you'll need them, or paperwork for a flight or hotel reservation next month or maybe just a bill that needs to be paid on a particular date.

The tickler file is like a reminder system for physical items, but you shouldn't solely rely on it for your reminders. Use this system to complement your calendar. If your calendar has an item scheduled such as 'David Bowie Concert', you'll know exactly where to look for the tickets.

If you don't fully trust your calendar, you can check the folder each day and see whether you need to do anything with the paperwork inside. At the beginning of each month, you can check the monthly file and reallocate any paperwork that needs to go into a different daily file.

Chapter 11

Further Productivity Techniques

In This Chapter

- Introducing the Pomodoro Technique
- Taking things a bit slower
- Keeping the chain going and developing new habits
- Working with Personal Kanbans

If you're the lazy sort, then the Getting Things Done (GTD) methodology (as described in Chapter 10) probably sounds like a whole lot of work. Are you looking for a simple technique that can assist you on your journey to greater efficiency and success? You could try the Pomodoro Technique or create your own Personal Kanban. This chapter talks you through both of these concepts, plus that classic piece of advice advocated by the hare and the tortoise – slow down to speed up.

As with any productivity system or technique, you need to commit to trying something out for a set period of time to get the benefits from using the system. Don't try out more than one at a time. Introduce only one into your life, and stick with it before trying something new.

The Pomodoro Technique

The Pomodoro Technique is a time-management technique created by Francesco Girillo in the late 1980s. The name *Pomodoro* is Italian for 'tomato', taking its name from the tomato kitchen timer used to track the time intervals. The Pomodoro Technique is a simple and effective way to improve your productivity. All it requires is a kitchen timer and your personal desire to get things done.

The basics of the technique are very simple. Take a look; in fact, why not give it a go right now:

1. **Choose a task you want to get done.**

   The task can be big or small, a daily task or a bigger, long-term project. It doesn't matter what you choose as long as it is something that you want to get done.

2. **Set the Pomodoro for 25 minutes.**

   Commit to sticking with the task for 25 minutes. Don't take a break or allow yourself to get distracted for 25 minutes.

3. **Work on the task until the timer rings.**

   Stay with the task for the full 25 minutes. Anything you think of that you need to do can wait until break time. If a thought comes into your head reminding you of something you need to do, capture it on paper and keep going until the timer rings.

4. **Record your Pomodoro.**

   When the timer rings, take a note of your Pomodoro and what you achieved in the 25 minutes. When I'm writing, I note how many words I wrote in 25 minutes. I average between 400 and 500 words in a 25-minute period.

5. **Take a short break.**

   The break is vital (isn't it great when someone says that to you?). Take five minutes to breathe, stretch, go to the bathroom or grab a cup of coffee. Use the break to refresh your mind and get ready for another Pomodoro.

6. **Start again.**

   Set the timer again, and go for another 25 minutes. After every four Pomodoros, take a longer break of 20 to 30 minutes.

Gaining from Pomodoros

The Pomodoro Technique is simple and easy to implement. This section lists some of the reasons you should make the Pomodoro Technique part of your productivity toolkit.

Working with time

The Pomodoro Technique teaches you to work with your time instead of constantly struggling to master it. If you regularly feel you're fighting time, constantly pushing to fit things in or get things done, try this technique, and you'll see how you can make time your ally. It helps you to use time to your advantage and make every minute matter.

Time can't be mastered. You have to create a partnership with it rather than try to control it. The Pomodoro Technique allows you to do just that: partner with your time to achieve your small daily goals.

Working with energy

Just like fighting against time, you get nowhere from fighting your energy. You should be aware of your own energy levels and patterns of energy throughout the day.

When you know your times for low or high energy, you can work it to your advantage. Never schedule high-energy tasks for the after lunch slump. Always tackle heavy cognitive tasks for first thing in the morning.

If you're having a period of low energy but still need to focus on an important task, consider using shorter Pomodoros of 15 minutes. Take a short break of 3 to 5 minutes and continue your task. Taking more regular breaks ensures that you don't tire too quickly.

Following are some ways to work with your energy levels:

- **Circadian rhythms:** Circadian rhythms are physical, mental and behavioural changes that follow a roughly 24-hour cycle, responding to light and darkness in an organism's environment. These changes naturally affect your energy levels and dictate whether you'll have a period of low or high energy. For most human adults, the first couple of hours in the morning are the most productive with early afternoon being the lowest point of energy.
- **Morning rituals:** Creating morning rituals helps you make the most of your circadian rhythms and gain advantage from your body's energy. Staying in bed late wastes valuable and productive morning time. Rising early works with your natural rhythm and allows you to get your best work done early.
- **Contexts:** Contexts is a condition set to a list to give you more information about when or where or how you want to do a task. A task may require the presence of a tool or a person to complete, so you assign the context of that tool or person next to that task, such as 'computer' or 'John'. When working with your energy, the context could be 'high energy' or 'low energy'. Refer to Chapter 10 for more detail about contexts.

- **Exercise:** To ensure higher energy more frequently, you know what you have to do: exercise. Richard Branson reckons he gets an extra four hours of productivity each day from working out in the morning.

Exercise is probably your single best productivity tool available. Make exercise a daily habit. Get out of bed an hour earlier in the morning to do a workout. This will increase your energy for the day and probably make you live longer.

Managing distractions

Another great benefit of the Pomodoro Technique is that it improves your focus. When the timer is set, you're less likely to wander off into Facebook or Twitter for a little distraction. You'll be more tempted to complete the Pomodoro before running off to find out what the rest of the world is doing. If you're busy with your work and you have an idea or you suddenly realise you forgot to pay the gardener, jot down the thought or idea and deal with it during your break after the timer has rung.

Who benefits from tomatoes?

The Pomodoro Technique can help different types of people in different ways; check out these examples:

- **Writers:** I have used the Pomodoro Technique to write this book. I know how many Pomodoros I need to complete to write each chapter and effectively the book. I can schedule the exact amount of time required to complete a chapter and know when I am on schedule. Using the technique in this way, I am calm and collected knowing that I can reach each deadline. It also reduces the stiffness I felt in my neck and shoulders from writing for too long without taking a break. I now stretch and do a quick yoga pose during my breaks to release the tension in my shoulders before starting again. I also drink more water, staying hydrated, as I am reminded at each break to fill up my glass.
- **Students:** Students experience many of the same benefits. The Pomodoro Technique helps minimise their distractions and keeps them focused on a particular task for a short period. It can also help a student figure out how long it takes to complete an average assignment or how long to study a chapter of a book. Breaking down large tasks into manageable chunks is a massive benefit for anyone studying a course.
- **Parents:** If you have trouble getting your kids to complete tasks, using the timer can be a great motivator. Give them a task to complete, such as tidying their room, and put on the timer. They can take a break when the timer sounds and do something enjoyable for five minutes. One or two Pomodoros should be enough to complete homework or to tidy a room.

Improving work-life balance

When you master the Pomodoro Technique, you become infinitely more creative and can complete tasks at a much faster and more efficient rate. Be gone the feeling of frustration and lack of accomplishment you used to get from procrastinating!

Because you'll be achieving more of your goals and getting more done, you won't have the need to think about what you're not getting done when you're out with family and friends. Your relationships should improve, and your life will ultimately become happier and more balanced.

Reaping the benefits of Pomodoros daily

Using the Pomodoro Technique comes with many benefits. It not only helps you to get more work done day to day, but it also helps you to improve the way you do your work by understanding more about how you work and what you can achieve each day.

Understanding how much effort a task requires

By starting to track how long your tasks take, you can begin to plan how you spend your time better and allocate the right amount of time per task.

Before I used the Pomodoro Technique, I didn't know how long it took me to write a chapter of a book. I wrote until I finished a chapter, never recording how long that took me or whether it was shorter or longer than the last time. Since tracking my work with Pomodoros, I have become more efficient than I ever thought possible. I know exactly how long I need to complete a section and always know whether I'm on track. Using this technique has massively reduced my stress caused by uncertainty. It has empowered me to understand my work and my abilities.

Managing day-to-day interruptions better

When you're working on your own time, you allow yourself to take breaks whenever you feel like it or task switch when the mood takes you. Before I started using the Pomodoro Technique, I often found myself doing a completely different task than I set out to do without even being conscious that I had switched tasks.

I'm not going to say this never happens anymore, but I can't remember the last time it did. It's easier to stay on track with the timer ticking in the background; the temptation to get to the end is high. And it's easy to delay distractions to the break because the break is never very far away.

Estimating the effort required for a given task

Understanding how much effort is involved in a task by tracking your time with Pomodoros and then being able to accurately assess how many Pomodoros it will take to complete next week's tasks or to complete a project is one of the more rewarding benefits of using the Pomodoro Technique.

Setting up a work or study timetable

When you understand how much effort a task takes, setting up a timetable becomes easier. The timetable accurately estimates how much time you need to complete your tasks. Having a schedule or timetable also creates boundaries between work and free time, helping create a better work-life balance.

Assisting you to reach your goals

The Pomodoro Technique helps you to reach your goals and objectives by helping you visualise your success more easily. With greater focus and direction, you get more of the right work done.

Slowing Down to Speed Up

Are you moving too fast, speeding through your work to get everything done? Modern life can make you think you need to move at the speed of light, do your work quickly and move on to the next job. Sometimes you may need to move quickly, but sometimes moving too quickly has a detrimental effect on outcomes. Maybe you need to slow down to speed up.

Getting things done quickly and racing through your work makes you feel like a super productive human. But often this speed can go against you, encouraging you to make errors and rash judgements in order to keep the pace. Wisdom shows that some things don't benefit from speed.

This section looks at some of those things that benefit from a tortoise-like approach.

Making decisive decisions

Decision making can be a tricky subject. Some will tell you to go with your gut and that your first instinct is always the right one. Others will tell you to take your time, to mull over all the options and definitely to sleep on it. There is truth in all suggestions; all have their merit and their appropriate time for implementation.

Effective decision making involves a number of steps:

1. Identify decision to be made.
2. Collect all relevant information.
3. Analyse the information collected.
4. Identify the options.
5. Assess the alternatives.
6. Decide on course of action.
7. Take action.

In reality, if you're going to work through this decision-making process, the more speed you engage, the less likely you're going to arrive at an ideal outcome.

- **Fast thinking:** Fast thinking and decision making use your instinct, but often your gut instinct is overshadowed by your prejudice and presumptions. Scientists have proven that even the most educated and aware individuals act from bias that they're not conscious of. Therefore, although your gut instinct may be right, it may also be strongly tainted with preconception and partiality.
- **Slow thinking:** Thinking slow has its benefits because it allows you to look at all scenarios and think clearly. It gives you time to challenge your bias and ensure that you're doing things for the right reasons. Major decisions should be given the maximum amount of time allocated to them but of course not leaving them to the last minute.

Benefitting from stillness

In a world that appears to move faster by the day, there is definitely a benefit to be earned from slowing down. But there is also benefit to be gained from stillness. Taking time out from the rat race to be still is a technique not only for monks in a monastery.

Everyone can benefit from quiet time to renew and go within. A lot of highly successful people have adopted meditation, people who understand that running at high speed for too long has many negatives associated with it. Stress is one of the biggest enemies; so many physical ailments are a result of too much stress on the body – skin conditions, headaches, backache, depression, anxiety, stomach problems . . . the list goes on.

You can use meditation and mindfulness to counteract the effects of stress. Meditation undoes the tightness of life, gives you an opportunity to unwind and come down from the adrenaline of the fast life and at the same time strengthens your body and your immune system.

'Don't Break the Chain'

'Don't break the chain' is another very simple technique that can have powerful results. You may have heard of Jerry Seinfeld, the American comic who had a very popular sitcom on NBC in which he played a neurotic comedian. But you probably didn't know that he is also known for suggesting this simple and effective productivity technique, 'Don't break the chain'.

Many years ago, a software developer by the name of Brad Issac was doing stand-up comedy sessions in his spare time. One evening, he came across Jerry Seinfeld, who was performing in the same club. Before Jerry went on stage, Brad knew he just had to speak to him and ask him for some advice. What advice would he have for a young comic starting out? Jerry's advice was not as expected but advice that Brad has found extremely beneficial ever since.

Seinfeld advised him that the way to become a better comic was to write better jokes. The way to write better jokes was to write every day. He also shared his own technique that he advised the young comic to try out: 'Don't break the chain'.

To use Seinfeld's method, all you need is a large wall calendar with a box for each day of the year and a big red marker. Hang the calendar in a prominent place in your office or home. If you're trying to write more, put a big red X on the day that you write. The idea is to continue each day, marking each day with a red X. His method is called 'Don't break the chain'. The more days you see joined with an X, the more difficult it will be to break the chain. Check out Figure 11-1 to see how this works.

Imagine how much you could achieve if you wrote a little every day. Just one hour a day of writing is the equivalent to one working day a week. Imagine if you dedicated one whole working day a week to writing?

You can use this method for many areas of life: exercise, meditation, journaling or any other positive habit you wish to create. It can be powerful for getting children to do their chores. Children love to mark things off, especially if you allow them to do it on your calendar and with a big red marker.

DON'T BREAK THE CHAIN

JANUARY

S	M	T	W	T	F	S
X	X	X	X	X	X	X
X	X	X	11	12	13	14
15	16	17	18	19	20	21
22	23	24	25	26	27	28
29	30	31				

FEBRUARY

S	M	T	W	T	F	S
			1	2	3	4
5	6	7	8	9	10	11
12	13	14	15	16	17	18
19	20	21	22	23	24	25
26	27	28				

MARCH

S	M	T	W	T	F	S
			1	2	3	4
5	6	7	8	9	10	11
12	13	14	15	16	17	18
19	20	21	22	23	24	25
26	27	28	29	30	31	

APRIL

S	M	T	W	T	F	S
						1
2	3	4	5	6	7	8
9	10	11	12	13	14	15
16	17	18	19	20	21	22
23	24	25	26	27	28	29
30						

MAY

S	M	T	W	T	F	S
	1	2	3	4	5	6
7	8	9	10	11	12	13
14	15	16	17	18	19	20
21	22	23	24	25	26	27
28	29	30	31			

JUNE

S	M	T	W	T	F	S
				1	2	3
4	5	6	7	8	9	10
11	12	13	14	15	16	17
18	19	20	21	22	23	24
25	26	27	28	29	30	

Figure 11-1: Don't break the chain!

Adopting New Habits

Seinfeld's 'Don't break the chain' is a habit-forming exercise (see previous section). It encourages you to repeat a daily task every day to achieve your goal.

To be successful, your daily habits must match up with your goal. If you meet a successful writer, he will have a daily habit of writing. A successful swimmer will swim daily, a runner runs daily, a dancer must dance daily – this is the reason they're successful. The secret to their success is that they have created habits that they repeat every day to make them who they are.

If you repeat the same tasks daily for over a month, the neural pathways in the brain that are fired up to complete the task will strengthen. Each time you repeat the task, they get stronger. They're reinforced each time until it becomes the norm. Not doing the task becomes the anomaly.

'Don't break the chain' is a system for helping you form a habit. Each red X is the result of you completing your habit for that day, and each time you mark that X, you're confirming that your neural pathways have been made stronger.

Other factors can also help you create the habit, such as the following points from my Habit Method. Following these tips will give you a much greater possibility of making your new habit work.

Starting with a plan

Be clear first of all about what it is you're trying to achieve. If you want to form a new habit of writing, be clear about what you want to write: a screen play or simply a blog? If you want to start a regular exercise practise, decide in advance what you're going to do and when.

Be clear about what success looks like. Set out the plan in advance, and you're more likely to succeed. A plan will help you make it work. The clearer you are about what you are going to do and when and where you're going to do it, the better.

Understanding your intentions

Understanding your motivation, the 'why' behind your new habit, will be of great value when trying to form it. You should be clear about why this new habit will benefit you and how it ties in with your vision for the future.

Understanding your intentions and connecting with them every day will reinforce your desire and commitment to succeed. The 'why' is essential for positive accomplishment.

Starting with small steps

Don't try too much too soon. If your intention is to write a new novel but you haven't been writing too much lately, perhaps committing to six hours a day is a little optimistic. You could start with an hour or even a half hour to get the ball rolling and create the momentum required to get a novel written. But slow and steady will win the race, especially when it comes to habit formation.

Using triggers to create a new habit

Have set times for your habits, and use a trigger to remind you to get going. Try first thing in the morning to get up and exercise. Try preparing your clothes the night before. Once you have set the trigger in motion, you're less likely to avoid it. If your trigger for your new habit can be an existing habit, such as rising early, once you get out of bed you know exercise comes next, or after your shower, you sit down to write. A trigger accelerates your chances of success.

Recording the benefits

Writing down how good you feel after your workout reinforces the benefits of exercise and imprints the advantages on your brain. Why would you ever skip a workout when you know how good it makes you feel?

Remind yourself regularly why you're doing the new habit and what the benefits are for you and your life. Write it in your journal and look at it often and especially if you lack motivation.

Avoiding failure

If you have tried to do something and failed, take some time to figure out why. If you understand why you failed, this helps you to work out what you need to do to make it work this time. If there are circumstances in your life that stand in your way, what can you do to avoid them? Bad habits, negative friends or too many commitments can all stand in the way of you reaching your goals. Take action and do what you can to make the circumstances work in your favour.

Personal Kanban

Personal Kanban is a simple mechanism for getting work done. Unlike other systems or techniques, it doesn't follow a rigid process. It's a template that allows you to visualise your work in process and helps you to stay in control. Personal Kanban is based on the principles and techniques of lean management (a system devised by Toyota in the 1980s, the core aims of which were to maximise customer value and to minimise waste).

Kanban is Japanese for 'visual sign' or 'card'. A Kanban system based on visual cues attempts to match inventory with demand to achieve higher levels of quality and flow. Also referred to as 'Just in Time', it aims at delivering only the materials required in the correct amounts at the correct time. A Personal Kanban helps you harness the power of visual information by using sticky notes on a whiteboard to create a visual picture of your work. Seeing how your work flows allows you to communicate status within your team and take action more quickly.

There are only two rules of Personal Kanban:

- **Rule 1: Visualise your work.** Visualising all your work is useful. People have a tendency to focus on the urgent and the deadlines that are within their sight daily. Often the larger, less urgent but equally important work gets ignored because that which shouts loudest stays within your vision. Visualising work gives it power, capturing all the work that needs doing can be empowering. Understanding the work that needs to be done gives you better awareness, and better awareness leads to better decisions.
- **Rule 2: Limit your work in progress (WIP).** Most modern-day workers have too much to do and will never have enough time to do it. The purpose of limiting work in progress is to help you to focus. To admit and accept that you can't do it all at once urges you to make decisions about priorities, asking yourself what should be done now and what comes later. You need to limit your work in progress to ensure that the work that you do is being done well.

Understanding the process

What you need to understand with Personal Kanban is that there is no process; it can change with the context. You may use a whiteboard and markers or a jotter and pen – the principles remain the same: visualise your work and limit the work in progress. You can use the Personal Kanban for visualising all kinds of work and projects that can vary in size and type. You can use it for almost anything that needs to get done.

Creating the basic Kanban

You can use the basic Kanban as a type of to-do list, allowing you to visualise the work that you have at the moment. You can't possibly do all the things on your to-do list now, so the Kanban allows you to separate your tasks in columns. Typical columns include *Backlog, Ready, Doing, On Hold* and *Done* (see Figure 11-2 for an example). You can use whatever titles best suit your environment and way of working.

- **Backlog:** The backlog column holds all the projects and tasks that haven't been started yet or planned. It includes stuff you need to do but maybe don't have the resources to get going yet. Keeping it visible means you won't forget about it, and you can make a decision at a later date as to its importance and urgency.

- **Ready:** This consists of all the projects and tasks ready to go but not started. They may be awaiting resources, but they're ready to go when you are.
- **Doing:** The work in progress, or WIP as it's often called, is the *Doing* column. This consists of all the tasks that are currently occupying your time. It's recommended that the *Doing* column has no more than three items at any one time. This ensures that you never suffer from congestion or overload. If you keep this column to three items, it will help you to focus and complete tasks before moving on to the next one.
- **On Hold:** Work may have to go on hold if you're waiting on someone else to complete something before you can continue. Having a column for on-hold items allows you to see how long things are being delayed because of other people or factors in the value stream.
- **Done:** This is the column everyone loves and the sense of satisfaction when the work is done. It's important to visualise the work done also, to appreciate the accomplishments and be clear about progress and effort.

As the work flows, you move it along the lanes. If you can visualise your work, you're better able to make decisions about your priorities. You can change priorities and make adjustments to represent the reality of a dynamic work environment, but you can rest assured that you're not forgetting anything because you've already captured it and it's in plain sight.

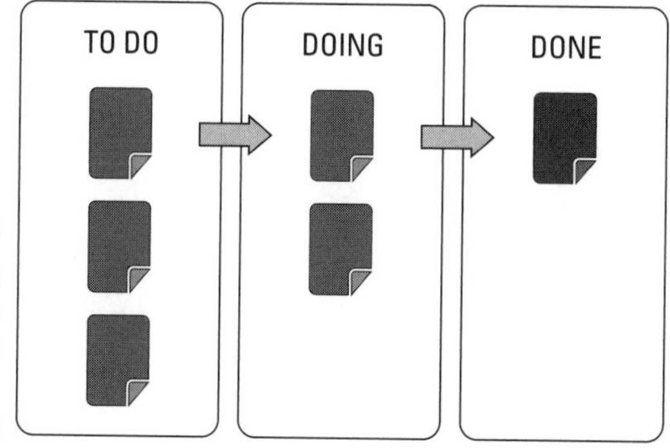

Figure 11-2: An example of Personal Kanban.

Illustration by John Wiley & Sons, Inc.

Moving along the Kanban

Movement happens when something changes or something gets done. You'll see the following in your Kanban.

- **Pull:** Work gets pulled along the Kanban when there's the capacity to do so. You don't want work pushed along because that can cause flooding and negative results. There needs to be sufficient pull, though, to keep work moving.
- **Constraints:** The work in progress field should have only three items in it at any one time. This constraint ensures that work will be done correctly and pulled along when the capacity is there. This ensures flow.
- **Flow:** As work is pulled along, it creates flow. Flow shows you how long it takes you to complete your work and allows you to see the patterns in the work. Flow is a positive state that everyone aspires to be in.
- **Bottleneck:** When things don't flow, you can have a bottleneck. Maybe work was on hold too long, or it got stuck in the *Doing* column, but when you can visualise it clearly, you can do something about it.

Part IV
Productivity at Work

Five Essentials for Staying Productive at Work

- Choose a team task management tool to store your team tasks and improve collaboration and productivity at work.
- In order to make the most of your time, start by tracking it. Time-tracking software will help you to understand where your time is going and to ensure that you use your time right from now on.
- Take a look at the big picture and use your calendar to plan and schedule your work to do. Scheduling is the number-one way to beat procrastination.
- Plan you MITs (most important tasks) each day. This will ensure that you get important work done each day and you are less likely to get distracted by time-wasting tasks.
- If you want to become a Productivity Superhero, take control of your inbox. Don't use your inbox as a to-do list, and learn the techniques of inbox zero.

Head to `www.dummies.com/extras/productivity` to discover the secrets of productive leaders.

In this part . . .

- Find out how to get down to business by creating productive teams.
- Get an introduction to task management systems.
- Understand how to use your calendar wisely.
- Discover and enjoy the benefits of technology management.
- Find tips on becoming a more productive freelancer.

Chapter 12

Getting Down to Business

In This Chapter

- Creating a productive team
- Turning meetings at work into something positive
- Exploring the efficiencies of using paper versus going paperless

Work environments aren't always as efficient as they should be. Most workers just don't have the time to spend on staying organised or filing effectively. Environment and process are just as important as what you do to produce high-quality end results. Having a cohesive and collaborative team to maximise performance is also important. This chapter is for those involved with teams: whether you are a manager or part of a team, you will learn how to build a productive team, run meetings effectively and create an efficient office, with paper or without.

Introducing the Productive Team

A team is a group of people who are working toward a common goal. Research shows that people are more likely to be productive if they're given the opportunity to work together in a social group setting and have the opportunity to get to know each other. For a team to work well, there must be trust, commitment and accountability. Alternatively, a gun to the head can also work, but I don't advocate that approach.

Some teams function well with a *flat structure* – that is, with no hierarchy and as a fully democratic unit. Most teams have a leader, however, and how a leader performs and behaves is crucial to the effectiveness of the team.

Leading by example

The behaviours a leader wants to see in a team must be behaviours and attitudes she adheres to herself. The old adage 'Do what I say, not what I do' carries no weight. A leader must walk the walk to gain the respect and trust of her team. If a leader behaves one way and expects the team to behave another way, she is on the road to failure.

The days of having one rule for management and another for the workers should be long gone. Yet in many organisations, team members participate in training to improve their productivity, performance and teamwork, and the leader doesn't attend. This behaviour is damaging to morale and isn't an effective long-term strategy. If you want your team to work productively, *you* must work productively. If you want to see trust, respect and collaboration, these traits should be visible in you.

Creating a high-performance team

A high-performance team needs a number of characteristics present in order to perform well and achieve superior results. These include having a common purpose and understanding the goals and priorities and roles of the team. There also needs to be trust between the team for cohesiveness and accountability to be present.

Knowing the goal

A high-performance team is clear about its goals and objectives. You can never be productive if you're unclear about your goals. Working hard doesn't achieve anything if you're working toward the wrong goals or someone else's goals. Get clear on the team's goals. Ask yourself:

- What are you trying to achieve?
- How will you know when you have been successful?

The clearer you are about the end goal, the more productive you can be every day.

Understanding priorities

Knowing your goals helps you understand your priorities. If you know what you're trying to achieve and the task you're doing is getting you closer to achieving it, then it's more than likely a priority. To make sure you're staying on task with your priorities, ask yourself regularly during the day whether what you're working on is getting you closer to your goals.

Identifying roles

Understanding your personal role in a team goes a long way to producing effective results. When people are clear about their role and responsibilities, they waste less time and take more dynamic action.

Fostering Trust

Trust is an essential component of a high-performance team. Team members need to be confident in each other's abilities to get things done. They need to be able to trust each other and hold each other accountable for what they say they will do.

Revisit goals regularly to make sure they're still relevant. Take time at least once a month to refocus the team and ensure maximum commitment and motivation.

Improving team communications

Collaboration is crucial for an effective team to function, and collaboration doesn't happen without high levels of effective communication. Communication is essential to not only get things done but get them done well and within a specified time frame. When you have a team that communicates successfully, it functions more efficiently and is more likely to reach its goals.

Team leaders need to create the environment for good communication to take place and encourage staff to use the appropriate channels of communication at the appropriate time.

Following are a number of ways in which you can improve team communications and function more effectively.

Curbing email

People rely too much on email, sending emails to everyone in the organisation to ensure that nobody gets left out. But email isn't always the right choice. Often, a face-to-face conversation can be a lot more productive or a short team meeting can avoid pages of email conversations. Teamwork can often be hindered by overreliance on email, encouraging people to spend too much time answering and forwarding emails rather than getting any actual work done. Teamwork can be a lot more efficient if you use a team tool, such as Asana or Basecamp, to hold all conversation relating to team tasks in one location. (Find out more about team tools in the section 'Utilising team tools'.)

Conducting meetings

All meetings are equal, but some meetings are more equal than others. Those of you who have read George Orwell's *Animal Farm* will understand the difference. Most meetings have the potential to be great, but too many are far from great. Hours of productivity are lost weekly to inefficient and unnecessary meetings.

When planning a team meeting, be sure your meeting is necessary to start with and then make sure you run it as effectively as possible. A meeting should be as long as you need but as short as possible. Have a think about your regular meetings and determine whether you can circulate updates to the team in a more efficient way.

You can find more on making the most of meeting time in the section 'Running Productive Meetings', later in this chapter.

Meeting face to face

Meeting face to face is a powerful mode of communication and usually one that gets more effective results than email or other electronic methods. Create a list of questions or tasks for your team on your computer, and then when the time comes to meet face to face, you can ask everyone at once instead of using email.

Don't use the face-to-face method too often. Interrupting people's work to ask them a question face to face isn't productive. As with most things in life, you have to strike a balance in work. If you're unsure what this balance is, discuss it with your team. You could suggest that team members set times they don't want to be disturbed, to allow time for getting the work done between meetings and other modes of communication.

Listening

Listening is essential for building trust and respect between team members and, of course, a fundamental part of effective communication. If every team member gets the opportunity to speak and be heard, you'll see higher levels of contribution and engagement.

Remind team members on a regular basis how important listening is. Leaders need to be good listeners, too, and lead by example.

If the team can communicate effectively, they will benefit from some of the advantages of having a communicative team. Following are some of the highlights when a team communicates well.

Creating trust

Trust is an essential ingredient for a team to function well. A lot of dysfunction in teams stems from a lack of trust between team members. If team members are unwilling to show vulnerability and be honest, you waste too much time trying to manage behaviours instead of working on the goals.

Reducing errors

Teams that interact well together and that have positive channels of communication avoid the errors that come from team members being ill-informed or unclear about their purpose or goals. Younger or newer members of a team are more likely to hide their lack of understanding. Clear and effective interaction with all team members supports more positive results.

Fostering input

A team works best when it has a diverse set of skills working together for a common goal. It's important to encourage input from all team members. Try to avoid the same dominant personalities giving the input and the quieter ones sitting back. Nurturing the relationships between team members can encourage the quieter personalities to give more input. Getting input from all members of the team gives a stronger output.

Reducing stress

Disorganisation and uncertainty cause stress. Clarity and efficiency reduce it. Investing time in team building and ensuring that effective processes are in place and means of communication are established will go a long way to creating a successful and productive team. See Chapter 6 for more on stress management.

Utilising team tools

Team collaboration tools are a great way to move from using email to more efficient management of team tasks and projects. Depending on your industry and your role in your job, you may have specific tools that you need to use for efficiency and the processes required. For example, sales professionals use sales software to manage their sales process, and technical support professionals have a support database to manage their customer queries.

If your job role doesn't require any specific tool for collaboration, I cover a few of the most popular team tools to improve team collaboration and communication in the sections that follow. All are mobile compatible and some have pretty amazing free versions so you can get productive without spending a cent. However, if you're willing to spend a little, premium versions give you extra features and awesome superpowers.

Asana

Asana is a tool for collaborating with your team around team tasks. Its tagline – 'Teamwork without email' – explains its goal. Asana aims to remove the incessant chatter on email around team tasks. By placing all team tasks in Asana and having all conversations about these tasks in the tool, you can not only rapidly and massively reduce the amount of time you spend in your email inbox but also improve your productivity.

Asana was founded by ex-Facebook employees who developed it to solve the problem of email overload in Facebook. They then went on to create a company out of it. Their mission is to 'Help humanity thrive by enabling all teams to work together effortlessly'. That's a pretty noble mission accompanied by some pretty great values. These guys are of the new generation of organisations that not only want to be profitable but also want to make a difference.

Trello

Trello also promotes the fact that it will reduce your email conversations and the need to use spreadsheets to manage projects.

Trello is based on a Kanban approach. A *Kanban* approach stems from the Toyota production method where visual cards on a physical board were used to signal steps in the manufacturing process. Columns on the board are known as *swim lanes*, representing different stages in your process. These swim lanes could represent simple steps like ready, doing, done.

For those of you who like visual tools, Trello is a good option because it helps you to visualize your team's progress in any task as you watch it progress on the Kanban board.

Basecamp

For over a decade, Basecamp has been the tried and trusted tool of many organisations. If you have one or many projects on the go, Basecamp claims it's the tool for you. The tool helps pull many people together by allowing internal and external stakeholders to access the system and see what tasks they are responsible for in a particular project. Basecamp allows you to communicate with everyone involved in the project effectively, share project files and allocate work. The internal calendar allows the team to visualise timelines and important events, and individual pages allow team members to see what work they're responsible for.

Uskape

Uskape is another collaborative team tool that allows you to work with your favorite apps or to use their built-in tools to connect the dots between your calendar, contacts, content and communications. The idea is to bring all your work together in one collaborative space and not have the hassle of juggling apps and searching through emails.

Getting team buy-in

Any of these team tools will help to improve team communications and enhance productivity and effectiveness. The biggest barrier to making these tools work is the commitment required. If the team doesn't buy into using the tool 100 per cent, the tool will eventually fail. Spending time choosing what you think may be the right tool is essential, but getting buy-in in advance is also important. Sell the benefits, and let the team members see how much easier their jobs and lives will be if they start to use it.

Getting the buy-in of the team leader or manager on the new tool is important. It can also help immensely if a few key influencers are advocates. If team members see that the team leader and other key individuals are using the tool and liking it, you'll be a lot closer to getting buy-in and commitment from the whole team.

Running Productive Meetings

Since the dawn of man, human beings have been gathering in groups to discuss how to hunt, how to build villages and how to go out and conquer others. Meetings have been a means to discuss progress, to share knowledge and to entertain communities.

To this day, meetings should and can be positive events. Unfortunately, through lack of attention, people have allowed them to become untamed monsters. Having meetings when they're not necessary and allowing them to drag on far longer than necessary have led to the risk of meetings being eliminated from some organisations and groups. The death of meetings wouldn't be a good thing, though, because the coming together of people face to face can yield many benefits. What people need to do is get smarter about meetings and ensure that when meetings are held they are necessary and the most effective means of communication under the circumstances.

In this section, I outline how to run productive meetings, from the planning stage to the actual meeting to the follow-up.

Planning

Before calling a meeting, you first have to do a lot of thinking and planning. Break the planning down into manageable sections by asking the following questions.

Why are we having this meeting?

The first question to ask is whether the meeting is really necessary. Can you come to a decision in another way? Meetings are useful when discussion leads to better decision making. A meeting encourages everyone to share ideas and possible alternatives. A group can be more intelligent that an individual, so a group may find better solutions to problems.

Meetings are beneficial when team building is required. At a team meeting, individual members may feel more motivated after leaving the room. A meeting can also foster more trust and respect and lead to a healthier, more cohesive team.

Who needs to be there?

Consider who you need at the meeting, who is essential and whether everyone you invite needs to be there for the whole meeting. You also need to think about who will chair the meeting and who will take notes:

- **The chair:** The chair of a meeting is an important role. The chair must keep the meeting on track and on time. The chair is responsible for managing personalities, keeping those who contribute too much under check and encouraging more contribution from those who contribute too little. The chair is responsible for ensuring that there's commitment to actions agreed and that follow-up will happen.
- **The note taker:** Someone must also be responsible for taking notes at the meeting. Meeting notes include the decisions taken and the actions required. It is the responsibility of the note taker to circulate the notes from the meeting to all attendees and ensure they are clear about the actions required of them.

Where should we have it?

The location of a meeting is also important. If you're having a team-building meeting, getting out of the office to a more relaxed environment will have better results. A brainstorming meeting to elicit more creative ideas for new products may also benefit from an artistic and creative environment. Make sure the meeting venue is booked and confirmed in plenty of time. If you have to discuss a conflict, a walk-and-talk meeting can be an effective way to minimise confrontation and get to a consensus more quickly.

Who should create the agenda?

An *agenda* is an outline planning document explaining what needs to be discussed at the meeting. The agenda can be prepared by anyone, but somebody needs to be assigned to create it. It can be an informal couple of lines jotted down to keep people on track, or if attending a more formal meeting, it should contain more detail on what you are trying to achieve from the meeting.

Too often, an agenda is thrown together just before a meeting is due to start. It often looks something like this:

AGENDA

- Website
- New hires
- Christmas party

All this agenda tells me is that we'll discuss those subjects. I don't know what outcomes are required from discussing these topics and what we want to achieve. A more effective agenda may read as follows:

> AGENDA
>
> - Website: Are we going to commit internal resources to the online purchasing system or outsource project?
> - New hires: How can we ensure our induction process prepares our new hires for the job?
> - Christmas party: Get suggestions for staff Christmas party and decide whether partners invited or not.

The second example agenda ensures that participants will be more prepared for the meeting. With a clear objective, the meeting discussions are more likely to stay on track, and it's less likely someone will initiate a lengthy off-topic discussion. For example, the more basic agenda might lead people to go off on a tangent about website graphics, as the agenda item 'Website' suggests that any website discussion would be allowed.

The order in which you discuss agenda items is also important to the success of a meeting. If a natural order to the way you discuss items on the agenda is in place, it's important to honour this, but you may want to think about the topics and whether they're likely to cause conflict or energise the room.

Prepare the chair

The person who chairs the meeting needs to be familiar with the agenda and the outcomes required from the agenda. The chair should speak to the person who prepared the agenda in advance of the meeting to ensure she understands the context and the objectives. The chair should also be familiar with all the company's ground rules when it comes to meetings. In the next section, I provide suggestions for ground rules that your company can adopt.

Take regular breaks if the meeting is going to be more than an hour. Breaks can help diffuse negative energy, keep people energised and on track and simply allow for the participants to be more comfortable and focused on the meeting agenda.

Parkinson's Law states that work expands to meet the time available. Don't allow too much time for meetings because you'll use it up. Give each agenda item an allocated time and try to stay on track. Reduce the overall time allocated to meetings to try to minimise any time wasted.

Running the meeting

With a clear agenda and a well-prepared chair, you're ready for a successful meeting. During the meeting, you want to ensure that all meeting participants have the opportunity to contribute and prevent anyone from dominating the discussions.

The following sections outlines ways for you to get the most out of your meeting.

Setting ground rules

Creating ground rules for all meetings in your organisation will have a positive impact on the effectiveness of those meetings. It will also create positive habits for all employees. Typical ground rules for meetings could include the following:

- Start and finish the meeting on time.
- Don't bring phones, laptops or other gadgets unless for approved note taking or presentations.
- Be present and engaged.
- Be honest.
- Be open to new ways of working and ideas.
- Respect others (all opinions are valid), but know you don't have to accept something you disagree with.
- Speak up and be heard.
- Come prepared.

Ground rules create a safe and productive environment. Choose your company ground rules and ensure that they're enforced at every meeting.

Staying on track

Having a clear agenda is the safest way to ensure that the meeting stays on track. With a clear purpose, the discussion should be focused on finding the right answers to the right questions. The chair is responsible for ensuring that the conversation stays on topic and that no one steers it away either accidentally or on purpose.

Sticking to the allotted time

Timekeeping is an essential part of any effective meeting. Everyone is busy. Some executives spend up to 80 per cent of their time in meetings, and they still have to get their job done. If a meeting runs over time, it can have a negative impact on many peoples' days. The meeting chair is responsible for making sure the time is respected, but all meeting attendees can do their part and keep an eye on the time to make sure the meeting ends on time.

Meetings should start on time regardless of whether all attendees are present. Starting meetings on time and staying within the allotted time are essential to making meetings productive and worthwhile for all involved.

Ensuring participants' comfort

If you want a meeting that gives you positive results, the participants need to be relaxed and comfortable. The meeting organiser should ensure a comfortable environment with the optimum temperature for the time of year and, if the meeting is to be a long one, provide plenty of fluids and snacks. Regular breaks are also important if the meeting is longer than an hour.

Generating positive contributions

The chair of the meeting should encourage the right sort of contribution from all who attend. Quieter people are often less likely to contribute, but they still need to be included and encouraged to share their ideas and opinions.

Circulate detailed agendas with outcomes required well before the meeting. This allows for people to think about their contributions and ideas and have them prepared in advance. Some people can't think on the spot and need time to put their thoughts and ideas together.

As well as encouraging everyone to speak, the chair may also need to curb the contributions of some. Some people like the sound of their own voices or just have something to say about everything. Some want to hog the limelight; others don't even know that their mouths are always open. It's important to make these people aware that their contribution is valid and desired but that all voices should be heard.

Establishing clear action points

Your attention may wander while you're in a meeting and you may miss one or two things that were said. That's normal. However, for these reasons, it's vital that the chair be good at summarising all actions agreed to ensure that everyone is clear and on board with action items going forward. The note taker will be responsible for taking note of all decisions taken and circulate them after the meeting.

Following up

One of the reasons meetings aren't effective is lack of follow-up. Lots of important people sit in a room for lots of time and make good decisions. Lots of these good decisions never get implemented. Sometimes this is due to a lack of clarity about what needs to be done. Other times, it is due to lack of ownership of an issue: The task was simply never assigned to anyone. To prevent this from happening, you need an agreed follow-up method.

Following are a few options for how you may follow up after a meeting and ensure that the decisions made are acted on.

Using minutes

Minutes are the historical records of a meeting, a full statement of who said what and who is responsible for actions agreed upon. Minutes are a time-consuming way to record the happenings in a meeting and should be used only when absolutely necessary.

Some organisations, political or perhaps voluntary, require minutes to be held for each meeting. Sometimes, where crucial decisions are being made in areas such as HR or safety, minutes are a good idea, but for most day-to-day meetings, they're not necessary.

The minute taker is responsible for circulating the minutes of the meeting after each meeting. In the minutes, there should be a detailed record of who is responsible for the completion of each task. Before the next meeting, the minute taker will again circulate the minutes along with the agenda of the upcoming meeting. The idea of this is to ensure that all follow-up actions have been carried out.

Working with an action list

Most work meetings don't need the detail of minutes. Simple notes with an action list will suffice. An action list is a summary of the decisions made and who is responsible for implementing them. The note taker is responsible for circulating the action list and reminding attendees that they are responsible for certain items on the list.

Operating with a task management tool

The most efficient way to follow up after a meeting is to use your task management tool in the meeting. Create an agenda as a project, and assign the items as they're discussed to the relevant person. Putting the tool on a screen ensures that everyone can visualise the items being discussed and can clearly see the outcomes agreed upon and the person responsible. If your tool is used effectively, the items agreed upon become part of each individual's task list and won't get forgotten about.

Asana recommends creating a project for all meeting agendas and has a great video describing how to do it at `https://asana.com/guide/more/examples/meetings`.

Getting creative

Remember that meetings don't have to be done the way you've always done them. It's okay to break the mould and change things around. Get creative with how you run your meetings. Change the venue; go outdoors. Try out the walk and talk or stand-up meetings. If you're not happy with the outcomes from your current meetings, shift the energy and do things a little differently. You may be quite pleased with the results.

Discovering Paper Productivity

Organising your paper can have a sizeable impact on your productivity. Clearing the clutter gives you a clean environment in which to think and work. It also reduces time spent looking for documents and limits the possibilities of something getting lost or misplaced.

What you can do with paper

Although many offices are moving toward paperless and reducing the amount of paper required to work an effective system, paper has its advantages. From doodling to brainstorming, tablets and software just don't cut the mustard. With all the note-taking apps and endless possibilities, pen and paper are still the chosen tools of many. Paper is sometimes the easiest and quickest way to take notes to explain ideas to others and be creative.

Filing (your finding system)

The purpose of a good filing system is to be able to find things when you need them. Filing effectively ensures that nothing gets lost and no time is lost when trying to retrieve a document.

When organising your paperwork, I suggest having both a reference filing system and an active filing system. Always separate the reference documents from the ones that are in use or represent a task to be completed. The following sections go into further detail about the two.

Reference filing

Reference filing is the stuff you put away in your filing cabinet. This is the paperwork you keep just in case you need it in the future or for compliance purposes. A simple A to Z filing system is always best. Whether it is projects, client names or suppliers, A to Z will ensure you know where to look and can find it in seconds.

If you attempt to adopt a more complex system, for example, organising first into areas of work, it can cause difficulties at a later stage. If the person who set up the filing system leaves the company, the people who remain may not think in the same way and find it difficult to maintain the original system. Having a simple A to Z system keeps things clear for everybody and eliminates any confusion.

Active filing

File work in progress, current work or work to be done in the near future in a separate filing system on your desk if possible. Use a desk file stand or hanging folders in a desk drawer to store your active folders. Your active filing system may include your expenses, travel documents or bills to be paid, for example. Label your files clearly with a label maker to make them easy to find. Buy manila tabbed folders and have a ready supply on hand to use when required.

Endless possibilities exist for folders that you can create. Be sure to always have as many as you need but as few as possible.

Streamlining to a Paperless Office

Since the emergence of the computer, there has been much talk of the paperless office. The prediction that computers would completely eradicate the need for paper hasn't yet been realised. And although the removal of paper from modern-day life is a point everyone can aim for, it probably won't be realised in the near future. This, however, shouldn't stop you for pitching in the direction of this noble goal.

Taking the time to research and plan a paperless move can be enormously worthwhile in the long term, not only for the impact you can have on the planet but also for the impact on your overall efficiency and productivity.

Evaluating the change

Deciding to move toward a paperless office is a big decision and gets bigger depending on the size of your organisation. For an individual to make that decision, it's easier to control the outcome, to set realistic boundaries and to tweak and change those boundaries according to the daily practicality.

When an organisation chooses to commit to paperless working, a lot more consequences of making the move come into play. It has to analyse numerous business processes that use paper and make changes to accommodate a paperless workflow.

The following sections list some of the elements to consider before rushing in to make the change.

Analysing the financial benefits

The first step to going paperless is to get clear about how much paper you currently use as an organisation and what the elimination of paper would mean financially to the organisation. Take into account any costs that will be incurred by making the changeover, such as time-changing processes or educating the workforce on the new practises. Also factor in any time saved from more efficient workflow processes and not having to walk to printers, get signatures and so on.

Identifying the impact

Before announcing a policy change to your organisation, get each department head to analyse the implications of a change. What processes would be affected and which ones may cause complications? Identifying the barriers and challenges in advance will help to make the move more fluid when it does come.

Agreeing on the goal

When each department understands the cost savings that can be made, it will make it easier for it to buy into the idea that this is a positive change. After identifying where changes in the workflow can be made, you can then set a more realistic goal based on your findings. This could be a 50 per cent reduction in paper usage by a particular date. This will give people something to aim toward and allow them time to adapt.

Drawing a line in the sand

A lot of organisations that have gone paperless drew a line in the sand and began from a given point forward. Trying to digitise past documentation is a massive job. It can be hugely beneficial for some organisations where document retrieval can take time, but unless this is you, you'd be wiser to spend your time on improving the systems for the future. If you decide to convert your past records to electronic, you may consider hiring some interns to carry out the process.

Looking into paperless storage benefits

Document management software has been around for years. The idea of turning cabinets of paper into secure, version-controlled storage systems emerged not long after the computer. The scope of what is possible is always expanding. Electronic storage enhances work areas such as accounting, legal, IT, insurance and healthcare, to name a few. Internal departments such as HR and compliance wouldn't function effectively without it.

Following are some of the benefits to paperless storage:

- **Effective information sharing:** The effective sharing of information has been a massive boost to the advancement of humanity. Electronic document management has enhanced and improved the collaboration with different people, offices and countries, enabling organisations to freely share information and allowing real-time communications around the world.
- **Maintaining accurate records:** Accurate records and version control are essential in certain job roles. Software documentation and ISO compliance require accurate version records for each document created. Working from an older document can have disastrous consequences. People are more likely to confuse paper documents; electronic document control is a more effective way to ensure that correct versions are in use at all time.
- **Improving organisational workflows:** A paperless office can improve processes and enhance operations. Removing the requirement for paper documentation can hugely improve many workflows. Processes are easier to follow, and therefore efficiency increases.
- **Reducing unnecessary costs:** Costs are reduced both in the reduction of labour time needed to file and store paper documentation and also in the physical cost of the paper and storage units. A paperless office still incurs costs for server space and document management software that improves the document storage experience, but both are outweighed by the saving gained.
- **Enhancing data security:** Data security is greatly enhanced by having a secure electronic system that can limit access rights and privileges. Maintaining documents securely stored in a document management system reduces the risk of inappropriate file access by unauthorized people.
- **Enabling disaster recovery:** Having files stored electronically enables a data recovery system to be set up. If all your files are paper-based and your office catches fire, you'd need to have a copy of every document offsite to recover your files. If you have an electronic filing system, backups of your data can be made much more easily and stored on a safe offsite server, facilitating the rapid recovery of your data in the case of a natural or other type of disaster.

Exploring the tools and technology of going paperless

For many years, the quest to go paperless was determined only by the latest software that was in development. Currently, hardware, software and cloud technology enable you to remove paper from the job.

Tablets

Tablets have made a massive improvement in how you can remove the need for paper. From medical professionals to wedding planners, the tablet has revolutionized their efficiency and eliminated their requirement for paper.

- **Medical records:** Many health professionals no longer use paper and instead take their patient notes on their tablets. Some have specialised software; others use standard software, such as spreadsheets or note-taking apps, to store their notes. This enables these health professionals to access past records more quickly and from any location.
- **Pilots:** Some airlines now issue their pilots iPads instead of loading them down with paper map books and charts. This makes finding information a lot more efficient for the pilots as well as hopefully improving safety.
- **Schools:** Many schools have made the switch to tablets. Children no longer have to lug around kilos of textbooks, saving their little backs and enabling them and teachers to share more information freely.
- **Sports teams:** Coaches and sports teams benefit from using tablets for sharing game tactics and information.
- **Retail industry:** Take a look at your local supermarket and you'll see a supervisor or manager walking around and checking the stock on his iPad.

Scanners

Although scanners have been around for some time, new technology is allowing people to scan large amounts of paper at once and also to scan paper on the move. This ensures that there is no excuse for leaving paper lying around.

- **Mobile scanners:** Mobile scanners are ideal for document digitisation on the move. A mobile scanner is perfect for in-vehicle scanning, hot desking, business meetings, and simply archiving documents at home.
- **Desktop scanners:** The standard desktop scanner allows digitalisation of documents in the office or at home. It's portable enough to move if required and generally doesn't take up too much space.
- **Heavy duty scanners:** When you have a lot of documentation to scan, you will want a scanner with fast scan speeds and a high-capacity automatic document feeder. If you have a high volume of paper that needs to be digitalized, you will need one of these. The other option is to outsource to a specialised company.

Software

You can choose from many software solutions to manage storage, depending on your organisational requirements. Ensure that the basics are covered and any further requirements that your company may have, such as the following:

- Basic document creation (Word, Excel, PDF)
- Scanning of paper documents
- Email backup
- Electronic notes backup
- CRM document generation
- Accounting software document generation
- Other proprietary systems

Cloud storage

One of the many benefits of cloud computing is the amount of costs it cuts for a business. There is no need for expensive servers to be installed in the office. This cuts hardware, software and energy costs and also, more basically, saves on space in an office.

Because information is not stored in any single location, it can be located from anywhere with any device, once it has an Internet connection.

- **Document storage:** You can store anything in the cloud today with services like Dropbox. Dropbox allows you to keep your files safe, synced and easy to share. Google Drive offers a similar service with same the facility to collaborate with others. These services are a must have if you intend to move into the paperless world.
- **Photo sites:** Photo sites like Picassa and Flickr offer free storage space. Simply set the settings to private and you are the only one who can view your photos. Also, by storing all your photos on one of these sites, rather than in multiple folders across your other cloud storage services, you will know where all your images are at all times, and you won't clog up your other cloud storage spaces like Dropbox or Google Drive with bulky photo files.

Accounting solutions

The cloud offers accounting solutions for both large and small business. Popular software programmes such as Sage and QuickBooks have their cloud versions, where purpose-built solutions such as Freshbooks and Wave are gaining popularity. Apps that can complement your cloud accounting solutions are Expensify and Shoeboxes to help you keep track of your receipts on the go.

Chapter 13

Task Management

In This Chapter

- Experiencing the power of lists
- Debunking the benefits of traditional to-do lists
- Finding the perfect task management system
- Letting an app track your time

Managing the work you need to do is always a challenge. You have to remember what needs to be done, prioritise it and then reprioritise it daily. Staying in control, on time, on target and on track are testing for everyone.

Task management has become a hot topic over the past number of years with first the introduction of team project management tools, helping teams stay on top of their projects, and then the introduction of the individual task management tools, enabling people to not only take control of their work tasks but also have a way to capture, organise and monitor the progress of their personal tasks. This chapter guides you through the nitty gritty.

Introducing the Power of Lists

The humble list has always been a useful tool to get things under control, to simplify more complex issues and to enable progress. People use lists to understand the world around them. People make lists of things they need to do, things they want to do, places they want to visit and people they need to see. Lists facilitate modern-day life. For example:

- **Shopping list:** How would you survive without the shopping list? Okay, so maybe you would instinctively go to the supermarket and buy food to eat, but without a list, you'd find yourself buying items you don't need or overshopping for the coming period. Shopping lists help you to plan in advance what is required and minimise time spent shopping as well as money spent on unnecessary items.

- **Event-planning list:** No successful event was ever planned without a list, and don't come to me with that spontaneous pool party you attended one summer break. Real-world events need planning and preparation, and what better way to do it than with a list? A list keeps track of all that is to be done and all that has been done.
- **To-do list:** The to-do list is man's best friend. Without a list of all the things you need to do, you'd be sitting directionless and with no idea of what to do next.

Saying Goodbye to the Traditional To-Do List

The traditional to-do list, while better than nothing, can have a negative effect on your happiness and productivity. The reason for this is that the to-do list is a list of stuff: stuff that hasn't been prioritised, stuff that you have no idea how long will take to complete and stuff that has sat there for many weeks. Another hard fact is that your to-do list will never be empty – well, at least not until the day you die; then it becomes someone else's problem.

For these reasons, to-do lists and happiness aren't compatible. With a never-ending to-do list, there is never any feeling of completion or achievement, and you'll forever feel dissatisfied. This is referred to as the *Zeigarnik effect* (see the nearby sidebar 'Bluma Zeigarnik and the not-so-dumb waiters' for why).

Bluma Zeigarnik and the not-so-dumb waiters

The Zeigarnik effect is commonly referred to as the tendency of the subconscious mind to remind you of a task that is incomplete until that task *is* complete.

Bluma Zeigarnik was a Lithuanian psychologist who wrote in the 1920s about the effects of leaving tasks incomplete. Some accounts say that she noticed the effect when watching waiters serve in a restaurant. Waiters would remember an order, however complicated, until the order was complete, but they would later find it difficult to remember the order. Zeigarnik did further studies giving both adults and children puzzles to complete then interrupting them during some of the tasks. The results showed that both adults and children remembered the tasks that hadn't been completed better than the ones that had been completed.

Some say that you must use this effect to your benefit. If there is something you're procrastinating on, simply get started; the Zeigarnik effect will haunt you until you complete it. But there is a way to use the Zeigarnik effect to your benefit while minimising the negative effects of the task hauntings. After you've committed to a task, you're more likely to finish it. And if you work with a task management system and also schedule the work to be done, you won't experience the negative hauntings.

Introducing the Benefits of Task Management

Task management is the to-do list 2.0. It's the next phase in capturing the work that needs to be done. It takes the work you need to do and categorises it. Most task management programs also allow you to prioritise tasks. The next phase is planning and scheduling the work to be done. You can find much more on scheduling in Chapter 14.

Taking your tasks and separating them into different projects or mini lists helps you to manage and prioritise your workload better. Storing all tasks relating to a certain job area or a certain project together allows you not to worry about these incomplete tasks until you're working on that project. Creating a resting place for each area of work outwits the Zeigarnik effect (see the nearby sidebar for more on this). After you've categorised a task and planned the work that needs to get done, your brain no longer has to carry this incomplete task in your short-term memory. Task management does the following:

- Captures work
- Makes clear how much work is involved
- Makes progress and workload easier to review
- Improves motivation by letting you visualise progress
- Breaks down larger projects into manageable tasks
- Reduces time wasted deciding what to do – your list is ready when you are

Team task management can have a powerful effect on team collaboration and productivity. Having a central location for team tasks that all the team has access to increases transparency and accountability, which has an immediate effect on efficiency and results. (See Chapter 12 for more on team tools.)

Choosing Your Task Management App

You can find many task management tools on the market, with new ones appearing daily. I currently use Todoist and Evernote to keep me productive. In this section, I also talk about Wunderlist, another popular tool recommended by productivity professionals. Note that these three are just a sampling of the thousands of other possibilities to consider. Many other team project management tools can be used effectively for personal use. Software such as Trello and Asana (see Chapter 12) are loved by many an individual.

Some tools will ebb and wane in popularity, but the concept remains that if you want to get more work done and be able to focus effectively on the right project at the right time, a task or project management tool is the way forward.

Choose a task management tool that you like the sound of and stick with it. They all work once you put a bit of effort into setting them up. If after about six weeks you feel the one you've chosen isn't improving your efficiency, you have my permission to try another one.

Todoist

Todoist.com has been around since 2007, but its 2015 updates caught my attention. It's a powerful personal task management solution that's available on PC, Mac, the web, iOS and Android. What won me over was its powerful plug-ins for email programmes such as Outlook, Gmail and Thunderbird, allowing you to add your tasks directly from your email, an essential feature if you want to achieve a clear inbox each week.

Todoist is simple and easy to use and allows you to use it in whatever mode suits your style. Its free version is good for personal users or those of you who don't do much work. The premium version is very affordable and advisable if you want a more robust task management system to help you get more done.

Projects

The first thing to do when you decide to use Todoist is to set up projects for the different areas of your work and life. Todoist has a number of standard projects and suggests ones like Work, Personal, Books to Read and Movies to Watch. You can delete these projects or rename them as you see fit. Include all the different areas of your work and your personal areas of responsibility.

You may want to create a project for your hobby or for garden and household chores. You can create subprojects for people who report to you or for people on your team. You can set it up in many ways; you just have to find the right way for you.

Breaking the big rocks

Big rocks are the big tasks you have to do. The name comes from the idea that if you think of your day as a bucket and you fill it up with sand, you won't fit any pebbles or big rocks into the bucket after that. But if you start by putting in the big rocks, then you can put some pebbles in around the big rocks and finally you will have lots of space in between for all the sand. If you start your day with the important big tasks, you will still have time for some smaller, less important tasks.

Tasks

You can add tasks directly into Todoist or from your email account. The important thing to remember when adding tasks is to associate them with a project. This will ensure that you have a realistic view of your work when you look at your overall tasks in a given project.

Recurring tasks

Todoist allows you to add recurring tasks that you can set to remind you on a particular day of the month. Monthly tasks, such as doing your expenses or accounts or ordering dog food, work well with a reminder because you don't do them regularly.

Labels

Labels allow you to add contexts to your tasks. (See Chapter 10 on GTD for more information on contexts.) Contexts give you more information about a task, such as when or where the tasks should be completed. The default contexts in Todoist include Coffee Shop, Low Energy and Travel. The labels allow you to assign tasks to certain contexts; for example, next time I am in a coffee shop, I will complete my coffee shop tasks. There are many tasks that don't need high energy or focus to complete; these tasks are low-energy tasks. When you are lacking energy, you can go to this list and still tick off a few tasks.

Filters

Todoist comes equipped with filters, too, allowing you to set different priorities on tasks. This can be used for setting your top three tasks for the day or your 'big rocks', as the big boys call them (see the nearby sidebar 'Breaking the big rocks')!

Evernote

With a tag line of 'Remember everything' and an elephant as its logo, I fell for Evernote the first time I laid eyes on it. I have a 'leaky brain', as my good friend Joel Zasflosky, founder of SimpleREV.com, calls it, so this was definitely the tool for me. I can remember irrelevant facts about *Star Wars* characters and Harry Potter spells, but I often forget my wedding anniversary or my children's schedules. Fortunately, Evernote has extended my brain, and with easy data retrieval, no one would even notice it didn't come straight from my own cranium.

Evernote is essentially a powerful note-taking app, but in recent years and many features later, you can use it as a place to store all your notes, research and ideas as well as a task management system. Evernote is available for Macs, PCs, the web, iOS and Android.

Notebooks

Evernote is set up with notebooks and notes. Each notebook represents an area of work or an area of your personal life. I have notebooks for books I'm writing, family chores, children's schedules, research for work and the list goes on.

If you intend to use both Todoist and Evernote, use the same project names for your notebooks. In this way, you keep your system streamlined and improve your efficiency when looking for information. Todoist is for getting daily tasks done, whereas Evernote is best for storing notes and research. You can cleverly combine them to create a productivity system that will knock your socks off when used effectively.

Notes

A note can contain a task, an image, an audio note, a checklist or a chapter of a book. These notes are stored inside your notebooks. This tool gives you a place to store everything and anything. Get creative and start your electronic curating.

Notebook Stacks

You can create Notebook Stacks to store your notebooks inside. Notebook Stacks are useful for creating high level areas of work, such as Work, Personal and Blog. Underneath these Notebook Stacks, you can have a number of notebooks, each one containing a number of notes.

Tags

Tagging is a useful feature that enables you to find what you're looking for in the months to come. Tags are like keywords, so, for example, when I'm in the supermarket and I want to make an almond cake, I search for 'almond' and all the notes that contain the word *almond* show in my search results. You can also use the tagging feature to put contexts on notes (see Chapter 10 on GTD and contexts).

Location

Think back on your last city break. Imagine you took a note of the restaurants you ate in, the sites you visited and the bars that had good night life. Two years later, you go again, you search for any notes that you made for that city, and *voilà* – you have information for your trip itinerary at your fingertips.

Web clipper

Another useful feature of Evernote is its *web clipper,* which enables you to attach a web document, image or webpage to a note to view at a later stage. This comes in handy when you're doing research for an article or assignment. You can capture the information, tag it and then put it in the right notebook so that you can access it later when you're ready to work.

Audio notes

Audio notes are convenient for meetings. Instead of taking notes or minutes, you can record the meeting to listen back to at a later time. You can also send the audio notes to someone who couldn't make the meeting. Or you can simply use them to remind yourself of something.

Note sharing

One of the premium features, note sharing can be valuable when collaborating on a project. It reduces the amount of time you have to spend on email sending documents back and forth. Using note sharing, you can share a notebook and allow your colleagues to edit it.

Notes links

When working on a collaborative project, such as a book or a course, it can be useful to use note links. This enables you to organise your notes better and give structure to your setup. Linking notes can be useful when you're using Evernote as an electronic filing cabinet. For example, you can scan a bill, pay the bill and link the receipt to the original bill.

Presentation mode

Presentation mode is a useful feature for meetings. If you have all the information you need for a meeting inside a note, you can present from Evernote. This saves you having to transfer the information to presentation software and enables you to open linked documents or update the information on the fly, visible to all at the meeting.

Wunderlist

Wunderlist is another popular and easy-to-use tool that has a simple and effective free version but also a premium version for task sharing and storing files. Its clean, intuitive approach to task management makes it another front-runner in the task management app decision race. Some prefer the design of Wunderlist and choose it for this reason, but its simplicity and ample features encourage them to stay. Wunderlist is available for free on Windows, Mac, the web, iOS and Android.

Wunderlist has all the following features:

- Lists
- Sub lists
- Notes
- Notifications
- Reminders
- Due dates
- Ability to turn emails into actions
- A premium version for those who want to share or collaborate on projects and a business version for larger collaboration with teams and colleagues

Wunderlist Pro

When you sign up for Wunderlist Pro, the premium version, it unlocks four features that can make your life a lot easier:

- **Sharing:** Wunderlist Pro enables you to begin sharing your tasks. This can be useful both for professional and personal life. Sharing home projects and grocery lists can help things run smoothly at home. Sharing projects and work to do can reduce the need for both email and meetings.
- **Files:** With the Pro edition, you can add unlimited files of all types – PDFs, videos, and audio files. This is a great way to keep everything belonging to a project in one place.
- **Unlimited subtasks:** You're allowed unlimited subtasks in the premium version. Breaking down tasks into subtasks can help to move work forward as larger tasks can be overwhelming and more difficult to complete than smaller subtasks.
- **Pro backgrounds:** Premium allows you to choose your background. This can make a big difference if you work better when things are aesthetically pleasing and visually comfortable.

Wunderlist Business

Wunderlist Business makes it easy to manage team projects all in one place. It's an effective tool for team communication and collaboration. It's another tool that discourages using email for team communication and encourages team interaction to take place within the app. Features include

- **Assigning:** You can assign tasks to your teammates and ensure that team members are accountable and work gets done.

- **Adding files:** In Wunderlist Business, you can add files to project lists. This keeps everything in one place, allowing team members to share documents and receive feedback more quickly.
- **Notes:** The notes feature enables clarification or extra information to be added to a task, ensuring that no ambiguity exists about what needs to happen.
- **Comments:** Comments encourage collaboration and discussion. This is the feature that reduces the need for email, keeping the conversations about projects all in one place.
- **Activity centre:** The activity centre keeps everyone in the loop when a colleague creates, completes or comments on a to-do. The activity centre is a list of all activity that takes place, allowing you to be aware of any updates or comments that may need your attention.
- **To-dos from email or web:** With Mail to Wunderlist and the Add to Wunderlist browser extensions, it's easy to create to-dos straight from your inbox and save anything you find on the web.

Keeping Track of Your Time

Time-tracking tools are a great way to see how much work you're actually getting done. They can help you gain perspective, spot inefficiencies in your day and become better at managing your time. They're also a great way to manage billable hours. This section covers some of the most widely used time-tracking tools.

Toggl

Toggl is simple to use, and you can set it up in minutes. It allows you to time all your work. If you forget to turn on the clock, you can add it in later. It is available on Windows or Mac and has supporting mobile versions.

Like most programmes, Toggl has a free limited version. The free version allows you to

- Track how you spend your time daily
- Give access for up to 5 people
- View Reports on time tracked
- Track unlimited projects and clients

If you upgrade to the premium version of the tool, you get more features, such as

- Unlimited team size access
- A feature to add billable rates so you can track what your time costs for each client
- The facility for rounding and decimals
- Project and task estimates

Tracking your time can be enlightening. Most people think they're being productive, but once they start tracking what they do, it uncovers a whole different story.

RescueTime

RescueTime allows you to understand your daily habits so you can focus and be more productive. It runs in the background on your computer and mobile devices without disturbing you, but it tracks time spent on applications and websites, giving you an accurate picture of your day. Some of the features of RescueTime can help you see what you're doing and adjust if necessary. Its standard features include

- **Time measurement:** You can measure your time when you want it. You are in complete control and can turn it off at any stage.
- **Weekly reports:** Weekly email reports give you an overview of your week so you can see how effective you're being and whether you're staying on track or things are getting in the way of your performance and productivity.

If you want to step up to the premium version, you can avail of the following features:

- **Alerts:** With RescueTime premium, you can set alerts to notify you of how much time you've spent on a particular project. This can help you to focus and ensure that you're staying on track.
- **Block distractions:** Block distracting websites by choosing an amount of time to focus, and RescueTime will block those websites.
- **Log highlights:** Log highlights about what you accomplished during the day.

RescueTime gives you an accurate picture of how you spend your time to help you become more productive every day. It enables you to set goals and achieve those goals. If you want to spend one hour a day on email and no more, you can set an alarm to tell you when you've spent more than one hour on it.

Chapter 14

Calendar Management

In This Chapter

- Planning the work to be done
- Discovering all the tricks and tools to using your calendar

The calendar is perhaps the most underutilised tool in your toolkit, yet it can be one of the most powerful. Many people use their calendars for planning daily activities, keeping track of events and reminding themselves of important festival dates, but after that the calendar remains empty. In this chapter, I show you how your calendar can be more than just a place to store events and meetings but a tool for getting organised, achieving your goals and living a more balanced and fulfilled life.

Using Your Calendar to Get Things Done

Many people argue that the calendar shouldn't be overloaded with all the work you need to do. Others say you should put all your tasks into your calendar so you can monitor your work and get it done. I lie somewhere in the middle. I have experienced the power of the calendar and found that planning the work I have to do in my calendar helps me to focus and get a lot more work done than I ever thought possible. The trick is to use your task manager for your tasks but to use your calendar to plan larger bodies of work, like projects and writing. You can find more on task management in Chapter 13.

Deciding what goes into the calendar

Anything that is date- or time-specific goes into the calendar – that means anything that needs to be done on or by a particular time or date. The thing is, most of your work eventually becomes time bound and needs to be completed. If it isn't time bound from the start and you don't put it into your calendar, chances are it will never get done.

The calendar: A timeline

The history of the calendar is long and complex. A couple of years ago, in 45 BC, Julius Caesar introduced a calendar that became widely used in many countries. Unfortunately, it didn't accurately calculate the length of the solar year, and from 1582, it was gradually replaced by the Gregorian calendar. The Gregorian calendar required the dropping of between 10 and 13 days from the calendar to accurately reflect the solar year. Imagine going to bed on the 2nd of September to wake up on the 12th; that would have turned out to be an extra-long lie in. Many countries adopted the Gregorian calendar in 1586, but many delayed in its adaptation.

Some of the most important examples of what you should put in your calendar include

- **Meetings:** All business meetings, both internal and external. These can even include coffee dates with friends or meetings with your family. All meetings should be noted and planned for in your calendar. By relying on your calendar and not on your mind to remember your meetings, you free up thinking time to get more creative in your meetings.
- **Medical appointments:** Dentist, doctor and specialist appointments fall into this category. It's best to leave extra time on either side of these appointments. More often than not, this type of meeting doesn't start on time and therefore has the tendency to run over time.
- **Holidays:** It's important to block off holiday time in your calendar as soon as possible. It's always good to see the big picture as clearly as possible and see what time is available to you during the year. Blocking off the holiday time encourages you to commit to taking a holiday rather than deciding you are too busy and keep pushing through.
- **The weekly review:** If you aren't doing a weekly review, as David Allen strongly suggests you should in his book *Getting Things Done: The Art of Stress-Free Productivity* (Penguin, 2002), then you're probably not as organised as you'd like to be. It's important to block out a period of time once per week to conduct the processing of all your inboxes and review your goals and priorities so you can feel in control of your workload and you can move things forward in the days, weeks, months and years ahead. Set aside an hour every week to get this done.
- **Exercise:** Exercise is such an important component of a productive and focused life. So many find it difficult to find the time to fit it in to their day. Using your calendar to plan your workouts will prompt you to stick to your schedule.
- **Strategic thinking time:** Not one executive I meet has enough time to do all the tasks required of him. What I notice more and more is that most managers are in reactive mode. They react to the work that comes their

way. Very little time is put into planning and even less time given to strategic thinking. If you're in a senior management position, part of your job is to spend time thinking about how your organisation or team can improve and grow.

Plan some strategic thinking time into your calendar each week. Even if you have to leave the office to go to a coffee shop or to a park, factor in the time and commit to it. It's as important to the business as doing accounts and shouldn't be left to chance.

- **Creative thinking time:** Just as many people spend too little time strategically thinking, people also don't give enough time to creative thinking. It's difficult to be creative in the typical office environment, a place where distraction and interruptions are part of every working hour. Put some creative thinking time in your calendar. Plan a trip to a museum or to a wide open space, sit back, relax and get creative.
- **Downtime:** Time for relaxation often gets left out. I've realised in recent years that if I don't schedule my downtime, it never happens. I've also realised that relaxation is part of my job. If I don't unwind, detach and relax, I don't perform as well as I should. Downtime is another one of those important things that should get airspace in the calendar.

Don't put all your to-dos into your calendar because you risk overloading it and reducing its efficacy. The fear is that if everything goes into the calendar, you'll feel overwhelmed, not complete the tasks you planned to do and get demotivated as a result. There are times when work gets shuffled along, avoided and ignored for more interesting or important tasks. This is why it's important to filter everything that you put into the calendar. If you can avoid putting in the small tasks, you'll benefit greatly from using the calendar daily.

Recognising the benefits of using a calendar

There are many benefits to using a calendar. Personally, I have benefited enormously. Since making a calendar part of my weekly planning process, I am achieving much more and ticking a lot more boxes. Following are several ways you benefit from using a calendar.

Beating procrastination

If you're like most people, you probably have a list of things you'd like to do but never find the time to do. Maybe you'd like to write a book, create a vegetable garden or start playing guitar. The chief reason for people never doing the things that they want to do with their lives is that they don't have time. They fill their days with daily tasks and convince themselves that they're too tired to spend their free time pursuing their goals and dreams.

The truth is, you have more time available than you realise. When you stop doing those things that waste time, such as watching TV or browsing social media, extra time comes from nowhere. Using the calendar has helped me to identify this time. It has helped me to become aware of all the hours in my day and use them more effectively. If there's something you've wanted to do for a long time, schedule some time into your calendar to get started. Once you make a start on something, you're much more likely to keep going.

Assisting focus

The calendar helps me to focus. When I have planned an activity and know how much time I need, entering it in to my calendar greatly assists my focus. I have to commit to completing this activity, so unless something more important crops up, that is what I will be doing at that time. Planning with the calendar helps me to get in touch with the big picture. When you can see what the overall goal is that you're trying to achieve, it is more motivating and inspiring to go get it.

Getting more organised

The calendar is also a way to get more organised. When your work is planned, you can visualise more clearly what needs to be done. This helps you to distribute your work more evenly throughout the week and keeps you more organised and in control.

Creating alignment with goals

A lot of people struggle to find the time to do everything they need to do. As time is a limited resource, you need to ensure that you're spending it on the right things. When people say they don't have time to reach their goals, often you'll find that they're spending time working on the wrong stuff or doing things that don't need to be done at all.

Planning your week in advance means you're less likely to let time-wasting tasks disturb your day. If you look back at the past week and work out how you spent your time, you'll soon see whether the tasks that you do each day are in alignment with your big goals and supporting their achievement. Make sure that you're making progress toward your goals and that you've scheduled time every day to help you make that progress.

Tracking your time

How long do you spend on Project A or on Client B? Your calendar can help you track billable hours. If you choose to use your calendar in this way, make sure you look back at the end of each week and adjust your calendar to represent exactly how your time was spent. You can also colour-code your projects or client time to make it easier to see how you spend your time.

Figuring Out How to Use Your Calendar

Every week after you do your mind dump (see Chapters 4 and 10 for more on the mind dump), take some time to plan the week ahead. Take everything that is date- or time-specific from your mind dump and add it to your calendar. Check over your task list and move anything that is time sensitive to your calendar.

When you plan the week ahead, it's a good practice to check over last week's schedule to ensure that it all got done and, if it didn't, find a time in the coming weeks to reschedule. You may want to use an electronic calendar so you can easily move a project from one day to the next or from one week to another as the case may be.

In the following sections, I cover aspects of using an electronic calendar and different options available and also give some suggestions for the old paper-based standby. I then show you ways that you can theme your calendar and also share it with others.

Checking out the views in your electronic calendar

When you first open your electronic, or digital, calendar, you're presented with a default view. The defaults applied can range anywhere from a daily view to a weekly view, but I suggest looking beyond those defaults to make sure you get the best look possible at your calendar. For example, when you're planning appointments that are further down the road, you're going to want to look at the monthly (or even yearly view) to make sure you don't double-book yourself somewhere along the line.

Here are several views you can choose from in your digital calendar settings along with some ideal times to use them:

- **Daily:** This view is most valuable after you've looked at some of the longer-range prospects. For example, when you first arrive at the office, you may want to check out what's going on for the rest of the week and then settle back to your daily view so you can focus on the day at hand.
- **Weekly:** This view is the one you should refer to first thing in the morning. It allows you to have a broader scope beyond the present day, yet it won't overwhelm you as much as a monthly view. In fact, a lot of people flip back and forth between daily and weekly view throughout their day, which is fine as long as your focus isn't taken away from the tasks at hand.

- **Monthly:** The monthly view gives a view of the month to come but doesn't allow you to see much detail. It can help with monthly planning but then you should switch back into your weekly or daily view to see more detail.
- **Yearly:** This view is ideal for longer-term planning, which includes holiday time and launching projects. It gives you an overview of your entire year at one glance, which is ideal for mapping things out as the year is either planned or progresses.

Alternating views on your calendar gives you more perspective than looking only at the day or the week that lies ahead. Managers often look at the bigger picture as opposed to the minutia on its own, and switching views in your calendar gives you the same ability. It's a tactic worth exploring, that's for sure.

Exploring calendar solutions

Whether you decide to stick with an all-digital solution, an all-paper solution or a hybrid of the two, there are no shortages of apps, services and products that you can use to help you better manage your calendar. The key is to be consistent across all platforms so you can do so efficiently and, most importantly, effectively. The following section explores the different calendar options that you can use.

Mac Calendar

For the Mac, you have several options. The most common is the stock Calendar app. Many long-time Mac users abandoned the stock app after years of unfulfilled expectations, but it's an effective calendar app that does its job well. You can also bring in calendars from a variety of other platforms, including Exchange, Facebook and Google.

When using Mac Calendar:

- **Make sure you use colours.** This is especially true if you start dragging in calendars from other sources.
- **Either use iCloud as your primary calendar or avoid it if you're bringing in Google Calendar.** You may wind up with duplicates that you didn't expect. If you've been using Google as your primary calendar service, then simply bring it in to Calendar and use it, leaving iCloud alone. ***Note:*** That means you have to enter your Google Calendar information on your iOS devices as well, but if it means fewer conflicts to start off, that's a small inconvenience.

Web-based calendars

The great thing about web-based calendars is that you can use them anywhere and on any platform. Even if a mobile app isn't available, thanks to responsive design of these web-based calendars, there's a good chance it will still look good and work well on mobile devices. Web-based calendars are great for work mobility, allowing you to work on your calendar wherever you are. And the Internet has plenty to offer in the way of solutions for calendar management.

Google Calendar is one of the most popular web-based calendars. Its integration tools are second to none. If you want the most complete and robust calendar solution available, you can't go wrong with Google Calendar.

When using Google Calendar:

- **Make sure to adjust the defaults that Google Calendar offers so they suit you best.** For example, leaving the option to have a pop-up remind you 10 minutes before each calendar event isn't all that helpful if you have to leave 30 minutes before to make the appointment in time. Adjust what you need as you need it – it will save you a ton of time later. Remove these reminders for calendar events in the office. If you're working at your desk, you shouldn't need reminders to tell you what to do next, and they may end up disturbing your focus.
- **Make sure to add context to anything you're adding in Google Calendar.** That means entering things in the Description field. Adding more information when first entering an event in your calendar will help inform you about the event later. You're at your most informed when you're first entering these events, not when you're looking at them later.

Windows calendars

The most common Windows calendar management tool is Outlook; you can use it alongside many web-based services, such as Doodle (for calendar arranging) and even Google Calendar.

Outlook offers a calendar component as part of its overall workflow, which includes emails and tasks. You can do pretty much everything with Outlook's calendar that you can with OS X Calendar and Google Calendar, so having it as your primary calendar solution can work very well.

When using Outlook:

- **Use colours to categorise your entries.** If you're syncing your Outlook calendar with other services or solutions, be sure to create uniformity with the colours across all platforms to avoid later confusion.
- **Although the temptation will be strong, don't add tasks that are not date-specific to your Outlook calendar.** Outlook does offer a to-do list component, so use the Task function rather than overload your calendar with items that aren't time-specific. The Task function may not be as robust as a lot of the other options out there, but using tasks rather than using your calendar is at least a step in the right direction.

iOS calendars

There is no shortage of iPhone and iPad calendar apps. However, there are more ineffective ones than effective ones. Three of the better ones are

- **Stock Calendar:** If you're using iCloud, then sticking with the stock Calendar app for iOS is just fine. With the reconfiguration of Notification Centre, having the stock app literally at your fingertips, with a swipe down of your thumb from any screen, makes it user-friendly and efficient.
- **Fantastical:** Fantastical is an iOS app from Flexibits. It's an award-winning calendar app designed for either the iPhone or iPad in mind. It's easy to use and a lot more aesthetically pleasing than most of the calendar solutions out there.
- **Agenda Calendar:** Agenda Calendar has a sleek design and theming options as well as the ability to send quick messages to the people that you have appointments with.

Android calendars

I'm not an Android user, but watching over my husband's shoulder shows me that there are a lot of apps to reckon with:

- **Google Calendar:** The old favourite by default, Google Calendar is easy to use and compatible with any platform.
- **aCalendar:** This calendar app is a bit more visual than Google Calendar, offering imagery for those who have birthdays. There's a lot of integration going on in aCalendar, and it makes for a decent alternative to Google Calendar.
- **ZenDay:** This app offers a unique view to your day, week and month. It has a rather unconventional user interface, but the fact that it allows for tasks to be added and then offers a review option for easy reference makes ZenDay an interesting one to explore.

Paper-based calendar options

I can't forget the old calendar standby: paper. Before digital calendars, paper calendars were it. In fact, many people, families and organizations still use them in one form or another. Heck, I'm one of those people. For those who are into using paper for your task and time management, as well as those who are looking at paper as a viable option, here are a couple for you to explore:

- **NeuYear:** This calendar was created by Jesse Phillips and can be used for yearly planning or monthly theming (see the next section, 'Theming your calendar', for more on this). It helps to be able to refer to it when making commitments and agreements with others that need to be done months in advance.

- **Moleskine:** This very popular brand is often associated with time management, and some varieties include a calendar option built into its pages. No matter what size you choose, you can make decent use of its built-in calendar.

Theming your calendar

Productivity expert Mike Vardy of `productivityist.com` recommends theming as a way to manage your weekly and daily calendars.

Mike maps out nine months in advance and chooses specific months to bring big ideas to life. This doesn't mean he doesn't take on other projects during those months, but the theme provides him with a plan for that month to move forward with. He sticks with the theme throughout the 28, 30 or 31 days of that month, and that means he has more of a chance to move things forward.

Although not everyone is lucky enough to work for himself or maybe doesn't have the capacity to move ideas forward, everyone can still use the theming approach to have a focus for each month.

Mike gives an example of how you could theme your months in a more personal way:

- January: Plan the year ahead.
- February: Focus on romance.
- March: Map out our garden.
- April: Plan the garden.
- May: Work on spring cleaning.
- June: Prepare kids for summer.
- July: Enjoy summer fun.
- August: Prepare for back to school.
- September: Catch up on reading.
- October: Do Autumn cleaning outdoors.
- November: Shop for the holidays.
- December: Focus on family time.

These are personal themes to give you an idea of how theming can work in any area of your life. You can use this theming principle at home or at the office. It just gives you a primary focus each month – and there's real value in that because with that focus you can really make big things happen.

To ensure that you check your calendar every day, get into the habit of opening your calendar before you open your email. Put a reminder on your wall beside your desk, and benefit from seeing what you have planned to work on each day rather than what others want you to do. If you're an Outlook user, you can set this up to happen automatically: select Options, then Advanced Options, start Outlook in this folder and browse to Calendar.

Sharing your calendar

If you work in a team environment, you're probably going to have to share your calendar at some stage. You may want to share your calendar with colleagues or even customers. It's important to understand which way to share is the most appropriate for the occasion.

- **Sharing your main calendar:** You can share your main calendar with someone so she can see your schedule. This is useful if you work with an assistant or need to give your teammates full access to your calendar. You can also share your calendar with everyone in your organisation (if you're brave enough) or only show your time blocked out as busy.
- **Creating a new calendar to share:** Another option is to create a new calendar that multiple people can edit, like a project calendar that everyone in that project group adds events to. Many organisations create a calendar for a meeting room so people can book a time to use the room. This calendar can be available to everyone to edit, or you can limit access to a meeting coordinator who has sole control over the calendar.
- **Editing your calendar:** When you add someone to your calendar, you can decide how others see your events and whether they can also make changes, like adding or editing events. In the case of the global calendar for your organisation, the meeting planner will have full access to the calendar, but everyone else will only have view access.
- **Sharing outside the company:** If you use a web-based calendar, you can share your calendar with someone outside the organisation by forwarding the URL of the calendar. You need to be careful about whom you share with in this circumstance, and it's also possible to limit what the person sees on your calendar.

Most of these features are available in most calendar solutions, so depending on what your sharing requirements are, you should be able to find the way to do it.

Chapter 15

Technology Management

In This Chapter

- Taking control of your email inbox
- Getting the most out of your tablet
- Using social media wisely
- Managing your electronic data

Each year, the rate at which technology seeps into our lives increases exponentially. Some see this as a bad thing, with traditional methods being lost while technology takes over. I'm not one of those people. I'm a technologist. I embrace every new advance and see these changes as enhancing the way things are done. Yes, we may occasionally lose out in face-to-face interaction and at times relationships may suffer, but the overall gains from the addition of technology, I believe, outweigh the negatives. The trick is to be the one in control. To manage technology like you would a Rottweiler. A Rottweiler is a beautifully loyal and gentle dog when managed correctly. Let her get the upper hand and she might just take it away from you . . . and this chapter helps you to avoid that situation!

Mastering Email Management

Email is a beneficial tool, one that has transformed the world of communication from the early nineties. Being able to communicate with a person from the other side of the world has had a massive impact on the evolution of business, politics and perhaps eventually the human race.

If email is so beneficial, why is it causing such stress, anxiety and unease in the business community? It causes chaos because, like the Rottweiler, people often let it get the upper hand, and it doesn't care whether they're keeping up or not. It will keep shovelling the new arrivals into your inbox whether you're ready for it or not.

Overcoming the misconception

You may assume that everybody knows how to deal with email. You may think email software is intuitive and easy to use. Not so. In my experience, after almost ten years looking at people's inboxes, most people don't use their email programme in an efficient way. Of all the people I meet and work with, not even 10 per cent have a way to manage their email efficiently. Regardless of how many emails you receive daily, you're expected to fit your email in along with all your other responsibilities. Email has become the most commonly used to-do list substitute, and this is not a sustainable approach for a productive worker.

Taking control of your inbox

It's time to take back the control, to create a daily habit that will help manage email overload. In the following sections, I take you through the steps to do just that.

Realising email is not a to-do list

The first step, or lesson, is to realize that email is not a to-do list. Your email inbox is a place for capturing your email and the tasks to be done inside your emails, but you should then take the work out of your inbox and organise it for action. If you leave email to sit in your inbox because you still have work to do from that email, you're headed for disorganisation and possibly total disorder. One of the problems with this approach is that you waste time looking back over your old emails deciding which one you're going to tackle next.

For a more efficient use of your time, touch things once. When you look at an email, decide what you need to do with it. Either schedule the work arising from it in your calendar or add that work to your task management system.

Scheduling time for your email

Unless your role demands otherwise, avoid leaving your email open all day, as this leaves you more susceptible to getting distracted by a new email or being tempted to have a quick look. Schedule times for processing your email each day. I suggest working with email early morning, again at maybe 11, after lunch, and before you go home. Of course, this schedule is just a suggestion and will differ per your job role. Some job roles allow you to take larger gaps between opening your email; others require more regular interaction. Managing your email in this way helps you to move away from the 'always on' culture and move toward an 'always in control' world.

Turning off notifications

Most people have a number of social media accounts, including Twitter, Facebook, LinkedIn and Google+. If you were to leave your notifications switched on for all these networks, you'd never get any focused work done. The benefit of switching off notifications is that you're no longer a slave to your email. You decide when you're going to your inbox: you're not dragged there by a sound, a changing mouse pointer or an envelope icon in the taskbar.

If you use Outlook, go to the File Menu, and click Options; a pop-up window appears. Click Mail and then go to the Message arrival area and un-tick all boxes under 'When new messages arrive'. In other email programmes, look for Mail Options and you'll find similar settings. Do the same on your smartphones and tablets. Switch off all alerts, and feel the Zen creep into your life.

Reducing incoming mail

Take a look at your inbox. How many of the emails you receive daily are of value? How many are from newsletters you don't read or mailing lists you don't need to be a part of? Instead of just deleting them as they arrive, take a few minutes to eliminate them from your inbox forever. Here are a couple of ways to declutter your inbox:

- **Manually unsubscribe.** At the bottom of each email newsletter you receive, you should see an Unsubscribe link. Even if you originally signed up to newsletters because they gave you free stuff, if you're now deleting the emails as they arrive, it's time to eliminate that clutter. Do yourself a favour and click Unsubscribe. And if you choose to unsubscribe to my newsletter, I promise I won't be offended. List holders prefer to have people signed up who are genuinely interested in their services.

  If you have internal mailing lists in your organisation, for example everyone@ourcompany.com or management@ourcompany.com, do an audit of how many of these mailing lists you're a member of and unsubscribe to as many as possible. Get your organisation to rethink this method of communication and ask whether people are receiving emails they don't need.

- **Use Unroll.Me (`unroll.me`) to unsubscribe for you.** If you're lazy like me, you may not want to click Unsubscribe for every one of your unwanted email subscriptions. For you, there's a cool service called Unroll.Me that unsubscribes for you.

  Unroll.Me shows you a list of all the newsletters and email lists that you're subscribed to. From one screen, you can unsubscribe from numerous newsletters and email lists. I have personally unsubscribed from over 200 lists with this service and continue to unsubscribe regularly.

  Note that Unroll.Me doesn't support every email client, but it does cover quite a few, so if yours is supported, I highly recommend signing up for an account.

Avoiding spam

Many organisations combat spam through high filters and expensive software solutions. If you work for yourself or your company can't afford these spam solutions, here are a number of tips to try to take control of your spam.

- Never respond to an email or open an attachment that makes you suspicious. If you do, the spammer will know that your account is active and you'll likely receive tons more spam as a result.
- Never click on a link inside a spam message, even if it says unsubscribe. Again, this will tell the spammer that you're real and worth hassling again!
- Switch off auto response messages, another way to alert spammers to the fact that your email is active.
- Never send personal details or bank details over email. Spammers often send emails, claiming to be a financial institution that wants to confirm your account details. This type of spam is called phishing, one of the more dangerous types of spam.
- Share your email address only with people you know.
- When you sign up for something online or buy something, make sure you're alert to any boxes that say 'we can share your information with third parties'.
- Never post your email address on a forum or on your website. Make sure to spell out your email address – for example, contactme[AT] ciaraconlon[DOT]com, or insert it as an image file.
- When you do receive a spam message, make sure you use your email software Junk or Spam mail facility to block sender. At least that email address will never spam you again.
- Make sure your antivirus software is up-to-date and is set to scan all incoming emails.

Another solution for managing spam is to use a programme like Sanebox (`sanebox.com`). Sanebox works with your email account by prioritising important emails and summarising the rest. It keeps your inbox nice and clean by moving unimportant email into different folders. These folders include SaneLater, SaneNews, SaneBlackHole and more. You don't have to worry about missing anything because you can check these folders at any time or at the end of each day. You're sent a daily digest summarising what's in your Sanebox folders.

Sanebox works by analysing your past email history and making decisions about what is important and what's not. You can use a number of folders, such as the following:

- **SaneLater:** SaneLater is the main folder that Sanebox sends all the email deemed unimportant to. If it gets an email wrong and sends an important email to SaneLater instead of leaving it in your inbox, you can train it by dragging the email back into your inbox.
- **SaneNews:** SaneNews is my favourite folder. After unsubscribing to newsletters you no longer want (see previous section), the ones that you do want will be moved to the SaneNews folder. This means that you can read the emails in that folder later when you're not under pressure for time.
- **SaneBlackHole:** All emails that look like spam are dumped into this folder.

You can also use *snooze folders,* allowing you to defer emails to a later day or time, such as Tomorrow, NextWeek or Vacation – pity that my vacation folder doesn't get as much use as I'd like.

Processing email to inbox zero

Inbox zero is a concept dreamt up by Merlin Mann of 43 Folders (`www.43folders.com`). The idea is to touch each email only once, deciding what to do with it there and then. Also, you want to set aside time each day to process your email instead of dipping in and out of your inbox throughout the day. As you check your email, start to plan and organise the work that lies inside each email.

If you plan the work in each email instead of leaving it laying in your inbox, you can clear out your inbox easily each day. When you reach inbox zero, it's not that all your work is done, it's that all your work is scheduled or organised into the correct project folders. People who master the habit feel more in control and organised.

Scheduling the email dash

If you want to learn how to bust some moves with your email, you have to be prepared to step outside your comfort zone and do things differently. You can't keep spending all your time doing the same thing and expect to have a clean, organised inbox. You need to schedule an email dash or two during the day.

The *email dash* involves scanning email and answering the emails that can be answered in less than two minutes. Spend ten minutes or so answering non-critical emails, and then process some of the emails left over. The idea is to keep trimming the fat, without it taking over your day. Processing your email involves using a system like Barbara Hemphill's FAT method – File, Act or Trash – or the more widely known 4 Ds:

- **Delegate:** You can delegate tasks in an email by forwarding it on to someone else or assigning a task directly to the person you're going to delegate to in your task management programme. If you use Outlook, you can assign a task and keep a copy of the task in your task list. Categorise these tasks as 'follow up' so you can make sure all delegated tasks have been completed by the end of each week.

- **Delete:** This doesn't need much explanation, but it does need encouragement. Use the delete button more frequently, and try to reduce the number of emails you need to deal with. I'm not suggesting you delete randomly but simply more often.

If you're one of those people who has never deleted an email in your life, you probably have a couple of thousand emails in your inbox. To get to inbox zero (see earlier section 'Processing email to inbox zero'), you need to bulk process your old email. Create a folder called Old Email and copy over any email older than one month. You can gradually process the emails in this folder to zero when you have time.

- **Defer:** If you need to defer a task, you need to either put it in your tasks management system in the correct project list (see Chapter 13 for more on task management) or in your calendar (see Chapter 14). You can directly schedule the work to be done by converting an email into a task directly from your email.
- **Do:** And don't forget to actually *do* some of the tasks. Any task that takes less than two minutes can be done straightaway. Alternatively, any task that requires immediate action needs to be attended to.

If you follow these instructions from the 4 Ds system, you'll have a clear inbox in a short space of time.

If an email is not actionable and you have no more work to do on the email, you may need to keep it for reference. Create a filing system for the emails you need to keep. The key is to have as many folders as you need but as few as possible. You don't need to create a folder for each client or each area of work; you can make do with a couple of folders. I use one main Reference folder but have folders for current projects (such as this one *For Dummies*).

Living life email-free

Another option to reduce the stress caused by email is to eliminate email from your life altogether. Yes, I know, I know!

Productivity expert Claire Burge (`claireburge.com`) has started a global no email movement inspiring people to eliminate this time waster from their lives. Claire believes social communication is different based on the platform. When you separate communication into task management systems or social media platforms, messages are automatically sorted and handled during times specified for those tasks. Claire doesn't recommend going cold turkey: she recommends starting by applying the principles of moving work out of your inbox and into a task management system. This will make work flow more easily and make you more productive.

Staying Productive with Your Tablet

Tablets can be a great way to stay productive on the move, allowing you to keep up-to-date with your work, but they can also be restrictive and frustrating if you don't get the setup right. One of the first things to consider is how you're going to input data. Then you have to figure out how to store your data and how to get the most productivity from your tablet apps. I explore all of these in the following sections.

Keyboards

Let's face it: keypads on tablets are not ideal. They're there to input information but won't help you get things done quickly. If you want to use your tablet for writing or inputting large amounts of information, you need a tablet keyboard. There are many keyboard options on the market. You can use the Bluetooth Apple keyboard for your iPad, but it isn't a great solution for portability. There's also Belkin, Logitech for all tablets or the Touchfire iPad keyboard that sits on top of your iPad onscreen keyboard.

Cloud storage

If you want to use your tablet as a productivity tool and actually get work done, you need a *cloud storage solution* to store your files remotely. This allows you to be able to transfer files from your tablet to your PC. The following are some of the most common.

Dropbox

Dropbox is a cloud storage solution that keeps your files safe, synced and easy to share. When you install the app, you can copy the files you want to access on your tablet to your Dropbox folder. These files are available to you on all devices – your computer, your tablet and your phone – if you install the Dropbox app on each. Set up a file structure that allows you to easily find files. Here are some ways you can use Dropbox that are most relevant to your productivity:

- **Backup:** You may want to simply use Dropbox for backing up your computer data, keeping a copy in the cloud in case of hardware failure or human error.
- **File sharing:** One of the more useful uses of Dropbox is to share files both with yourself and with others. Sharing files with yourself may sound strange but what you're doing is sharing files with your other devices. After you install the Dropbox app to all devices, you can readily access your data on any device and work on it.

- **Extending your hard drive:** If your hard drive is running out of space, you can use Dropbox as an extension of your hard drive, giving you the extra space you need but also giving you other useful features. You can store music, photos or videos as these file sizes are rather large, and many computers may not have the capacity.
- **Current project folders:** Another handy tip is to put your current project folders in Dropbox to ensure that you have these project files available to you wherever you are but also shared and accessible to other members of your team in the case of your absence.

Google Drive

Google Drive is a similar service to Dropbox, but it has heaps more free storage space – 15GB as opposed to the 2GB Dropbox gives you for nothing. Although 15GB sounds amazing, you're sharing it with your Gmail and your other Google apps. One of the benefits of Google Drive is the built-in office suite where you can edit documents, spreadsheets and so forth on your tablet.

AirDrop

AirDrop is a neat way to share files between your iOS devices. You can download a file on your iPad and share it with your Mac when you're in range. You can also share with your friends who use an iOS device.

Cool productivity apps

If you have a tablet, you of course need some cool apps. And to make sure you're getting the most out of your tablet, I suggest a selection of apps from the following sections.

Task management

A task management app is essential to keep you productive and on top of your tasks and projects. (See Chapter 13 for more details on task management.)

- **Todoist:** Todoist is my app of choice, and it's simple to use for day-to-day tasks. It works across platforms, is aesthetically pleasing and is easy to set up. Email add-ins let you create tasks directly from your email, helping you to clear your email more quickly and reach inbox zero more regularly.
- **Wunderlist:** Another great app for task management. Wunderlist has all the bells and not too many whistles to distract you. It will help you stay in control and organised.
- **Remember the Milk:** This one is worth a mention for its name alone, but its name isn't the only cool thing about this app. It's another easy-to-use app that will put an end to your procrastination.

- **Things:** Things is an Apple child and runs only on Mac, iPhone, iPad or the Apple Watch. Things doesn't have a free version, but don't let this put you off. It's one-time fee is probably better value that the recurring fees the other guys charge. And if you think you'll stick with the free version of the other apps, you're mistaken. Once you start feeling the love from your task management app and start saving hours and stress, you won't think twice about upgrading to the premium version.

Whichever one you choose, stick to one app until you get the hang of it and benefit from it.

Note taking

The following note-taking apps allow you to store all notes, ideas, and cool things you want to be reminded of. You can sort your notes into different categories, covering all areas of your work and life.

- **Evernote:** 'A place for everything and everything in its place', just like Momma used to say. Evernote is a non-negotiable part of the kit if you want to get productive. It's a note-taking app that can function as a task manager, audio note taker and presentation programme. You can organise your whole life with Evernote and even go paperless if you dare.
- **OneNote:** If you're a Microsoft Office user, you may want to use OneNote. OneNote is a powerful note programme with all the same functions as Evernote – audio notes, web clipper – you can embed anything into a note. Move email directly to OneNote and keep your inbox clear. OneNote is heavily featured with so many capabilities, but perhaps this is also one of its downsides, because, as you know, sometimes less is more.

Mind mapping

A mind-mapping app is a powerful tool for brainstorming, planning and creative thinking. Here are few of the many on the market today:

- **SimpleMind:** SimpleMind is available on Mac, Windows and Android. It's an uncomplicated tool that allows you to organise your thoughts in a clear way. It's ideal for brainstorming because you can get your thoughts out quickly with its easy-to-use features. It doesn't take long to organise the branches and nodes of your mind map.
- **MindNode:** MindNode is another mind-mapping tool I have on my iPad. I find MindNode easier to use for preparing presentations, because you can organise the nodes in a more visual way, and the potential for colour and outlining is broader. It does take a little longer than other tools to get the same result.

- **iMindMap:** This mind-mapping tool was developed by Tony Buzan (the guy who popularized brainstorming). iMindMap is one of the more expensive options, but it does have cool features, such as images and different fonts and icons to make your mind maps more visually creative and easier to remember if you're using your iMindMap for studying or creating presentations.

Presentations

If you need to create presentations, you're in luck: a lot of cool apps can help you create visually appealing presentations that don't take a week to produce. Say goodbye to reading endless words on a slide and make space for colourful, visual storytelling.

- **Prezi:** Prezi, one of the first presentation apps to rock the world, allows you to create, edit, present and watch presentations wherever you are. Prezi is cloud-based, so it takes the stress out of making sure you have the right computer or memory stick with you when you leave the office. Prezi is used by sales teams, CEOs and students. The cool thing about Prezi is that it allows you to show your audience the big picture and then zoom into each section, keeping your audience engaged as they always know where you are in your presentation. This is definitely one to try out.
- **Keynote:** Keynote is Apple's presentation offering. It's easy to use and has lots of templates to help you pull together a presentation in no time. So if you're lacking inspiration, a prompt will help get you going. You can add charts, animations or video to make your story more compelling.
- **Haiku Deck:** My app of choice currently is Haiku Deck. With this app, you can create stunning presentations in minutes. And if you don't have inspiration, Haiku Deck supplies you with images that wow and a font that is easy to read and engaging.

Photography and video

As the cameras get better on smartphones and tablets, photography becomes an important function. Photography is no longer tainted by having to download photos and buy expensive software to be able to edit it. Photography apps have enabled the mere mortal to take great photos, and if you aren't in the group of people who take great photos, these apps will help you fake it 'til you make it.

- **Snapseed:** Snapseed is a powerful editing app that's free and easy to use. It has adjustment tools for improving colour and exposure, along with effects and filters to pimp your photographs.
- **Over:** Over is a cool little app for putting text overlay on your photos. You can add quotes or names to your images and upload them to Twitter or Facebook. It's very easy to use and great fun, too.

- **Capture:** Capture enables you to take a video on your iPad and upload it immediately to your YouTube account; you can make edits, add keywords and upload, taking all the stress out of sharing and uploading videos.

Writing

One of the reasons you bought a tablet is to write on it, I'm sure, but as I pointed out at the beginning of this section, the tablet isn't always designed for perfect data input. After you get a good keyboard, the following apps will help make the job much easier.

- **Google Docs:** If you're a Googlite, all you need to do is download the Google Docs app to allow you full access to your documents and spreadsheets. If not, you can still set up a Google account to benefit from the app, edit existing documents or create new ones and stay productive on the go.
- **Byword:** If blogging is your thing, you may want to look at Byword. Byword is a writing app that gives you what you need to write *Markdown* and rich text. Markdown is a simple way for non-programming types to write in an easy-to-read format that can be converted directly into HTML for the web.

  HTML (HyperText Markup Language) allows you to add 'tags' to the text that then tells the browser how to display the text or graphics in the document.
- **WordPress:** If you have a WordPress blog, you can download the WordPress app to allow you to access your blog dashboard from your tablet, add new blog posts, edit existing ones and stay up-to-date at all times.
- **Notability:** This app allows you to combine handwriting, photos and typing to capture your thoughts and create the best ideas. You can scale, rotate or recolour these notes to get the results you want. You can share these beautiful notes via Dropbox, Google Drive, email or AirDrop. What I love about this app is the ability to annotate documents and suggest changes and edits with a big red marker, or even pink if the mood takes you.
- **Penultimate:** Penultimate is a handwriting app for the iPad. Using the app feels like you're doodling in a paper notebook. You can write, sketch or scribble. Add a stylus and you can write like a pro. Penultimate is part of the Evernote group so you can save and retrieve your doodles using Evernote's powerful search.
- **Evernote:** Evernote is also an option for writing. I have worked on a book with a colleague writing in Evernote, which allowed us to create a shared notebook and both edit our separate chapters wherever or whenever we wanted to.

Staying in Control of Social Media

One of the biggest distractions in life (aside from your little darlings) is social media. There's a universe of information out there: updates on all the people you know and every person they know. And it's all accessible to you right now. It's overwhelming just thinking about it. Facebook, Twitter, Instagram – which ones do you choose, and how many can you keep up with? I help you straighten it all out in the following sections.

Understanding your motivation

Do you use social media sites to stay in touch with friends or family or as a marketing tool for your business? Remind yourself first of the why and figure out the purpose of your social media accounts. As long as your objective is being delivered and you're suffering no negative repercussions from having these accounts, fire ahead. If, on the other hand, you're spending too much time online or it's making you feel inadequate or getting in the way of your work, you need to think again.

Setting up boundaries

When it comes to social media – whether you use it for personal or professional use – you have to set up some boundaries. Limit yourself to time, place or purpose. There is no one-size-fits-all method. Your limits depend on what is appropriate for your life and your job role.

- **Setting time limits:** Limit your time online, only allowing yourself an hour or two a day. This should be ample time to connect with all your family and friends or to post any updates you may have for your business.
- **Keeping to place limits:** You could decide to access social media only when you're at home, thus keeping your work environment safe from the distractions.
- **Staying within software limits:** If you don't trust yourself to stay within your time or place limits, use software to keep you on the straight and narrow by blocking your access to certain websites at certain times of the day. LeechBlock, StayFocused and Strict Workflow are all free browser extensions that allow you to be stricter with yourself and limit your access to the big, wild world out there.
- **Turning off notifications:** Eliminate the distractions of notifications. To turn off notifications, go into Facebook, Twitter, LinkedIn, Instagram, Google+ and all your other accounts, go to Settings and turn off push

notifications to your phone. No, I don't want to know when Will Smith follows me on Twitter. No, I don't care if Gerard Butler liked my new profile picture – okay, well, maybe that deserves a look, but I'll see it when I go there.

Recent studies show that marriages are suffering due to excessive social media use. Instead of focusing on what you need to give up, focus on the positive; ask yourself what you'll gain from changing the way you interact with social media.

Assessing the ROI

A lot of people use social media for their businesses, fooling themselves that browsing the web is one of the responsibilities of their jobs. This may be true for some of you, but for most, it's not what makes you money. Yes, social media is important. And, yes, it's something you need to do some of the time, but it can do no harm to do a social media audit and assess which sites are creating a return on your time investment and which ones are for pure pleasure. Following are a couple of ways you can do just that.

Taking stock

Start by creating a spreadsheet with all the sites you have a presence on. Create columns for the name of the site, the URL and the purpose of the site. Get clear about your objectives and motivation. Add another column with time spent per week. And just to be safe on your estimate, add another 10 per cent.

Questions to ask yourself include the following:

- What am I (or my company) trying to achieve through social media?
- Who is my target audience, and which sites do they use?
- How much time do I have to spend on social media?
- Do I have analytics for my social media with good data?
- What results am I getting from my campaigns?
- Which methods are currently working for us?
- Which methods are not working for us?

After you've answered these questions, then comes the difficult piece: Which accounts are you going to give up? It's a waste of time and money to maintain accounts that your target market doesn't use.

Maintaining desired profiles

Spend some time checking the profiles you decide to keep. Are they complete and accurate, and are they giving the right impression of your brand? Take a look at your competitors' profiles to see whether they're presenting themselves in a better light than you are. Make any updates required.

- Are my profiles well branded? Do they represent me or my company in the correct way?
- Are my profiles well linked to/from my website and other media? Do I use every opportunity to advertise my profiles?
- Am I integrating my offline marketing with my online? When marketing, do I include my online profiles in my marketing material?
- Is my content sufficiently engaging? Am I creating content my target audience would enjoy or benefit from?
- Am I posting frequently enough? Check out popular competitors' profiles to see how often they are posting.
- Are people interacting with my content? Am I receiving comments, likes and shares with my content?

Managing Electronic Files

Have you ever spent more time than you care to remember searching for a file that you thought you knew the location of? Effective electronic file management can have a big impact on your productivity. Getting organised needs to extend to your electronic world. Throwing all your files on your desktop isn't the way to do it. In the following sections, I fill you in on digital file storage and take a look at document management systems.

Digital file storage

Your digital file storage is as important as your paper file storage and really breaks down into five areas. Deciding how to structure and organise your files, giving each file an appropriate name, throwing out what you no longer need, streamlining the process by filing as you go and creating backups that you can rely on are all essential to creating an organised, efficient and effective digital system for your files. Read on for more details.

Setting up a file structure

The first part to file storage is to decide on a file structure in advance and have everyone in your organisation follow it. Following a basic hierarchy with folders and subfolders is best practise. To keep the structure consistent across projects and teams, create an empty folder template that people can copy each time they have a new project.

Individuals can rename the New Project folder to the project name and add subfolders when required. It's best not to create too many levels of folders, though, because that can become confusing and counterproductive. Always create as many as you need but as few as possible.

Be careful about file duplication. For example, say you receive an invoice from a client that you place inside the Accounts/2016 subfolder, which has a subfolder called Invoices. A colleague receives the same invoice and files it under Clients/Client 1/Invoices. If you notice places where duplication could occur, rethink your file structure and eliminate the folders that threaten duplication.

When it comes to accounts, you need to get clear about folder direction. Should you put the Accounts folder inside the 2016 folder or the 2016 folder inside the Accounts folder? You have to answer this question based on the priority in your work environment. Which folder is searched for more regularly, and what works better for the department involved?

Naming

The naming of folders can also be a point of confusion. Keep naming structures simple. If multiple versions of a file exist, each one needs to include the date and ideally the initials of the last person to save the file in the file name. Make the file names clear and comprehensible – for example, 1115_Dummies_Chapter2_CC.doc and not Chapter2.doc.

Avoid using underscores or AA to move files up the filing structure. Doing so is common practice for files that are most in use, but this can cause confusion and lead to duplication of folders. For example, if someone can't find the file called _Projects, he may end up creating another folder called Projects.

Purging

To maintain a system of files that's easy to use where files are easy to find, you must also make purging a regular occurrence. Recycling and shredding files that are no longer of use are common practices with paper filing, and as such, deleting files that are no longer required should be a common practice with your digital information.

Don't delete files without checking the data management legislation in your country. Some countries require you to maintain records for seven years. Make sure that you have a place to store this old documentation that you need to save for legal reasons.

Filing as you go

An ideal way to stay organised is to file as you go. Don't get into bad habits of saving files on the desktop or in other folders to organise at a later stage. This only creates a disorganised mess, one I'm sure many of you are familiar with. Take the plunge and commit to getting your electronic data in order, and while doing so, commit to never leave a random file alone and out of place on your desktop again.

Backing it all up

After you've created an organised filing system to die for, you've got to make sure you don't lose it. Add a backup routine to your daily practice. There are many ways that you can automate your file backup – for example Dropbox or Skydrive, which are free online storage services that automatically sync selected files and folders to the cloud. Having a properly operating filing structure will ensure maximum efficiency and control and more efficient backups.

Document management systems

If your goal is to go paperless, you may want to look into a document management system that can capture all your paper documents and file them electronically for you.

Some organisations may want to scan existing paper files to create an effective search facility of all their documentation. Governments, the legal industry and healthcare have a more critical need to store their documents for the long term whilst always being accessible at all times. Other organisations may be happy to keep their historic files in paper but choose to keep all future documentation in electronic format to make the search and retrieval of files more efficient.

Whichever way you lean, here are three areas to consider:

- **Compliance:** Paper-based systems are difficult to maintain for compliance and quality management systems. Increasingly, there's a need to create more robust systems to manage important data. With electronic forms and processes, electronic systems can reduce the cost of compliance and audits for an organisation.
- **Security:** For an organisation with large amounts of data, security should be a priority. Maintaining the integrity and the safety of this data can be done more easily with a document management system. With automated backups, you're less likely to lose any data when it's safe inside your system.
- **Hardware:** To move toward a paperless office, you'll need a heavy duty scanner that can scan multiple files at once and a shredder to shred the documents you no longer need.

Chapter 16

The Productive Freelancer

In This Chapter

- Setting up as a freelancer
- Finding out how, when and what to outsource
- Creating and managing a virtual team

Working as a freelancer can be a rewarding career change. No more boss to disturb your creative flow, no workmates disturbing your focus. But with the freedom of freelancing comes a particular set of challenges. That boss no longer checking up on you may mean you relax a little more than you should. The workmates who interrupt you sometimes helped you to brainstorm and get motivated. As a freelancer, when your productivity drops, your income does, too. In this chapter, I show you how to be a productive freelancer and never have to do water cooler chit chat again.

Getting the Basics Right

Whether you're setting out for the first time or are a seasoned freelancer, getting the basics right is key. From creating a productive work environment to setting boundaries to scheduling your work, this section has you covered.

Creating a productive work environment

As a freelancer, you want to create an environment that fosters both creativity and productivity. Many people think that clean, organised surroundings aren't compatible with creativity, but this isn't so. Having a clean, organised and pleasant workplace allows you the freedom to focus on whatever work project you need to focus on.

Following are specific ways to create a work environment that is conducive to getting things done.

Deciding where to set up shop

Choosing the right workspace makes all the difference when you're pushed to your limits to deliver work on time. Your workspace must be the right temperature, airy and bright. It must also have minimal distractions and be comfortable enough to allow you to work for long periods of time without longing for your chaise lounge.

Your workspace should ideally be somewhere that doesn't have people moving through it or isn't a place that others need to use at any stage during the day. Ensuring that others respect your workspace will be a challenge; the easiest way to encourage this is to have a door, and close it. Any colour of door will do, as long as it has space on it to hang a Do Not Disturb sign. If you don't have that luxury of closing a door, consider buying a screen that visually blocks you away from the rest of the house.

Choosing the office furniture

Don't skimp on office furniture. Your backside is going to get familiar with your office chair, so make sure it's comfortable. Consider ergonomics, the height of the chair, and the distance from your screen. You may want to invest in a kneeler chair, which helps to keep the spine straight. Also, make sure your monitor is at the correct height to minimise eye and neck strain.

Other things to consider are a wrist rest if you use a mouse and another one for your keyboard. These are gel pads that help prevent wrist strain. People often overlook the simple things, but with a simple addition of a few cushions for different parts of the body, you can minimise any discomfort and hopefully prevent any repetitive strain or pain.

Next up: your desk. You want a desk that is big enough for the work that you do. Trying to do work with insufficient space only causes frustration and reduces your productivity well before you get distracted by social media. You may want to consider a standing desk or a desk whose height can be adjusted. Standing desks can be useful for the post-lunch slump or for people who suffer from lower back pain from sitting too much. If you don't have the oodles of cash required for a standing desk, put a box or mini table on top of your existing desk, and voilà – the homemade standing desk.

Maintaining a clutter-free desk

Your desk is where it all happens, so make sure it's a place that you enjoy spending time. You want to put some thought into setting up your work zone. To make sure your desk stays clutter-free, use an in-tray for any paperwork and make sure you place all documents in the in-tray to process. Don't leave any documents on your desk. Also, use your drawers wisely, and place items that you use regularly in your top drawer. The less used an item, the further away from your desk it can be. Respect your work desk and try to keep it clutter-free at all times.

Creating sufficient storage space

Everything needs a home, so make sure you have a place for everything. Clutter is created when you fail to make a decision about something, usually because you don't know where to put it. Take the time to create a home for everything, either by allocating an existing storage space or buying new storage solutions.

After you find a home for your supplies, label boxes so you can easily find what you need. Keep filing cabinets close enough to your desk so you have no excuse not to file your documents straightaway. If you're lacking storage, head out to your local store and pick up some shelves or filing boxes to help you stay organised.

Take notice of the things you leave lying around. They're probably items that don't have a home or the home they do have is impractical. Rethink the situation, and get the right storage needed.

Keeping a paper-free zone

Maintaining a simple filing system will help you keep your paperwork under control. You need a filing system for both reference items and active projects, and never the twain shall meet. Keeping your reference and active files separate helps you to stay in control.

The best and simplest method I've found for filing is to use an A to Z filing system with hanging files and everything labelled clearly. On your desk, set up an active filing system for your work in progress, and put these files in a desk file stand. You can create a new folder for each new project. Use manila folders and label them clearly with a labeller. Leaving papers lying around on the desk is distracting and may disturb your laser-sharp focus. When papers are no longer needed, put them in the recycle bin or shred them if they contain confidential data.

Inventing boundaries for your working day

When you work for yourself, you have no set working hours and no one to tell you when you should and shouldn't work. This can be both liberating and restraining all at the same time. For this reason, it's good to set some boundaries, such as the ones I cover in the following sections, to ensure that you don't get burnt out before you've earned your first pay cheque.

Choosing the times that work

Based on your past productivity performance, decide what working hours work best for you. If you tend to work effectively in the evenings and your home environment allows it, you don't need to fall into the social norm of a 9 to 5 workday. Avoiding the 9 to 5 is probably one of the reasons you went out on your own in the first place. The beauty of being self-employed is that you can watch box sets on your iPad in bed every morning if the mood takes you. Of course, you'll have to offset that with working late into the evening if that's the timetable that suits you best.

Try to stick to a routine for your working hours – whether it be morning, afternoon or evening. You're more likely to get more work done if you have set hours for work. Research shows that early risers are usually more productive, and if you get up at the same time each day, you'll have a well-rested body that will perform better.

Don't be fooled into thinking that the middle of the night is the only time that you can work creatively or productively, when only yourself and the owls are not sleeping. Most people work well at this time if they're capable of staying awake. The reason for this is the stillness of the night combined with the reduction in distractions. To be creative at any time of the day, you need to recreate these conditions for maximum productivity.

Communicating to your posse

Make sure your friends and family know when you're working. If your office is at home, it can be difficult for people to absorb the fact that you are, in fact, working. Communicate it once, twice, three times if necessary, and if they still don't get the message, stop answering the phone and the door during work hours.

If you're constantly distracted by the people who live with you, communication is also key to success. Tell those old enough to understand the importance of quiet time. If the bodies that are distracting you are too young to realise, try to get older members of the family to keep them busy while you work.

Minimising the distractions

As I write this chapter, I'm listening to Hozier, blocking out the sounds going on around me. Earphones are a wonderful invention, allowing you to sift into a relaxed and focused state with your preferred music playing in the background. Get yourself a playlist that motivates you and helps you relax and focus on your work. Turn off the TV and close your browser. Switch off notifications from your email, calendar and social media accounts.

My preferred way to focus is to use GrooveOtter.com. GrooveOtter is based on the Pomodoro Technique and encourages you to focus for periods of 25 or 45 minutes and then take a 3-minute break. Working in this way encourages you to stay working on the job at hand until the timer sounds and you can take a break. Keeping time-wasting activities to your breaks makes for much more focused work going on.

Scheduling your work

Scheduling work can help you move projects forward that previously didn't have air time. Use your calendar to schedule all the work you need to do (check out Chapter 14 for some great tips on using a calendar). If you allocate time for each project you're working on, you'll continue to make progress daily. Remember to take into account your preferred working hours, and schedule work accordingly. You also need to factor in that the rest of the world probably works from 9 to 5, so as long as you can interact with your customers and suppliers at some stage during the day, you should be good to go.

Increasingly, we're all working in a global workplace. You need to bear in mind that 9 to 5 in Shanghai or Vancouver doesn't happen at the same time as it does in Dublin or London.

Try theming your days. For example, you tackle admin on Mondays, existing client work on Tuesdays, Wednesdays and Thursdays, and business development on Fridays. Maintaining some sort of schedule will help you to stay on track and not allow the distractions to encroach on your days.

Outsourcing Like a Pro

Many entrepreneurs think they can do it all – the accounts, the graphic design, the website maintenance, the marketing, the sales . . . oh, and the stuff they get paid to do. This isn't a sustainable strategy. Although finances may not allow you to hire someone when you go out on your own at first, the quicker you do it, the quicker you'll grow. In this section, I cover the do's and don'ts of outsourcing, from knowing when to outsource to what and how.

Deciding when to outsource

Outsourcing is important for your business to not only survive but also grow and thrive. Many reasons exist for why you should be outsourcing. Here are a few key examples of when outsourcing should be part of your growth strategy.

- **When what you want done isn't one of your core competencies:** Don't outsource just because you don't like doing the job. If it's a core competency, keep the job in-house. If someone else would do it better and in half the time, guess what? It's a job to outsource.
- **When the role is required only one or two times a year:** If you do a project work that may need external input a couple of times a year, it's a good idea to outsource it and not be tempted to come up with a more permanent arrangement.
- **When you need extra hands on deck:** When you're at maximum capacity and need help to complete a project on time, it can be wise to get more help. Often those who work alone come to a point where they have more work than they can do themselves. The question then comes, should they hire or outsource? You can collaborate on the project or outsource parts of it. Outsourcing will probably be more economical.
- **When it costs less to get someone else to do it:** Often times, a job would cost you less to get someone else to do it, such as attempting to set up your own blog when you are far from an expert. If this is the case, don't waste your time trying to do it yourself; use your time more effectively.
- **When times are tough and you definitely won't be hiring:** Sometimes, you'll be so busy that hiring someone full time may look like an attractive option. Fixed costs are never good for a freelancer. Stick to a more flexible model, especially when times are tough.

Knowing what to outsource

If you've decided that you need to outsource some of your work, the next question you need to ask is what to outsource. The answer to that question is anything that doesn't generate income. Your job is to do the work that people pay you for. Everything else can be outsourced. Outsourcing will make a substantial difference to your productivity and to your bottom line. You may still need to go to the gym for the other bottom line.

The types of jobs that you may need to outsource fall into three categories:

- **High-expertise functions:** This category includes tasks that need to be done by the experts, such as lawyers, accountants and auditors, or any highly technical role, video creation and editing and other specialised tasks. It's best not to try learning expert tasks from scratch. Although learning something new can be great fun or something you've always wanted to do, ideally you should leave the expert work to the experts.
- **Expertise-favoured functions:** Sure, you can do your own PR, marketing, sales and bookkeeping, but is that the best use of you time? How much time do these tasks take daily? Weekly? Would that time be better spent serving your customers and earning more money? How much do you earn per hour versus how much you pay out per hour? Do the calculations and you'll quickly see whether it's worth your time to hand over the extracurricular tasks.
- **Repetitive, administrative tasks:** These tasks are the ones that ideally someone else should be doing. They include managing calendars, booking flights, invoicing clients, making payments, moderating blog comments, answering calls, creating documents and reports and much more. If you can offload these types of repetitive tasks to someone else, not only will you free up time to do your job but the tasks will also get done more effectively because the person you hired likely won't be in as much of a rush to complete them as you were.

Becoming a Virtual CEO

Chris Ducker, an online serial entrepreneur, calls himself the 'Virtual CEO'. In 2009, he was working 14-hour days, and he realised that he was spending way too much time working *in* his business and not *on* his business. In 2010, he set a goal to replace himself in his business where possible. He achieved his goal within a year and started another business called Virtual Staff Finder. He now works a six-hour day, and Fridays have become part of his weekend. Chris recommends starting with his three lists to freedom, which were featured in his bestselling book *Virtual Freedom* (BenBella Books, 2014), to help understand what you really should be working on day to day as a business owner.

To complete your own three lists of freedom, grab a sheet of paper and a pen. Draw two lines down the centre of the page to create three columns. In the three columns, put the following:

- **Things you hate doing every day:** Think of the jobs that you try to avoid, the ones that make you wish you'd never gone out on your own – you know, the ones that sit on your to-do list until the last minute. Write these down in the first column.

- **Things you can't do yourself:** These are tasks that are beyond your skill set. Maybe the accounting, the graphic design or the techy stuff. Make a list of things that need doing but that you don't have the skill set to do yourself. Be honest here; it's okay to not be good at everything. Fill up the second column with these items.
- **Things you shouldn't be doing:** Which jobs do you do that you shouldn't be doing? They may be jobs that would benefit from a little more expertise, or they may be jobs that are so mundane and repetitive that a monkey could do them. Write all of these down in the third column.

By creating these three lists, you get a clear picture of the tasks that only you should be doing. This is an excellent starting point for deciding what has to go. This will then become your road map to start working with virtual staff and delegating effectively (see the next section). When you complete these three lists, you can continue by batching tasks together. Which tasks can be done by the same person? Which tasks require expertise beyond the general virtual assistant and most importantly which tasks can you do yourself?

Building Your Virtual Team

The way people work today has changed. Many people are no longer chained to desks in dull buildings. Flexible and virtual working has become more normal in the modern organisation. As a freelancer or entrepreneur, it's easier than ever to create a virtual team around you to complete all the tasks you need done in your virtual organisation. I make a few suggestions in the following sections.

The virtual assistant (VA)

There are many types of virtual assistants. There are the VAs who answer your calls and manage your calendar and the VAs who write your blog posts and handle your Twitter feed. It's important to get clear about what tasks you need carried out and to get the right person for the job. Don't be tempted to get your VA to do it all. Some will be tech-savvy while others may be better at accounting and bookkeeping. Just as you'll gain from playing to your strengths, don't expect your VA to be good at everything. For this reason, it's okay to have more than one virtual assistant to handle different parts of the job.

The IT geek

Let's face it: you're probably not as tech-savvy as you'd like to be, or if you are, do you do it as well or as fast as the professionals? If you're an incompetent when it comes to computers, like Jen from *The IT Crowd,* take a reality pill and outsource. Or maybe you're more authentic, like *The IT Crowd*'s computer genius Moss. If so, you may still benefit from giving your IT work to someone who specialises in that sort of thing, freeing you up to be more creative, strategic or whatever it is you're good at.

The social media guru

Do you get distracted by social media? If you answered no, I don't believe you. Social media is great for business, but it's far too easy to get sidetracked and lose valuable time tweeting and posting away. The other disadvantage of doing it yourself is a lack of strategy. Few entrepreneurs have a well thought-out social media strategy. A good strategy includes using the right voice, targeting the right people for your product or service and posting the appropriate content at the right time. If you get a social media expert on board, it doesn't mean you can never tweet again. It just means your tweets will be more melodic and heard by the right choir.

The marketing maven

Marketing is one of those subjects people think they can tackle themselves but then tend to fail at miserably. A marketing strategy is crucial to aid growth and development. Without a strategy, efforts are often haphazard and untargeted. A marketing expert can really put wind in your sales and get you the results that you want. You may not need a permanent marketing person on the team, but getting advice upfront will do a lot to set you on the right path. A marketing expert can help you create the strategy to spearhead your success. Don't overlook the marketing maven.

The finance specialist

Leave the money stuff to the money experts. If you're a web and graphic designer, you don't need to ruin your buzz by sitting in front of figures you probably don't understand. That's not to say you should hand over all responsibility and close your eyes to the cash. It's important you stay in control, but let the specialists do the heavy work that you can oversee.

Finance is a complicated area if you're not trained in it. You may be missing out on tax breaks or failing to make your returns correctly. Take my advice, and take the finance specialist's advice.

The blogging buff

It's okay to outsource some of your writing, too. Whether you do this depends on who you are and how much your blogging is part of your strategy. A professional with good copywriting skills could write blog posts with the correct grammar targeting the correct audience. However, if you don't want to hand over your fountain pen just yet, consider hiring somebody to edit and review your blog posts. You could also get her to moderate comments and research and suggest new content for future blog posts.

The video whizz

If you're an Internet entrepreneur, this role is essential. Creating video and audio content is part of the remit. There are many programmes that allow for amateurs to record and edit video, but if you're not a professional, it never looks as good. It also means you can spend more time creating awesome content and not worrying about the editing.

Managing the Virtual Team

Managing a virtual team can have its challenges – geographical distance and time zones to name just two. The following sections walk you through some steps you can take to make sure you make the most of your new relationships and that you put measures in place to ensure efficient communication and maximum productivity.

Communicating clearly

The more time you spend setting expectation and clarifying your needs and requirements upfront, the better the results will be from these new relationships. People focus better when they know exactly what they're trying to achieve, so your virtual team will be no different. You can't just expect them to know what you want without you telling them. Create open channels of communication to allow for any queries or questions. Set times to regularly discuss updates, challenges or suggestions. Keep the dialogue going to ensure that your team delivers the job you need doing.

Giving sufficient training

Set some time aside to train your team into your ways and systems. The time you spend upfront will be repaid tenfold in the future. The reason you're hiring a virtual team is because you don't' have enough time to do it all, so don't fall into the trap of not having enough time to train them in to your way of working. Lack of training will cost you in the long run.

Documenting procedures

A great way to allow someone to take over some of your tasks is to document the processes and procedures. Sounds like a pain, I know, but it will pay off. You may decide to get your new assistant to do this; in fact, you may even use it as part of the training process. As you train your assistant on the way you want things done, he can take notes and write up a work procedure as to how the job should be done. These procedures will help your new assistant to be more efficient and to think of work in a new way. If you get him thinking in terms of efficient processes from the beginning, he's more likely to maximize his performance and work effectively from day one.

Sharing information virtually

Set yourself up with a task management system to share projects and tasks. You can use Asana, Trello or any software that allows you to share and assign tasks. Doing so keeps everyone connected and communicating. It also allows you to make updates or comments on what you want done without having to call or email your assistant. You can also create a common storage area in Dropbox or Google Docs for sharing files and documents. Have this information piece decided on upfront so that you can hit the ground running as soon as you hire your new team.

Setting up virtual meetings

Having regular virtual meetings at the start helps build rapport and creates a solid working relationship between you and your team. You may want to schedule a monthly meeting to ensure that everyone is happy and all is moving along well. A Skype call can work well for this. If you feel it would be beneficial for the extended team to connect and meet each other, you can do a Skype group call or use Google Hangouts. GoToMeeting is another option that has a more formal setup for a conference call.

Using Skype

Skype is useful for free video and audio calls. Skype group calls can be tricky, though. Skype claims that you can connect with up to 25 people on a group call, but in reality large numbers on group calls appear to be something few have achieved before someone gets knocked out of the call. Skype's premium version claims to accommodate up to 250 on one call. I'm not sure anyone has achieved this, but it seems like a lofty goal to me. On the other hand, Skype is very affordable as a stand-alone offer, or you can get it included in your Microsoft 365 plan.

Hanging out with Google

Google Hangouts is a great option for up to ten people. Its connectivity is usually quite robust, and you can see each other and share screens. You will need a Gmail account to take part. You can broadcast your call to more people if you want to use a webinar, but you can have only ten active participants. Because your Google account links to YouTube, you can also leave a recording of the call on a YouTube account, which can be useful for people who may have missed the webinar.

Going to GoToMeeting

GoToMeeting is a paid service and allows up to 100 users on the call at once. It's more affordable and possibly easier to set up than its paid counterparts, but it isn't necessarily the most reliable or best quality. GoToMeeting makes it easy for people in different countries to dial in and join a call without too much stress, and this can be done with toll-free numbers to ensure that the people dialling in don't have to pay for the call.

Part V

Personal Productivity

Morning Routine	
Name	
Breakfast	☐
Wash	☐
Brush teeth	☐
Make bed	☐
Pyjamas under pillow	☐
Get dressed	☐
Lunch in bag	☐
School bag	☐
Coat on	☐
Shoes on	☐

Find seven household routines for an easier life in a free article at www.dummies.com/extras/productivity.

In this part . . .

- Find out how to become more productive at home.
- Discover how to clear the clutter once and for all.
- Understand how to become a more productive student.

Chapter 17

Productivity at Home

In This Chapter

- Becoming a productive parent
- Getting in tune with your work-life balance
- Raising productive children
- Putting together a home office

Many people are highly productive at work, but their home life is a completely different story. Staying organised at home is as important as being organised at work. If you come home to a cluttered and disorganised space, you can't feel relaxed and at peace.

Your time away from work should be comfortable and stress-free. Creating an organised and calm environment at home will help make it a perfect place to spend time with family and friends and renew and re-energise for another day or week at work.

Productivity for Parents

Being organised at home is something not many have achieved but many crave. I know a lot of parents who are desperate for more structure and order at home. Whether or not both parents work, staying productive at home is important both for your sanity and for your children's upbringing. When two parents work, it can be difficult to spend your precious time with your kids in the evening or on weekends tidying and organising. If you do put aside some time to getting organised, everyone will benefit. When you have an organised home space, you'll feel more relaxed and in control, and you'll give your kids a great example.

Scheduling to fit it all in

Few people think of scheduling their home life. Putting times on home life may seem too controlled or structured. Many think that work should be a controlled environment, not home; home should be spontaneous and carefree. That was my naïve approach to parenting when I had my first son at 24. I vowed never to be a stuffy parent, missing out on life's experiences to stick to routines and good habits. I realised many years later that I made life difficult for myself. I learnt that having routines and structure in your life can be liberating.

There's no getting away from the fact that the washing has to be done, the dinners cooked, and the floors swept. Creating routines for these jobs ensures that you don't have to waste time thinking about them or perhaps feeling guilty that the jobs aren't done.

Scheduling the days

Many people do all their cleaning chores on a Saturday morning; this can work well if you don't have sport or other commitments on a Saturday morning. If you have a family, Saturday mornings will most likely be filled with football, hockey, swimming or other obligations. If this is the case, try to schedule your chores for during the week. If you can clean the bathroom on Monday and give the kitchen a deep clean on Tuesday, you free yourself up on weekends to have fun and spend time with your family.

Planning the fun

Planning the fun may seem like a strange phenomenon, but sometimes in the busy schedules of modern life, people tend to lose out on having fun. Plan some fun time into your calendar. For example, schedule cinema trips and picnics with the kids or with friends. Make sure you have at least one fun activity in your calendar each week. Remember that what gets scheduled gets done, and you're much more likely to do the things that are written in your calendar than the ones planned in your head.

Budgeting: Keeping tabs on the spending

Budget is a word nobody likes to hear. Budgets are restrictive and restraining. They're definitely not fun to plan and usually tell you things you don't want to admit. But here's the grown-up piece of advice: you need to have a budget. No matter how much money you earn, you need to budget. You need to know how much life is costing you and whether you're spending your hard-earned cash on the right things. Becoming more organised with your spending habits, will help you feel more in control and ensure you that your finances aren't a source of stress in your life.

Taking your head out of the sand

The ostrich is said to bury its head in the sand. It doesn't. If any animal put its head in the sand, it wouldn't be able to breathe. That's exactly what would happen to people if they try to bury their heads in an attempt to ignore the reality. The truth is, if you don't have enough money to wine and dine and buy new clothes each week but you still do, you'll end up suffocating yourself with debt, cutting off the life force and creating an uncomfortable and stressful life.

To get in control of your spending, you first have to know what's going on. Get clear about your income and expenses and start building a budget. You can use one of the many free budgeting apps and templates online, or check out Microsoft Excel's free templates for budgeting. These templates are available and included in Excel.

Making clever choices

After you start to track your spending, you can see where your money is going and make educated choices about what to spend your money on. If you buy yourself a double soy hazelnut latte with cream each day, that is absolutely fine, as long as you're aware of how much this daily treat is costing you and what you're giving up to fund this little indulgence.

A lot of the spending people do is in small amounts, but it adds up quickly. Have you ever taken 50 pounds from the bank machine to find it gone a couple of hours later and don't really know how it disappeared? This is the type of spending that can get you into trouble. That's not to say that you can no longer spend your hard-earned cash on whatever you want. The trick is to spend it on whatever you want *mindfully.* That way every choice you make is with awareness of the value you get and the consequences of that spend.

Creating the habit of tracking spending

Tracking expenses can be tedious, and if it isn't something you're accustomed to doing, it can be difficult to get into the habit. Like any habit, you first want to get clear about what you need to do and why you're doing it. Remind yourself of the benefits of tracking your spending and then commit to entering in a notebook or an app each time you spend some money.

Using a tracking app, such as Budgt or Mint, is a useful way to record all your daily spending, but you may find it easier to save your receipts for each day and enter your spending once a day instead of opening the app every time you spend. You can also write down your spending in a notebook and enter it into a spreadsheet once a day.

Whatever method you choose to track your spending, make sure you stick to the one method and don't confuse yourself by tracking in different places.

Keep all receipts in a pocket of your wallet, but don't let them build up for days or weeks or you'll be discouraged to track at all.

Download a tracking app, such as Budgt, Mint or Pocket Expense or one of your choice and get started.

Deciding how much you can spend

When it comes to figuring out how much you should budget, some advise using the *50/20/30 rule*. With this rule, you budget to spend 50 per cent of your income on your fixed costs, like rent, electricity and bills; 20 per cent should then go on your saving goals – whether that is to save for a holiday or work on your pension; the 30 per cent left over is your discretionary spending for things like groceries, entertainment and presents. This distribution depends on what you earn and what your expenses are. If you have a child in college, your expenses will be more than usual, but if you're saving for a child's future education, you should probably save a larger proportion of your income.

Budgeting isn't about doing without; it's about conscious spending.

Deciding how much you can save

Whatever your income size, you should try to save something each week, no matter how small. Take this money from your main account before you start the discretionary spending. Try to find areas that you may be overspending. Check all your bills, such as phone, electricity and insurance and see whether you can save from switching providers. These savings could fatten up your savings account each month. And that latte, if you multiply the price by 365, I'm sure you'll rethink that expense to put more toward your savings or your annual holiday.

Planning meals and shopping

Planning meals was never something I was much good at. The positive part of not planning meals is that you probably get to eat what you feel like every day. The negative side is that you spend more and eat more, which isn't ideal for anyone.

Planning once a week

Taking some time once a week to plan seven meals isn't a difficult task. With a few cookbooks for inspiration or a quick browse online, you can quickly come up with a few new idea to intermix with your family favourites. By doing this you can also use common ingredients that will be more economical and easier on the chef. For example, you could roast butternut squash on Monday and freeze half of it for a meal later in the week.

Shopping once a week

If you have a solid plan in place, shopping is much faster and easier. You won't dump food at the end of the week because you didn't have a plan for it. Ideally, you should buy your fresh fruit and vegetables locally and more frequently than weekly, but if the bulk of your ingredients are in your cupboards, you're good to go and less likely to opt for convenience food on the way home from work.

Planning shopping times

Why not go shopping at unorthodox times to benefit from empty supermarkets and short cashier lines. Traditionally, people shop closer to the weekend, with payday usually on a Thursday or Friday, so the supermarkets are full to capacity, making a trip to the supermarket an unpleasant experience. If payday doesn't determine the times of your shopping, consider an alternative time and day to benefit from the less busy aisles.

Shopping at peak times adds up to 60 minutes to your shopping trip, wastes unnecessary time, and probably causes you unnecessary stress. Be brave and vary your routine to see the benefits.

Focusing Your Attention on Work-Life Balance

Traditionally, organisations see work and their employees' personal lives as competing priorities. Where one gets attention, the other loses out. In recent years, however, this isn't the case. Organisations are beginning to reap the benefits of the alternative workplace and flexible working.

Working from home and flexible hours are no longer a fad, and more and more managers are seeing the business case as well as the benefit to the worker. Businesses benefit from increased productivity, reduced sick leave and costs and the preservation of difficult-to-find talent. They also benefit from more engaged, relaxed employees who are better able to manage the multitude of roles and responsibilities that modern life brings.

Defining what work-life balance means to you

Work-life balance is different for every person. Whether you have children or elderly parents to look after, are married or live alone, *balance* is an important word. Having time for relaxation, hobbies, friends and family is important to feel truly happy and fulfilled.

Discovering your balance

What does balance mean to you? Do you want to work a full week and spend sufficient time with family and friends, or would you need to reduce your working hours to fit it all in?

Whatever your ideal scenario, the first step is understanding yourself and your needs. Just because your sister works three days a week and is happy doesn't mean the same setup will work for you. It's not about how many hours you work; it's about identifying the areas of your life that need attention and ensuring that you're being fulfilled in all areas. If you work a long week, chances are the other areas of your life are suffering. For example, maybe your relationship isn't getting the attention it deserves or your kids are feeling a little left out.

Identifying your priorities

A good place to start is with your priorities – not your work priorities but your big-picture priorities. Think about the different areas of your life that need attention. Following are some examples:

- Family
- Friends
- Children
- Career
- Personal development
- Health
- Voluntary/community contribution
- Spiritual growth
- Fun
- Travel

Are you spending enough, if any, time developing these different parts of your life? Which areas have been neglected? Which ones are getting too much of your time? You don't have to spend time on each area, but you need to get some degree of satisfaction from other areas of your life. The question is, currently in this phase of your life, what is priority for you?

Your priorities may be spending time with your children, family and friends while also developing your career and having fun. If this is the case, what needs to change for you to be fulfilled? See the sections 'Identifying what needs to change' and 'Doing anything but not everything', later in the chapter, to help you answer this question.

Understanding shifting priorities

Think of a set of scales. It's always ready to shift to maintain equilibrium. Life is just like this; your priorities today may not be your priorities tomorrow. You need to be able to adapt and change to suit your shifting needs. Know that this is perfectly acceptable and part of life. To understand this is to accept life's ebb and flow. When you push against something, you cause tension; when you go with the flow and stay flexible, you can adjust and bend with the wind.

Identifying what needs to change

When you're clear about your priorities, it's easier to see what needs to change. The keys to changing what needs to change are learning to be flexible and uncovering time-wasting activities and then not engaging in those as often.

Learning to be flexible

If you want to make changes in your life, you have to be open to doing things differently both in work and at home. Don't do things a certain way just because you've always done them that way. Consider whether a different way would be better, and be open to alternatives. For example, if you're looking for ways to change up your work hours, try working from 7 to 3 or 11 to 7, if possible.

Stop going with the status quo, and make life work for you!

Uncovering time-wasting activities

We all waste time daily – oodles of it actually. Sometimes you may not be aware of how much time you're wasting – in meetings, watching TV, mindlessly browsing the Internet or reacting to every email that comes your way. You can become more conscious of how you spend your time by creating a timesheet. Enter in everything you do during the day, and review each week. Are you engaging in activities that don't merit your time and attention? What can you reduce or eliminate from your weekly schedule? The timesheet may also help you to identify those things that you're not spending enough time on.

Doing anything but not everything

Anything is possible. Remember that you can work hard, play hard *and* be good a parent and that achieving your dreams is well within your reach. But it's vital that you don't try to do everything. What happens when you try to do everything? You do few things well. Doing too much usually ends up in burnout.

Overdoing it

Doing too much is a tendency of high performers and high achievers. There's always something more you can do to improve and to prove yourself. Overdoing it is also a tendency of caring people who do too much out of kindness and compassion. Either way, whatever your motivation, it rarely ends well.

Stress, depression or heart attack is not something you want to add to your curriculum, but too many people have at least suffered from stress because they're trying to do it all. Stress needs to be managed. When it begins to cause strain, stress has health repercussions.

One of the best ways to manage stress is to exercise. Reduced stress, increased health and enhanced wellbeing are all commonly experienced benefits that come from moderate amounts of exercise. Exercise is a definitive way to get more out of life.

Underdoing it

If you want to be successful in life, there are times when you'll need to stretch yourself, go outside your comfort zone and make time for new projects and challenges. If you do this in a measured way, it won't cause the stress and anxiety that overdoing it can cause.

After you identify your priorities (see earlier in this chapter), you may notice that certain areas of your life need attention. Start by eliminating the things that aren't priorities and waste your time and start to introduce the things that you need to do more of, little by little. Once you start to make positive changes, your confidence will increase and you'll find yourself capable of so much more.

Asking for help

Finding balance sometimes requires asking for help. It's rarely possible to do it all yourself and have an effective work-life balance. If your immediate family can't help you due to other commitments, you may need to get someone else to help. If you want to have a successful career and be a good parent, you can hand over some jobs, such as cleaning or tending the garden without anything suffering too much.

Don't try to start everything at once. Introduce new activities one by one and wait until you've comfortably created a new habit before introducing a second change. If you do too much at once, your chances of success will be slim.

Identifying work priorities

If you want to change the way you currently do things, chances are you can free up some time by being more focused at work. Don't be offended when I tell you that you could probably save up to an hour a day when you work more effectively with your email, plan your day and become clearer on your daily priorities. These are the areas that cause most office workers to waste hours daily doing things inefficiently.

Getting clear goals

The clearer you are about what you want to achieve, the more likely you are to be focused on the right things and stay on track each day. When the work you do daily is aligned with your overall work goals, you can rest assured that you're being productive.

Communicating clearly

To be sure you're doing the right things at the right time, you must communicate regularly with your boss and your team. Lack of communication can result in the wrong work being carried out, wasting everybody's time and causing frustration. Communicate clearly and regularly.

Limiting interruptions

When you're clear about your priorities, you're more likely to be able to deal with interruptions assertively. Interruptions can really disturb your flow and limit the amount of work you're capable of. Being clear about your priorities and what you need to do will minimise the amount of times you allow someone to intrude on your time and space.

Letting people know that you're busy and that you'll get back to them in an hour or later that day isn't bad manners or bad management. If you don't push back on people, you'll never get your priorities done, leaving you with work to do when it should be family time or time to enjoy yourself.

A good way to push back is to ask yourself the question, 'If I say yes to this person or to this project, what am I saying no to?' Often, it's family that suffers. Your children don't get the bedtime story promised because you have to complete a report, or your partner has to eat dinner alone, again. Now is the time to make your priorities *the* priority and stop working on other people's priorities.

Plan the work you want to get done each day, estimate the time you'll need and put it in your calendar. If you're clear about how long each task will take, you'll see if you have time to attend to other people's requests while still getting your work done.

Raising Productive Children

Raising productive children may seem a little more challenging than becoming productive yourself, especially if your offspring regularly shed their belongings and clothes like snake skins around the house. Children may not mimic your every move and buy into your plans, but they do absorb what you do. Children are much more likely to become productive adults if you have exhibited productive and organised behaviours right through their childhood. So if you are disorganised chaos, think what you are doing to your children and get your act together quickly before your disorder affects another generation.

Teaching children positive habits

The first step in teaching children positive habits is to practise them yourself. If you exhibit the behaviours you're trying to teach, you're twice as likely to have success. I guess you probably want your children to pick up after themselves, make their beds, tidy their rooms, eat healthy foods, stay hydrated, exercise regularly and not overindulge in electronic time. Sound about right?

How many of these habits have you mastered? It's no use lecturing your child about too much 'screen time' when you spend every waking moment with your head buried in your phone or tablet. Before even trying to foster good habits in your children, you need to create the habits for yourself. (See Chapter 5 on how to create new habits.)

Passing on your gift

The ability to create positive habits and be productive is in fact a gift. It's a wonderful gift that your children may never thank you for, but you can feel proud and satisfied to see your children as productive, happy and successful adults. Being organised and living in a clutter-free environment brings with it many advantage. These are advantages that both parent and child can profit from. Calm, controlled structure and routine build a positive environment in which your child can grow and develop. It is, in fact, the ideal environment to flourish.

Creating a new habit won't happen from hearing others talk about it. Neither will it happen by just observing others do that activity daily. The way to form a habit is to practise it, regularly, daily if possible.

Creating the motivation

Adults are motivated to start a new habit because the outcome inspires them. If there was no positive outcome to creating this new habit, they wouldn't bother. Even when a positive goal or outcome exists, some people don't bother. Habits are as difficult to create as they are to break.

So what motivates a child to tidy his room? Some children are naturally motivated and like the reward of a clean room. Others don't care, and telling them their mother or father will be happy with them if they tidy it probably won't be enough to inspire them to get busy. You need to help them find the motivation. One way to do that is to offer a reward that will stimulate them to take action.

Offering an incentive

Offering an incentive or reward is the best way to stimulate kids and to help them see the attractiveness of this new habit. If you want to teach kids to pick up after themselves, offer an incentive by creating a game that rewards them with each new level reached. Each toy or item of clothing picked up can be a point; after a number of points, they unlock a new level of the game that brings with it a reward or a treat.

Older kids may not be interested in a game, so encouraging them with a reward that is attractive and age appropriate may be your best bet.

At the ages of 8 and 10, I challenged my two youngest boys, who share a room, to keep their room tidy for a month. I had tried other tactics to no avail, so I decided to use a substantial monetary reward to motivate them. (Who says money doesn't motivate?)

Every evening for a month, they had to make sure their bedroom was organised before they got into bed. Every evening for a month, I was surprised to see a clean floor and an organised bedroom. On Day 31, after the money had changed hands, something changed. My younger boy continued to pick up his clothes and keep everything organised. The older boy reverted to old habits instantly, the carrot removed, the bounty pocketed, the motivation was gone.

The lesson here is that not all tactics will work for all children. The myth that it takes 21 days to form a habit isn't based on scientific evidence. It may work for some but not for others. Some children will be more difficult to convince, and although I can't pay my older son every month for keeping his bedroom clean, I do think he benefited from the month of tidiness. Some day in the future, he may crave the cleanliness again.

Sharing chores for one and all

From a young age, children should help with the chores. Not every chore is age appropriate, but every child can have an appropriate chore. In the following sections, I show how to make a master chore list, assign the work to be done daily, weekly and monthly, and allocate who's responsible for each chore.

Making a list of chores

Start by making a list of all the chores that need doing in the house. You can create three columns, one daily, one weekly and one monthly. Figure 17-1 shows a sample chore list.

Daily	Weekly	Monthly
Pick up toys/misc	Clean bathroom	Dust light shades
Laundry	Clean bedroom	Wash cushion covers
Recycling	Weed garden	Wash windows
Dinner dishes	Water plants	Vacuum under furniture
Unpack dishwasher	Dusting	Defrost freezer
Sweeping	Mop floors	Clean fridge
Vacuuming	Take out bins	Check smoke detectors
Wipe down surfaces	Clean microwave	Mow lawn
Collect mail	Shopping	Rake lawn

Figure 17-1: Master chore list.

If you live alone, you may have to do laundry only once a week. If you're like me and have three boys who play sport, you'll have the washing machine on a couple of times a day. Write your list to suit your lifestyle and your requirements. You may also like to create a fourth and fifth list for quarterly and yearly tasks, such as clearing out the garage or the attic. After you've created the list, you can then think practically about what days you should do the weekly tasks and how you can share the workload.

Be realistic and don't try to be a superhero. Get help from family, and if there is still too much for everyone's schedule, consider getting outside help. A cleaner or housekeeper is a valuable addition to any busy household, so if the funds allow, it's a clever investment.

Allocating the work

From a very young age, children can put away their toys in toy boxes. School-age children can do a lot more jobs, such as help setting the table for dinner, keeping their bedrooms in order, sweeping floors or unpacking the dishwasher. Teenagers should be sharing the weekly chores: vacuuming, clearing the kitchen and even helping with the laundry and cooking from time to time. Giving your children chores isn't to make slaves out of them, but having age-appropriate chores helps to teach them responsibility and lessons that will stand to them in later life. It also helps take the burden away from one person and helps make for a happier household over all.

Refer to the weekly chore list from Figure 17-1 with all the daily and weekly jobs listed in the first column. Each member of the family should be responsible for some job or chore each day. Don't overload anyone with too much work; try to be realistic from the outset. If you overload at the outset, you're setting yourself up for failure.

Figure 17-2 shows a sample chore list. This list was created in Excel and allows you to edit and change the person responsible if required. You can use a list in Excel or print one out and place it on the fridge or in another communal area.

Discuss chores in advance with all the family. Explain how you need help keeping the house in order and agree on jobs with everybody. Make sure you get buy-in before you post the list.

FOR THE WEEK OF: 04/01/2016	MON 4		TUE 5		WED 6	
TASK	WHO	DONE	WHO	DONE	WHO	DONE
Pick up toys/misc	Everyone	☑	Everyone	☐	Everyone	☐
Laundry	Ciara	☐		☐	Ciara	☐
Take out trash		☐		☐		☐
Dinner dishes	Everyone	☐	Everyone	☐	Everyone	☐
Sweep	Kai	☐	Troy	☐	Kai	☐
Vacuum	Jordan	☐		☐	Jordan	☐
Water plants	Troy	☐	Kai	☐	Troy	☐
Clean bathroom		☐		☐	Ockie	☐

Figure 17-2: The weekly chore list.

Remember to mix up the chores and not to give someone the same chore every day. This can become tedious, which I'm sure you're fully aware of. Variety helps to lessen the boredom that can be caused by repetition.

Creating a daily routines checklist

Do you ever feel like a parrot, repeating the same instructions over and over, which often fall on deaf ears? A way to overcome this frustrating condition is to create a daily routine checklist for your kids. Giving them a checklist to complete each morning means that you don't have to keep yelling at them to do all the things they need to do. From the age children can read until they are 10 or 11, they should enjoy ticking the boxes. In my experience, they don't need to receive any further reward than the feeling of achievement and independence this checklist gives them. See Figure 17-3 for sample checklists to get you started.

Morning Routine	
Name	
Breakfast	☐
Wash	☐
Brush teeth	☐
Make bed	☐
Pyjamas under pillow	☐
Get dressed	☐
Lunch in bag	☐
School bag	☐
Coat on	☐
Shoes on	☐

Bedtime Routine	
Wash	☐
Brush teeth	☐
Pick up clothes	☐
Pick up toys	☐
Put on pyjamas	☐
Kiss Mom	☐
Kiss Dad	☐

Figure 17-3: Morning and bedtime routine checklists.

Add to these checklists as you see fit. For example, if you bathe your children each night or shower them each morning, change the list accordingly. Encourage your children to complete the checklist each day. If you find resistance, you may want to encourage them with a treat or reward for a week of checked boxes.

Give plenty of praise when the job is done. Don't punish for non-completion. This activity needs to remain a positive one with no negative repercussions.

Storing the kids' stuff

Keeping children's toys organised can be a challenging job, especially if you have more than one child. If you want your children to tidy up after themselves and want to live in an organised, clean environment, you have to make it easy for them. It's your job to provide them with everything they need to be able to be organised. Tidying up isn't a nice job for anyone, but even less for kids, especially if they don't know where to put things.

Using the wardrobe

Not every wardrobe has a magical world on the other side, but most children's wardrobes do possess an alternative world, one that is unrecognizable to most adults. To maintain a workable wardrobe, it must have enough space to fit all the child's clothes. You then need to show how to hang up and fold clothes. This isn't an obvious skill. You can't assume a child will know how to fold a t-shirt or hang a pair of jeans or even which item should go where. Some people like to hang T-shirts; some hang only shirts, dresses, skirts and slacks. Before you start to expect a tidy room from your children, make sure you're clear about the standards you want them to keep:

- **Hanging clothes:** Explain to your children which items of clothing should be hung in the wardrobe. Show them how the item goes on the hanger and, if you want to go a step farther, which way the hanger should hang. Don't be too fussy at the start, and just try to let them get to grips with getting the piece of clothing off the floor and into the wardrobe. Then you can perfect their technique. Always praise the effort, even if the outcome isn't exactly how you would like it.

  Hanging clothes is easier for a children than folding so if you have the space, allow younger children to hang as much as possible. If your child is visual, she may enjoy colour coordinating her wardrobe. Don't force this on children who doesn't see this naturally. This is adding another layer of complexity to an unwanted chore.

- **Folding clothes:** Folding is a skill you must teach children. My three boys all still suffer trying to fold their clothes. I won't embarrass them by saying their ages, but you would expect the eldest to have it by now! Being the eldest, I omitted to show him many skills, assuming that he would absorb my knowledge and skills (not that I had many in the household department back then). He regularly reminds me when tasks aren't completed to my standard how I never showed him how. If you want your children to master a chore, you need to give them the skills before you expect them to do the job.

Organising and storing toys

Whether you have a playroom or keep your children's toys in their bedroom, you'll want to invest in plenty of robust toy boxes to store the toys. Categorise toys into different types and label the toy boxes accordingly. For example, if your children play with cars or other vehicles, put a big sticky label with CARS written on it. Keep labels clear, and consider adding an image to labels so that young children can understand what toys go where and partake in the cleaning ritual.

Having the toy boxes to keep the toys in is a great start, but you'll also want the furniture to hold those toy boxes. A wall of self-installed shelving is a great idea so you can create the heights and widths that you require to fit all the toys, games and books that your children have.

Sufficient storage is key to keeping an organised and tidy space. If you don't have the facility to make your own shelving, go to the furniture shop with a tape measure. Make sure you buy shelving that will fit your toy boxes.

Keep a number of boxes of toys out of reach of the children so that when they're bored you can produce some toys that they haven't played with in a while. This advice my mother-in-law gave me has been a life saver many times.

Organising the Home Office

A home office is an important part of any household and one that often doesn't get too much attention. Having an area of your house that's dedicated to household accounts and planning will do wonders to help get you more organised at home.

Many people have an organised working environment, but when it comes to the household they're disorganised and sometimes even chaotic. It's important to follow through on both fronts. Disorder affects your performance, and you carry the guilt of disorder with you always, sometimes unbeknown to yourself. Get your house in order to be your best.

Creating the space

Whether you work from home or have a home office purely to look after the family accounts, it is useful to create an environment that you enjoy working in. Also you want one that doesn't feel like borrowed space. Lots of people set up shop on the kitchen table to be disturbed each time there's a requirement to eat. This isn't functional or productive. The frustration of having to clear off each time may lead to you avoiding the jobs altogether.

Choose the room

The first step to creating your office space is to decide what room you're going to set up shop in. If you intend to work, study or write from home, you'll need a quieter space, one where you can close a door or have some privacy. The more private your workspace, the better you'll be able to focus and ultimately get more done.

Be sure to put a little thought into the space that you choose. Is the desk close to a window? Being close to a window is great to get light but not so great when the sun is shining. Bright sunlight will inhibit your ability to use a screen, and even if you are working on paper it may heat up too much to make it sustainable. On the flipside, working in a dark, dreary space will do nothing for your productivity.

Consider the temperature of the room in winter time. Does the room get too cold to spend time there? These questions aren't as important if you are using the room only for family accounts and budgets. These activities don't necessarily require long periods of sitting – that is, of course, if you keep your accounts up-to-date. The most important thing is that you like the space you've created and that you won't begin to avoid the task because of the space.

Choose your times

A home office has many considerations. Will it be possible to work when other people are in the house, or will the office be for times when nobody is home? Be clear about the logistics of your office and don't tell yourself you'll work in the afternoon if you know the afternoon will be hectic with the kids home. Be realistic from the start and don't set yourself in for frustration.

Choose your furniture

Invest well in office furniture. If you intend to spend a lot of time at your desk, your chair should be comfortable and your desk sufficiently big for the work you will be doing. If you suffer from back pain, you could consider investing in a kneeler chair, which helps to keep the spine straight, or you could look into a standing desk. Standing desks can be expensive so you may want make your own with a box on top of your existing desk.

When choosing furniture for your home office, consider the design of your home and try to get furniture that is in keeping with the existing style of your home.

Create sufficient storage space

To keep your home office clean and organised, allow sufficient storage space so that everything has a home. If you have a place for everything, you will feel more organised and in control. Label boxes so you know where to find things. Keep a filing cabinet close to your desk so that filing becomes an easy task that you will no longer avoid.

Investing in storage solutions

Put some planning into your storage solutions. Don't run off to your local office supplier and buy the first filing cabinet you see. Think about your requirements. Do you have many files? Or do you need to keep a lot of books close by to help you with the research for your writing? Take a look at everything that needs to go into your home office before you go shopping. Make an intelligent estimate of the storage that you'll require. The rule is always to have as much as you need but as little as possible. Having too much storage can drive you to the other side of the fence, encouraging you to fill what you have and accumulate stuff you don't need.

Organise your paper

To keep your paperwork organised, a simple filing system will help. You will need a filing system for both reference items and active projects. Keep your reference and filing separate. Create a simple A to Z filing system with hanging files in your filing cabinet. On your desk, set up an active filing system for your work in progress and put these files in a step file organiser. Use manila A4 folders and label them clearly with a labeller. Never leave papers lying around on your desk, and when papers are no longer needed make sure you recycle them or shred them if they contain confidential data.

The filing cabinet

There are many styles and sizes of filing cabinets. For a home office solution, you shouldn't need anything too big or elaborate. Filing cabinets can be pricy, too, so culling the files that you have can do your pocket a favour. Before you buy a new filing cabinet, spend some time going through all your files. Recycle any older files that are no longer relevant. Find out the auditing requirements in your country and get rid of any files that are older than needed.

Consider scanning newer files to store electronically and also asking your service providers to give you bills and statements online. (See the later section 'Keeping electronic information' for more ideas.) Not only will you be saving yourself money and grief, but you will also be saving the environment.

If you can reduce the amount of files that you have to one drawer, you can buy a miniature filing cabinet or a filing box, which should have enough space for a family's accounts. Keep your filing solution close to your desk. If it isn't accessible, you'll tend not to file regularly, creating a clutter problem and more work for yourself. If you can keep it within range, you're much more likely to do it day by day:

- **Hanging files:** Get hanging files and manila folders to organise documents inside them.
- **Manila folders:** Buy tabbed manila folders to store your documents. The tabs are for the labels to help you find what you're looking for more quickly.
- **Labels:** Put labels on all your manila folders. Place the label on the back of the tab so the documents can never cover the label.

File your folders from A to Z, keeping things simple and easy to retrieve, and return back to them place.

The bookshelf

The bookshelf can be for the typical books, magazines and folders, and it can also store photo boxes, stationery boxes and other relevant office stuff. The bookshelf can be an aesthetic addition to your office and could also contain the odd family photo or plant to bring some life to your office.

The office equipment

The printer, scanner and phone will also need a perch. If your desk is large enough, it may host the printer and phone, but you don't want the equipment to take over your workspace. Having a cluttered desk only disturbs your focus and concentration. Consider a separate cabinet for the printer. Search for office solutions online, and you can visualize the different options. Some desks come with a space for the printer underneath, but make sure your desk is still comfortable and has space to work.

Maintaining a clutter-free desk

In order to maintain a clutter-free desk, you will need an in-tray for any paperwork that hasn't been processed and make sure all documents are placed in the in-tray. Do not leave any documents lying around on your desk. After you've processed them, use a step file organiser or folders and file any documents that are active or belong to current projects.

Use your drawers wisely. Place items you use regularly in your top drawer; the less used an item, the further away from your desk it can be. Respect your work desk and try to keep it free of clutter at all times.

Keeping electronic information

You may decide that a lot of the information you keep, such as family medical information, food diaries, school calendars and even your identity numbers, would be more useful electronically. This information may be useful to have at hand whenever you need it. There are many apps that can store your medical information for you, such as Family medical manager or Family medical history. There are apps for food diaries, such as MyFitnessPal or MyPlate, and possibly anything else you can think of. Or rather than have a different app for each part of your life, you could use a general note-taking app, like Evernote, OneNote and Simplenote, to keep everything in one place to be accessed by you from any device.

Using note-taking apps

Note-taking apps can be useful to help you organise your information. As life gets busier and more complicated and you become responsible for more things, you need to remember lots of information. The more information you ask your brain to remember, the less processing space you have for coming up with great ideas. Using a note-taking app allows you to

- Capture all your ideas when you have them and file them away in an accessible manner, to be retrieved whenever you're ready to use them.
- Store information that you may need regularly or not so regularly. This information can be accessed and retrieved from any device wherever you are.
- Create a central area to share information with other people. Create shared to-do lists, checklists or collaborative projects.

Electronic note-taking apps have the benefit of being in the cloud, stored on a server on the Internet, which makes them available from any access point to the Internet. They also have the added benefit of being secure in the cloud with the option of keeping a copy locally.

Storing your stuff online

If you don't have your information in a cloud-based programme, consider using a cloud-based document storage, such as Dropbox, Google Docs or Box. If you don't feel comfortable in the cloud, remember to do regular back-ups. Losing information is a productivity nightmare.

Chapter 18

Creating a Clutter-Free World

In This Chapter

- Living clutter-free with fewer possessions
- Discovering decluttering techniques
- Figuring out how to keep things in order

More and more people are realising that the accumulation of stuff doesn't make for a happy life. The workweek is long, and the weekends are spent shopping for things that the media convince people they need. Houses are full of clutter and junk that never gets used, and lives are emptier than ever. It's time to stop the wheel and get off. In this chapter, I help you embrace a life of simplicity, declutter from house to office and establish and maintain order throughout your life.

Living a Life of Simplicity

How often have you heard someone say he lives a happy, simple life? Simplicity and happiness are often linked. The fewer possessions you have, the less stress and complications you have. On the other hand, the more you have, the more complex your life becomes. In the following sections, you discover how to rid your life of stuff you don't need, live consciously, develop an attitude of gratitude and take on a minimalist approach.

Ridding your life of stuff

The first step to living a life of simplicity is to rid your life of the stuff you've accumulated over the years. I mean, how many pairs of shoes do you really need? Could they be put to better use by passing some of them on? Out of all the ornaments, jewellery and paintings that adorn your surroundings and your bodies, how much of it do you really need? If you had only one bag to fill with all your possessions, what would you take? Which jewellery would you take with you, and which pieces could you do without?

When you start to think about living more simply, you often realise you have many clothes, shoes, books, CDs and possessions than you really need. Ridding your life of these extra possessions brings freedom and a lightness to your life. It also feels good to donate items and let others benefit from your unused possessions and also just to have less. It's a type of freedom that can't be explained, only experienced.

Living consciously: The power of one

Conscious living is a goal to aspire to. It means you understand that everything you do and everything you purchase has a consequence. If you think consciously and don't accept life the way it is, you can consciously make a difference. Change starts with the power of one. Each one person can make a difference, a difference that matters. One can inspire another to change, and a pattern may emerge.

But the key is believing you can make a difference. Never be discouraged from doing what you believe in because you think it won't make a difference. If you doubt your ability to make a difference, doing good deeds can be challenging. If you understand that each choice you make does have an impact, if you choose walking over driving your car to the shops, that contribution may seem to be just a drop in the ocean, but each person's contribution can make a difference.

Following are some ways you can make a difference:

- **Shopping locally:** Buying local produce is good not only for your health but also for the environment. When you shop locally, you're generally buying fruit and vegetables that are in season and you avoid buying the imported goods that need to be transported into the country. Eating tomatoes that were grown in your country reduces the number of tomatoes that need to use fossil fuels to be transported.
- **Recycling:** Every item you recycle reduces the strain on the planet from producing new goods. It also avoids the item being dumped in a landfill. Recycling is a habit that everyone needs to foster. It's easy to get lazy and toss recyclables into the general trash, but every action has an impact and every act contributes to an outcome, either positive or negative. Become more conscious of your actions, and make the outcome positive.
- **Composting:** Composting provides a way of reducing the amount of waste that needs to be disposed of and also converting waste into a product that's useful for gardening. Composting is a great way to get children involved in a process that's good for the environment and their ethical education.

Focussing on gratitude

Gratitude is the simple act of giving thanks. It's a powerful emotion that helps you see the good in all things. It's difficult to feel sad or sorry for yourself when you're feeling grateful. Many scientific studies are uncovering the powerful effects of daily gratitude. Studies show a reduction in depression and anxiety and an increase in happiness and well-being. Gratitude can help you to appreciate the simple things in life and not be always looking outside for sources of happiness. Here are some ways you can implement the idea of gratitude into your daily life.

Focus on outcome over income

To live an uncluttered, simple life, you need to focus your attention on the positive outcomes that your actions lead to rather than the quantity of income that you can get. Money doesn't bring happiness. After you acquire the income you need to fulfil all your needs, more money, bigger houses and cars and the possessions that more money brings doesn't equate to more happiness.

Focus on the experiences that you want in life rather than on the money that you think will get your there, and be grateful for what you have achieved thus far.

Look internally, not externally

Many unhappy people spend their lives comparing themselves to others. They judge themselves by both the quantity and quality of possessions they have in comparison to their friends, families and neighbours. This is never a good thing to do. Comparing yourself and your possessions to others and what they have can bring with it a sense of lacking that can never be fulfilled. Someone else will always have more wealth, more friends, more business . . . more everything. Happiness never comes from looking outside.

Happiness comes from within. Focus your attention inside, and create your happiness without the external possessions and belongings.

Keep a gratitude journal

One way to make sure you stay focused on gratitude is to make a daily list of what you're grateful for. You may choose to keep these lists in a journal, app or on sticky notes – whatever you choose, make a list every day. Include simple but wonderful gifts like your sight and hearing. You may want to give thanks for your children, your family and maybe even your pets. There's no end to the things you can be grateful for, and when you focus your attention on the multitude of gifts you've been given, it shifts your attention away from the things you feel you lack or need more of.

Living life to the min

The minimalist movement began in the art world in the late fifties. The fifties was a time of Abstract Impressionism where artists sought to express their personal emotions through art. The minimalist movement sought to take the personal expression out of the art and claimed that the art shouldn't refer to anything but itself. Stripping the art of the artists' interpretation creates freedom for the audience to interpret what they may.

On the Minimalist's website (`theminimalists.com`), Joshua Field and Ryan Nicodemus describe minimalism as a tool that can assist you in finding freedom:

> 'Freedom from fear. Freedom from worry. Freedom from overwhelm. Freedom from guilt. Freedom from depression. Freedom from the trappings of the consumer culture we've built our lives around. Real freedom'.

Create the positive habit switch

When you have a negative thought or feel sorry for yourself because things aren't exactly as you want them, make a conscious decision to change that thought and think of something positive, something you can be grateful for. This can be a powerful way to keep your spirits up and give you more energy and enthusiasm for life.

Following the minimalist movement

Minimalism is the act of stripping away what is unnecessary. Living life with less but with as much as you need. The philosophy is to question what's important, eliminate what you don't need and make space for the important things in life.

Typical minimalist values

There is no rule book to following the minimalist movement because the result will be different for each person. Some people may choose to remove the unnecessary items from their homes; others may reduce the size of their homes. And some may decide to stop driving and refuse to take airplane flights to lessen their impact on the Earth; others may simply choose to travel less. Whatever steps you choose, the values of people who practise minimalism usually include those in the following sections.

Experiencing freedom from materialism

One of the core minimalist values is to experience freedom from materialism, not to get caught up in the race to possess more. Too many people link their happiness to the accumulation of goods. Minimalism seeks to link happiness to different values, such as spending time with family and friends, doing good and pursuing the things that make a difference and make you happy. More money clearly doesn't buy happiness. Sometimes money can give people the freedom to live the life they want, but to pursue money for money's sake rarely leads to a happy and fulfilled life.

Living in the moment

Living in the moment is a lesson everyone can learn from. To live your life always thinking about what tomorrow will bring, wishing your life away, won't make for a happy life. It is important to realise that your life is *now* – not tomorrow and definitely not last week. What's happened in the past can't be changed. You can learn from mistakes you've made, but you shouldn't linger on your mistakes or bother with regrets.

When you worry, you're thinking about things that haven't yet happened and may never happen. Future worries are pointless. Far too much time is spent contemplating that which may never come to be. Yes, you need to plan for the future and ensure that your future needs are accounted for, but to spend your limited time thinking and worrying isn't a good use of your time.

Spending your time focused on the now is the more productive use of your time. Focus on the here and now, pay attention to the people around you, give them your attention when they speak and be able to give your work the focus and attention it deserves.

Pursuing your purpose

Life should be lived, passions pursued and dreams realised. Living your life to pursue the dreams of others isn't much of a life. Spending your days working in a job you don't love to earn money to buy things you don't really need isn't the most clever plan. It's more important to be passionate about your job, even if it doesn't pay as well as the next one.

Happiness is more important than stuff. Minimalists put more value on freedom and happiness than on income and stuff.

Consuming less

The Western world has become addicted to spending. Shopping has become a pastime. To shop for pleasure rather than necessity is a social norm. People have become convinced that they have a need for so many items they previously never knew existed. They buy more, bigger, better because they can. Mindless consumption isn't good for your psyche or the planet.

Minimalism is about consuming less, focusing on the essential and foregoing what isn't. It's not about never purchasing anything, and neither is it about spending less. Minimalists would rather buy quality than quantity, buying once rather than many times. Overall, it's clear for personal satisfaction and the health of the planet: people need to consume less.

Clearing the distractions

Living a life full of distractions – TV, social media and email – fills your head with unnecessary clutter. Only when you're free of these shallow distractions can you live a life of meaning. I'm not saying these items have no place in life, but their overuse and the addictions that they cause can keep you from being truly free.

Minimise these distractions and fill their place with more meaningful activities. Rather than spend an hour watching a TV show, read or play a game with your children. Rather than spend an hour looking at other people's lives on Facebook, call a friend for a catch-up. Life can be full of beautiful moments if you can minimise the mindless distractions.

Reclaim your time

Living with less and focusing on the important things in life should shift your time and attention to what matters. Reclaim your time from the unimportant to focus on the important. No more multitasking and racing around to get stuff done. Stop and prioritise what's really important. Single-tasking and slowing down are often more productive than trying to achieve everything all at once. Minimalism is about shifting your attention to what matters, spending the precious time you've been given in life on things of value.

Benefits of minimalism

The benefits of becoming minimalist range from inner freedom to protecting the planet. Other benefits include

- Less stress
- More money
- Less cleaning
- More peace
- More time

If you want to benefit from the many advantages of minimalism, start with awareness. Become aware of all the places you consume when you don't need to. You can then become conscious of unnecessary spending. Seeing a few extra coins in your wallet at the end of the week may motivate you to explore this thing a little more.

Devising your declutter plan

The first step to decluttering is to create a plan. Think about what rooms and areas need to be tackled in your house and your office. Writing things down will help you to commit to your plan and get it done. Use the headings in the following list:

- **Zones to declutter:** Write down all the areas in your house and office that need to be attacked. Break it down into smaller areas if the job is too large. Write down wardrobes, cupboards and junk zones to be addressed.
- **Desired outcome:** Be clear why you're decluttering. Think about the desired effect of decluttering, how it will affect you and your family and how you'll feel about yourself after it's done.
- **Start date:** Commit to a date to get started.
- **Prior actions:** What needs to happen before you can begin? Do you need more storage solutions, bags or boxes? To help you stay on task, try to have everything ready to go before you get started. Stopping to go to the shop may break the momentum and give you a way out before you're done.
- **Deadlines:** Whether you need to set deadlines depends on your past history. If you're the type to start and never finish, then you should give yourself deadlines to get some of the work done. If you have years of accumulated clutter, the idea of getting started will probably feel overwhelming. In this case, you may need to call in a friend for moral support. A buddy will keep you motivated and on track. Be realistic and realise that you won't get it all done in a week.

Once you have your declutter plan ready to go, here are a few simple decluttering tips that can be used for all zones.

- **Give yourself a time-based goal.** Starting out with the goal to clean out the garage on Saturday is a noble goal and probably one you'll fail at miserably. The reason I say that is because the task is too big for one person for one day. Setting unrealistic goals often results in disappointment, frustration and probably discouragement to finish the job.

  By setting a time-based goal, you allow yourself a certain amount of time to work on the garage. If it isn't 100 per cent complete when you finish, that won't be a problem because the result is that you made progress, and if progress is your goal, you'll be happy and motivated to continue some other day.
- **Challenge yourself with small tasks.** Another way to set yourself achievable tasks is to give yourself small goals, such as clearing out one drawer or clearing one shelf each evening after work. Each small task you undertake helps you move closer to your overall goal. Celebrate each small success. Each job done gets you closer to your goal of a clean, organised and comfortable environment to live in.
- **Have a supply of boxes and bags.** Have plenty of boxes and bags on hand to put your rubbish into. Label each box to help you clear. Examples include recycling, donating and normal rubbish. Having somewhere to immediately place your stuff will encourage you to keep going.
- **Schedule time in your calendar.** Schedule time for the task. Don't keep saying 'I will

(continued)

(continued)

get around to it'. Commit by blocking out a couple of hours or a day to tackle an area. If you schedule the time, you're more likely to achieve your goal.

- **Ask the question 'Is it useful or beautiful?'** When you struggle to throw things out, a good question to ask yourself is, 'Is it useful or beautiful?' You'll find that so many of the things you hold on to are neither. If it's neither useful nor beautiful, it's time to say adios.

Give away or donate at least one item this week that you no longer need. It may be something you've been holding on to, not ready to let go. Raise the courage to say goodbye and experience the freedom of detachment from your stuff.

Don't get caught up trying to follow someone else's minimalist path. Your journey is personal. It's more important to be conscious of your impact on your life and the planet than to have only 100 possessions.

Decluttering Your Home and Office

Decluttering is a simple activity that can have a powerful and uplifting impact on your life. Even if you don't want to live life as a minimalist (see previous section), you can benefit from removing the extra items from your life or simply organising the stuff that you do have. It's not important where you start, only that you do start. Choose a room of the house or even an area in that room and go full-steam ahead.

Clearing the bedroom

The bedroom is a good place to start the decluttering process because you spend so much of your life there. Your bedroom should be a place of peace, a haven in your busy world. If that's not the case, make a plan to clear out anything that doesn't belong there, minimise the stuff you have and organise what's left over.

Downsizing your wardrobe

Work through your wardrobe, and pass along anything you haven't worn in the last year. Some people hold on to clothes of different sizes, thinking they may one day wear them again. However, if you're holding on to clothes that are bigger than you currently are, that doesn't say much about your faith in yourself. In fact, you're basically saying that you know you can't maintain your current weight and that you expect to be larger again in the future. This is a bad idea, and I suggest you get rid of the larger sizes now. Next time your trousers get a little tight, let that be a trigger to start watching what you eat rather than jumping into the next size up.

On the other hand, if you're holding on to clothes that are a couple of sizes smaller to motivate you to lose weight, you have to be realistic. If you've had these clothes for the past five years, perhaps it's time to let them go. If you've recently gained weight and want to get back into your clothes, then your smaller sized clothes will encourage you to keep to your diet and exercise plan. But if it's 12 months down the line, you should consider letting go and starting again. In short, you must be realistic with yourself. There's no harm in starting fresh. You could always reward yourself with some new clothes after you lose some weight.

Using hangers

Hangers are important; be sure you're using the right hangers for your clothes. Wire hangers aren't ideal for jackets or coats and will only cause frustration. Invest in strong wooden hangers for heavy items of clothing. You should also consider whether you want to use trouser hangers or to hang trousers and skirt hangers to keep skirts crease-free. Having the right trappings will keep things in order and reduce frustration. You may think I'm crazy now, but you'll thank me once you have a wardrobe filled with good-quality uniform hangers that get the job done.

Arranging the colours

Colour coordinating may sound like a job for a fashion designer and not a busy executive trying to keep her room tidy. But give it a go before you knock it. Start at one end of your wardrobe and hang your jackets and shirts from dark to light, start with black then greys, navy, blues and so on, as you work through your wardrobe. You do this, of course, after you've decluttered, donated and recycled the clothes you no longer wear. Keep trousers separate and arrange them accordingly.

Deciding when to expand storage

When wardrobe number one doesn't fit everything in, you may be tempted to buy another wardrobe. But buying more storage isn't always the optimum solution. Take an objective look at what you do own. If you were emigrating, what would you take with you and what would you leave behind? Try to reduce your load by donating the items that you definitely wouldn't take to a new country.

I'm obviously not recommending you throw out all your jumpers because you may emigrate to a sunny country, but get rid of the things that don't merit that journey. When you've downsized as much as you can and you still don't have room in the wardrobe, then you can go buy another wardrobe to fit it all in if you still need the space.

Looking under the bed

Are there monsters under your bed? We've all found a furry friend at some stage during our lives – the apple or peach that grew hair and a beard. A clear, dust-free under-bed experience is important for both health and well-being. Some people like to use the space under the bed for storage. I'm not one of these people. I believe the energy should flow freely under your bed, and storage boxes are another place for dust to settle. Find somewhere else to store your shoes and other stuff that you've shoved out of sight.

Stacking up on shelves

Just like I'm not a fan of under-the-bed storage, I don't think shelves are a good idea in the bedroom. Wherever you put a shelf, you will fill it with books, ornaments, photos and more. Do you really need these things in your sleeping quarters? Keep your bedroom as minimal as possible. The less clutter and stuff lying around, the better you'll sleep.

Digging out the drawers

Drawers are the worst offenders for enticing people to hoard. I bet it's safe to say that the contents of all the drawers in your house wouldn't fit inside your car. The truth is, a lot of what's inside your drawers is stuff you'd dump if you were moving house. Drawers are clutter zones. Although you may think that out of sight is out of mind, that stuff still lurks somewhere in your subconscious. The knowledge that there's stuff that needs to be sorted through and possibly dumped is always there, disturbing your perfect peace.

Clearing the garage

If you're lucky enough to have a garage, you're probably unlucky enough to have dumped a lot of stuff there over the years. Garages and attics are generally dumping zones, a place to put the stuff you don't know where to put.

Clearing out the garage can be a big job and may not be possible to do in one day. It also likely isn't a one-person job. The best way to tackle a garage is to set aside a few hours to work on it each week. And call on your spouse or kids to give you a hand. If the garage is filled with everybody's belongings, having everyone close by can be helpful so each person can deal with his or her items. Also, having your kids help sets a good example that hoarding shouldn't be an option, and that you should keep only what you need.

Good shelving is essential in the garage with plenty of containers to store the items you need to keep. Consider hanging spades, brooms and brushes on hooks on the wall. Hooks can be a great way to store tools and can reduce the amount of items kept on the floor. Browse the Internet for ideas of how you can best design your garage to suit your storage requirements. Whether it's garden tools or outdoor toys and bikes, there is a way to maximise the space that you have.

Clearing the attic

The attic is a similar place to the garage for some – it's somewhere to put the Christmas decorations, the baby stuff and all the things you don't use and probably don't need. Clearing out an attic will uncover many things, including good and bad memories. The attic is not somewhere to tackle when you are in a rush. Schedule plenty of time and get someone to help.

The attic is usually the least accessible space in your home. If you don't have your attic converted with permanent stairs, it's probably a pain to go find something that you've stored there. For this reason, use the attic for long-term storage of items that you don't need to regularly access.

Clearing the office

A lot of organisations have adopted a clean-desk policy to encourage workers to stay organised and keep the environment in a state that is conducive to productivity rather than chaos. The problem with this policy is that most people stick their files, folders and other paperwork into their drawers to get it off the desk, but this isn't enough. Out of sight doesn't always mean out of mind. Having everything organised is important, and it's better to have things organised and on display than disorder behind doors.

Cleaning off the desk

Having a clean desk is definitely a good thing; the less on display and in your line of sight, the better. Stuff lying around can disturb your focus and your ability to work at your best. Maintain a clean desk as much as possible. Take a look at the stuff on your desk and ask yourself whether everything there does have a home. Often, clutter is simply a sign of a homeless item. You may not be quite sure where something belongs so you leave it lying around. If everything has a home that is obvious, practical and accessible, your desk will always be tidy. Okay, maybe that's a little optimistic – your desk will at least be more organised.

Filing it all away

Keep your filing simple. A simple A to Z system with hanging files and folders can cope with a lot. If you need to file regularly and refer to files, keep them close by. If your filing cabinet is on the other side of the room, you can guarantee more files lying around. If it's in arms' reach, you can keep the filing up-to-date without breaking a sweat.

A desk file stand is ideal for storing paper-based work in progress. If you have working files, filing them away in a filing cabinet to be retrieved regularly isn't very practical. The most rational way to deal with these files is to have actionable work on your desk in folders, labelled in a file stand. These folders will be dynamic and ever changing as projects come and go. Another useful way to use the desk file stand is to have a folder for each person you report to or are responsible for. This allows you to capture any paperwork to be passed on to each of them in an efficient and neat manner.

Tidying up the desk accessories

Keep your accessories tidy with a desk tidy. Don't overload it. Only have what is essential on a day-to-day basis. Alternatively, you can use a tray inside your top drawer for stationery and accessories. This keeps your paper clips, staples, and pens organised and out of sight.

Avoiding wall charts

Unless wall charts are crucial to your job, try to avoid them. Too many charts, posters or 'wall candy' can distract your attention from your work. The cleaner and less cluttered, the better!

Maintaining the Order

After you've done the decluttering and have everything in order, you may be worried about how to maintain that order. In this section, I provide some tips to help you keep your organised life . . . organised.

Buy quality

If you want to minimise the quantity of objects you own, the best way to do this is to buy the best of everything. That may not be so easy to do when you don't have much money, but you'll find it works out better in the long run.

When you buy cheap clothes or other objects, you tend to buy more so you usually don't save any money in the long run. Good things make you feel better. And having fewer but better items to choose from makes getting ready in the morning easier and quicker.

Use a list

Never buy anything that isn't on your shopping list. Even when you go clothes shopping, make a plan before you go. Shopping on impulse usually doesn't bring good results. When people buy without a plan, they buy bargains; they get blinded by the savings and forget about the actual money they have to spend. Using a list will help you avoid impulse buying and make you think before you act.

Think 'one in two out'

When you do need to buy something or if you simply like the look of something, follow the 'one in two out' philosophy. If you buy a new pair of shoes, for example, donate two existing pairs. This trick is great to help you remain clutter-free; it also contributes to gradually minimising the belongings you do have.

Convince the stakeholders

Staying clutter-free can be difficult when not everyone sees things the way you do. You may have a partner who is a hoarder or a child who likes to keep broken bits of toys. The way to tackle these challenges is to stay positive, communicate and don't complain.

Stay positive

Keep a positive attitude and remain calm. That's easier said than done, I know, but getting angry with the family doesn't work. Forcing others to keep things the way you like them isn't a long-term strategy for harmony and happiness. Do as much as you can and remind them regularly of the benefits. Be consistent with children, and give them chores to stay tidy and clutter-free.

Communicate

With children, you can tell them what to do; with your spouse, not so much, nor is it advisable. However, you can communicate calmly and clearly and explain your wishes. People often assume that others know what they want them to do, or they expect them to know how much disorder and clutter upsets them. Don't assume. Use your voice, and calmly let your family know what you want and talk about how you think you can achieve it.

Don't complain

If nobody is hearing you, moaning and complaining aren't going to help. Instead, take action, and make it easy for the people in your house to get organised by providing the storage solutions for them.

For example, if your husband drops nails and screws on the sitting room mantelpiece every evening after work, buy a little wooden box to hold the screws. If your teenage son drops football gear in the entrance hallway every evening, buy a box to enable him to dump his stuff inside. You may need a couple of air fresheners to offset the smell, but at least it will look tidier. Life is too short to spend time arguing about clutter, so stop complaining and take action. Make it easier for your family to be tidy rather than untidy, and don't sweat about the rest.

Practise the clean sweep

Create a nightly habit of a clean sweep where everyone in the family must start at the front door and walk right through the house collecting his or her belongings. If you can create this habit, you'll keep things orderly and make it easier to stay on track. Provide your spouse and kids with a basket, if necessary, to collect their possessions and take them to their room. They then, of course, must empty the basket and have it ready for the next evening's clean sweep.

Make decluttering a daily habit, and you'll never have to live with clutter again.

Chapter 19

Productivity for Students

In This Chapter

- Choosing the right tools
- Understanding how to schedule your time
- Creating positive and productive habits
- Creating a solid network for life

Going from school to college can be a difficult transition. Gone is the hand-holding through every decision in your life; now it's time to take responsibility for your actions. The best advice you can take as a student is to get organised from day one. Being organised will save you so much grief and stress as the years pass on. This advice holds true whether you're straight out of school or have been out for a while and going back to college part time or full time.

In this chapter, I show you how to organise your notes, schedule your time and create positive and productive habits for your success as a student.

Taking and Storing Notes

Whether you prefer taking handwritten notes or electronic ones, it's best to be consistent. Using the same note-taking method prevents you from losing notes or having to duplicate work trying to transfer all notes to the same format.

Working with paper

Lots of people prefer to handwrite their notes. There's a special connection between the pen and the paper, one which you're allowed to be part of for a little while. Handwritten notes are usually faster and allow you to doodle while listening. You can choose from a couple of methods for writing out lecture notes. Decide on the method that best suits your style and subject you are studying and stick with it.

If you use paper for note taking, be sure to clearly label your pages with date, subject and name of lecturer.

The outline method

The outline method is probably the most used form of note taking. It's based on a hierarchy of notes and uses bullet points. It uses indents to structure and indicate importance. The closest information to the left margin is generally the top level, and as you create subtopics, you indent them with bullet points. See Figure 19-1 for an example.

Taking notes in this manner can help when reviewing information. A negative of this method is that you need time to sort out your structure, so if a lecture is moving too quickly, it can mess you up. This can be a good method to use if taking notes on a laptop or tablet, though, because it's easier to readjust hierarchy and edit as you go.

Sample Outline Notes

Note Taking

- Cornell method
  - Note taking
  - Cues
  - Summaries
- Mind mapping
  - Main topic
  - Subtopics
  - Linking

Figure 19-1: Outline note method.

The Cornell method

The Cornell system was devised by Walter Pauk at Cornell University. It's a simple method that helps you record notes that will be useful when it comes time to study. The Cornell system requires you to split your page into three sections: the main section of the page is for note taking, the margin is for questions and cue words, and a section at the bottom of the page is left for a summary. See an example of this method in Figure 19-2.

During the lecture, you should focus on capturing the notes in the note-taking area. Shortly after the lecture, write questions and cues in the margin area. The margin area can also contain key points of the lecture, dates or other information that will make it easier for you to study. You can use these questions and cues in the margin to quiz yourself while covering the note area with another book or paper. The summary area of the page helps you to figure out what is on each page without having to read over all the notes.

The Cornell method is a do-it-once, do-it-right method of note taking. It saves you time by not having to rewrite notes at a later stage and hopefully helping you learn as you go.

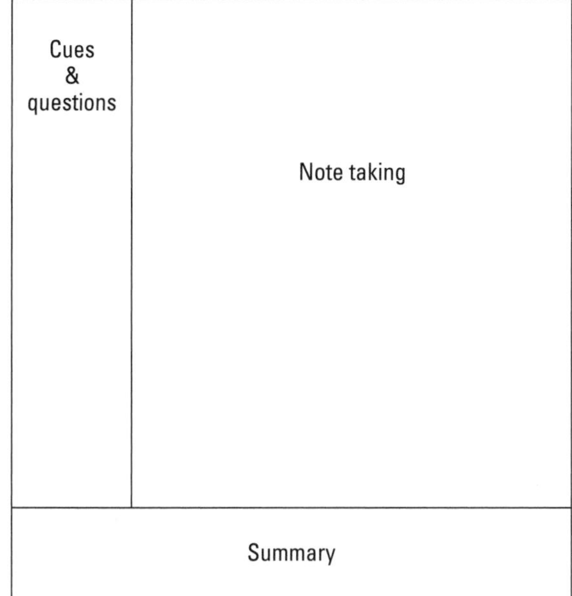

Figure 19-2: The Cornell note-taking method.

Mind-mapping method

Mind mapping is a wonderful visual method of note taking, which should also help you to absorb the information as you work. Mind mapping was first introduced by Tony Buzan in the 1960s. He was frustrated with traditional note-taking techniques, so he devised mind mapping as a way to create a visual map of ideas, laid out in a radial format around a central thought. According to Buzan, a mind map is very similar to a brain cell and works on similar principles: linking, associating, transferring and storing images. For that reason, it makes sense to take notes in the same way the brain works.

Here are a few of the benefits to using the mind-mapping method for study notes:

- Mind maps are visual images with coloured branches that appeal to the brain.
- Keywords save you time and help you study for exams. Recording information in this way helps to remove the overwhelming feeling of trying

to learn and recall reams of text. Your mind map will help you recall the most important information and trigger the rest.

- Ideas flow through making your mind map. Your brain actively makes links between ideas, adds connections, puts thoughts in order and generates further creative ideas.

Figure 19-3 provides an example of the mind map note-taking method.

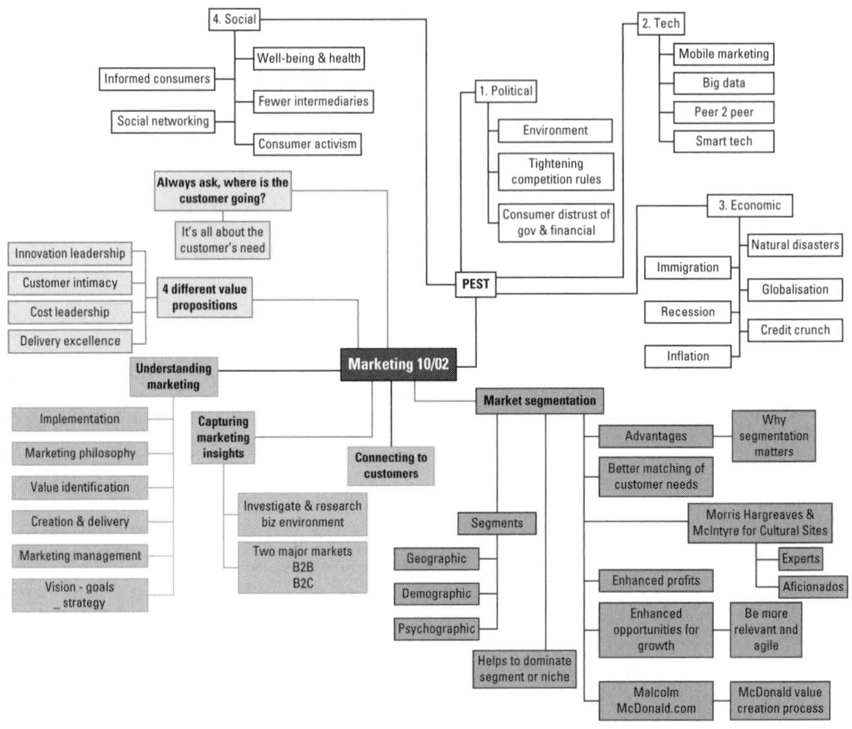

Figure 19-3: Mind mapping.

The flow method

Flow-based note taking, devised by Scott Young, is described as a powerful technique to accelerate your learning while listening. The method is different to the traditional linear, hierarchical note-taking systems for the following reasons:

- You emphasise the important details and omit or downplay the irrelevant.
- You write down notes according to your mental picture of the subject, going back to add details and moving into new sections as you learn.

- You transcribe information in a completely original way from the way it's presented.
- You create a new set of ideas and understandings, based on the original lecture.

The goal of the flow method is not to merely transcribe what you've heard in a lecture but to learn as you listen. Learning as you go sounds like a very productive method to me.

The flow method starts out similar to mind mapping, making visual notes that link to each other. The concept is to make notes in your own words and not to use the lecturer's words. You can add in new ideas if they come. The idea is learning, so if you get ideas as you go, all the better. Also you want to connect ideas backward and link back to earlier notes.

You can also make a place on each page for references made during your lecture that you want to follow up on later, such as a book or video that was mentioned. Making a space for these references on the page will help you to find them easily and means you won't miss out or forget any nuggets of information given in your lectures.

Getting the gear together

Paper isn't the only thing you will need for note taking and organising your notes; following is a list of equipment you need to ensure you are prepared and ready to go.

- **Highlighters:** Highlighters can be helpful, but you don't want to overuse them. One mistake many students make is highlighting important information. What they find, though, is that most of the notes they took have important information, so they end up with a page full of highlighter. Not so helpful.
- **Pens:** Of course, any pen will do, but writing is so much more pleasant when you have a nice pen. Even the colour of the pen can have an effect on how you work. Invest in a couple of good pens before you start. They don't have to be designer pens, but spending a couple of extra cents on pens that write well and feel comfortable in your hand can make life more pleasant and notes easier to take.
- **Plastic pockets for your binder:** If you decide to go the paper route, you need a way to file your notes. Doing it straight after a lecture is a good habit to get into. You can choose either to file the pages directly into your ring binder or put the notes in a plastic pocket. Plastic pockets are great if you'll be referencing the notes often because they will keep your notes from getting damaged. If you plan to reference the notes only for the odd assignment and for your exam study, you can probably do without the plastic pockets. It will save you a bit of money, and it will be better for the environment.

- **Dividers:** To keep your notes organised and easy to find, label your notes clearly and invest in dividers to divide the folder into different subjects or subtopics within a particular subject. The more organised and structured you are, the less stress and hassle you'll have when it comes time to study.
- **Audio recorder:** If you're an auditory learner, you may want to take an audio recording of your lecture so you can listen back when it comes time to study. It's always a good idea to get the college or lecturer's permission to do this in advance, to ensure that they are okay with you recording the lecture. You can also use a recorder to record your thoughts directly after the lecture. You may have some thoughts on what you heard, and recording them as soon as possible will help you not to forget.

Taking notes electronically

Research shows that manually transcribing notes makes for better students, but not when the students have a tendency to lose their paper notes or the dog eats them. The benefits of working with electronic notes are numerous and can have positive effects for many learners. If you decide to go this route, you can choose from many programmes to create and store your notes. Evernote, OneNote and Google Docs are popular choices for students. Each can help to organise the multitude of notes that students have to take during their stretch at college.

The benefits of going electronic

Although I still like paper and sometimes remember more from writing notes with a pen rather than a keyboard, the benefits of having notes electronically and organised in whatever programme you choose to use far outweigh the benefits of paper. These benefits include

- **Accessibility:** Having your notes available to you wherever you are is a blessing. You never know when you'll have time to work on a paper or when a killer idea will strike and you want to add it to previously completed work. Keeping your notes electronically allows you to access your work wherever you are and whenever you want.
- **Safety:** No more dogs eating homework. Electronic notes are safe and secure online. Most of the time, you won't even have to manually save your notes because a lot of cloud-based solutions auto-save work. Don't take my word, though; check it out for yourself.
- **Order:** The structure and order created by having everything organised and saved online can put you in a very fortuitous position starting out as a student. Don't underestimate the impact this can have on your ability to achieve and be successful.

Using Evernote

Evernote allows you to create notebooks where you store your notes. You can also create notebooks within notebooks, so, for example, you can create a notebook for a subject and another notebook inside for the subtopics within the subject. See Figure 19-4.

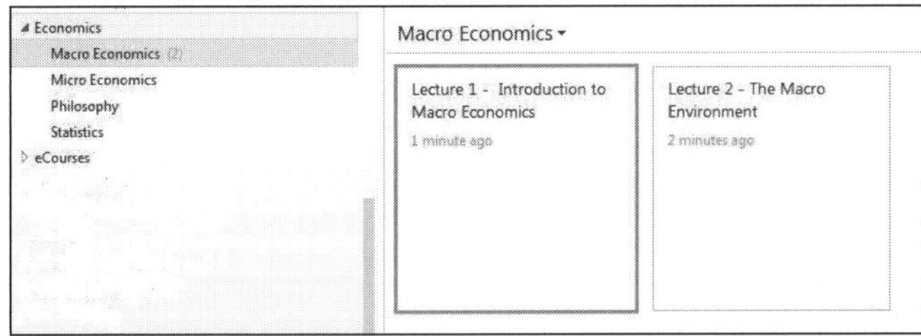

Figure 19-4: Notebooks in Evernote.

Source: Ciara Conlon

Evernote has many other features that make it useful for students to store information and research, such as the following:

- **Web clipper:** Evernote's web clipper tool allows you to capture information from a website in the format of a complete webpage, the URL or even a screenshot. This feature is useful for researching a project or paper because you can grab information that you may find useful to work on at a later stage. There's no limit to the amount of info you can capture that may or may not come in handy later.
- **Sharing notebooks:** Evernote also allows you to share notebooks, which can be useful when you're collaborating on a project or paper. To avail of this feature, one of the sharers needs to be a premium user, and that person can then share the notebook with the other person.
- **Capturing images:** Nowadays, most all phones have good cameras, but if you capture an image and want to use it months later, it can be annoying and time-consuming to try to find the one you're looking for. Evernote allows you to capture a photo, tag it and save it in a notebook for use later.
- **Capturing audio:** Sometimes you may want to take a break from transcribing notes and allow the technology to do the work for you. Try capturing a lecture or meeting discussion with audio notes. You can then tag and save the note in the right folder for later use.

Getting it down with OneNote

OneNote is another popular choice for students, allowing students to create sections for their subjects and pages within those sections to write notes. You can also add audio and images or embed other files within these pages, which makes OneNote a useful storage location for all relevant files for each lecture or body of learning. Check out OneNote's user interface in Figure 19-5.

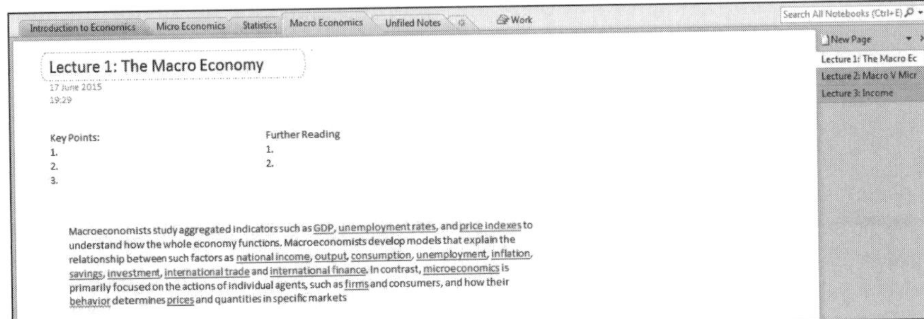

Figure 19-5: OneNote in action.

Source: Ciara Conlon

Google Docs

Google Docs is another cloud-based solution great for both collaboration or for individual use. Using a cloud solution for your documents, spreadsheets and presentations will ensure that you never get caught out, forget to bring an assignment to class or lose a file again.

When you use a *cloud-based solution,* you are storing your documents and files on a protected server on the Internet. A cloud-based programme allows you to store your files and access them from any device once you have your account login details. If you have a Google account, you can also benefit from email, calendar and cloud-based storage for all your stuff using Google Docs.

Scheduling Your Time

Your time is your most precious resource and something you may not have a lot of depending on the course you decide to study. Making the most of your time is easier said than done, but scheduling the work that needs to be done will help you maximise the time that you do have. I explore a few effective ways to schedule your time in the following sections.

Making use of your calendar

Whether you've ever used a calendar before, now is the time where it can really come in handy. A calendar is a great tool for planning time for doing assignments and studying as well as keeping track of your deadlines whenever you're given an assignment. Marking everything you need to do and when it needs done in your calendar is crucial to avoiding stress and staying organised so you can complete your assignments on time.

Most students leave papers to submit to the last minute, cramming work the night before with caffeine-fuelled productive bursts. This pattern is neither sustainable nor good for your health. Using a calendar to plan and create time for completing assignments is a much better plan.

Whether you choose to use a wall planner, pocket planner or electronic calendar to enter in all important dates throughout the year – all your assignment deadlines, exams and, of course, parties – scheduling everything into your calendar is a great habit that will help you make the most of you time and get lots done.

Planning sessions

Take time out each month to look at an overview of your month or at least the next couple of weeks. Consider how many papers you need to hand in. Think about what other responsibilities you have. Taking a step back to look at the big picture is useful every couple of weeks. This will help you to see how much time you should be scheduling each week for study and assignments.

You should also plan your free time and exercise time into your schedule to ensure that they get done. Don't forget there are only 24 hours in a day, and you should be sleeping for at least 7 of them, so don't overcommit to jobs or hobbies that will take up a lot of your time.

Creating Good Habits

Good habits will get you places. The more positive and productive habits you have, the easier your life will be. Habits enable you to reach your goals. Habits also lighten the cognitive load on your brain to make decisions daily. If you can get into the habit of doing certain tasks and chores at the same time each day, your brain will automate the action and make life a lot easier for you. You foster many habits during your time as a student, but here are a number of the top habits that productive students share. If you can create a couple of these, you're well on your way to becoming the A student you always wanted to be.

Go to class

It may sound obvious, but lots of students through the years haven't copped on to this one. As a college student, it's so easy to skip class. The great thing is that nobody is going to call your parents. The downside of this is that nobody is going to call your parents. It can take some first-year students a while to realise that this is a bad thing. If you skip too much class, the onus is on you to catch up. But in reality, you probably won't do the extra work to catch up, which means you'll probably fail first year. Believe me, I have experience with this. Two different economics lectures at 9 a.m. that never saw my face meant that I had to go home early from my summer working holiday in London to re-sit my economics exams. Bummer.

Try to go to as many classes as possible and pay attention. Take notes and ask questions. Try using the flow method (see the earlier section in this chapter) to help you learn as you take notes, which minimises the amount of work you have to do at a later stage. That sounds like a better plan to me.

Take part in something active

The most successful people in this world are by and large physically fit. To be able to achieve great things in life, you need to have a healthy body and a healthy mind. The first step to both of these is to get active. Whatever sport you choose to practise, do it daily. A small daily habit is healthier than a weekly blowout. If you don't already have a daily habit, see Chapter 6 for more on how to create the habit of exercise.

Why is exercise so important? Daily exercise oxygenates your brain, making you even cleverer than you already are. Exercise helps you to focus, gives you more energy and helps you to manage any stress or anxiety that may creep in as the year progresses.

Exercise doesn't have to be running or going to the gym. Dancing, swimming, karate or any sport or activity that increases your heart rate and makes you sweat will do. Exercise is good for your heart and soul, so if you can weave exercise into every day, you'll be healthier, happier and more successful.

If you get involved with sport early on in your college career, you'll likely become friends with other people who play sport. Sporty people are often more engaged students and ultimately more successful. Get in with the good crowd early.

Surround yourself with people who understand the Latin term *mens sana in corpore sano* (a healthy mind in a healthy body) and who will support and encourage you to stay active and stay productive.

Get a reasonable amount of sleep

Now, if you're a student leaving home for the first time, getting enough sleep is going to be difficult – so many parties, so much life outside your dorm room. Try to have a few early nights during the week to catch up on late nights on the weekend. Sleep is very important; believe me. The benefits are numerous; here are just a few:

- Sleep is a natural beauty treatment. People who are sleep deprived look and feel older.
- Lack of sleep is often linked with hunger and weight gain.
- There is truth in the old saying 'Sleep on it' – people make better decisions after a good night's sleep.
- Sleep helps you to remember, so staying up cramming all night is never a good idea.
- Lack of sleep makes it difficult to focus and get things done.
- If you don't sleep enough, you won't have the energy to work out, meaning you'll be unhealthy and likely put on more weight.
- Lack of sleep makes you irritable and more likely to engage in conflict.
- Lack of sleep affects your immune system and diminishes your ability to fend off viruses and bacteria.

Create an ideas notebook

When your mind is being exercised, you may find you get a lot of ideas. You may also find that you don't have time to act on them or explore them further. If you keep an ideas notebook with you at all times, you can capture those ideas to be worked on at a later stage. Who knows, you may come up with the next Facebook idea or maybe just a pair of socks that don't smell.

Have a place for everything

Get organised at home – whether you live on or off campus. Keep all your books and folders in one place. If you don't have a shelf, ask your parents or the owner of your accommodation to install a shelf for your books.

It goes without saying: you need a desk. Whether you choose to do most of your work in the college library or in your room, you need your own desk. At times, you'll need to do work at home, and having a setup that is conducive to working will be very beneficial and more encouraging if you need to get stuff done.

Keeping things tidy and in place removes any potential anxiety or stress that can be caused from disorganisation and clutter.

Getting the Budget Right

Unless you're one of a lucky few, money will likely be tight when you're a student, and what you don't want to do is sacrifice study time for work time. Here are some tips for getting the budget right from the start and managing your money well.

Staying in control of your finances helps you to feel more organised and ensures that you are not feeling stressed by financial worries. The fewer things you have to worry about, the more you're able to focus on your studies.

Listing your expenses

The first step to creating a budget is to list your expenses. Start by writing down all the things you need to spend money on. Create a spreadsheet in Microsoft Outlook or Google Sheets and add columns for all the different expenses you have. Examples include accommodation, travel, electricity, telephone and any other monthly expenses. If you're just starting in college, you may not be sure what these are going to cost you. Ask around, and someone will likely be able to give you a good estimate of the costs. Your new landlord may be able to tell you what past tenants have paid. Have the spreadsheet ready to populate when you get your first bill.

Work out how much you have left over after you spend on essentials. Rent, travel and other bills have to be paid before you decide on your discretionary spending. Your discretionary spending includes food and entertainment. Of course, food is essential, but you can spend hugely different amounts on food depending on what your budget is. If the figures aren't as sweet as you'd like, you may have to consider cutting back. Figure 19-6 shows a typical student budgeting sheet.

		Jan	Feb	March	April	May	June	July	Aug	Sept	Oct	Nov	Dec
FUNDING/INCOME													
From Employment													
From Parents													
From Student Loans													
From Scholarships													
From Grants													
Other													
Total FUNDING/INCOME	0	0	0	0	0	0	0	0	0	0	0	0	0
EXPENSES													
Tuition													
Housing/Rent													
Loan Payments													
Computer and Other Equipment													
Dorm/House Furnishings													
Books													
School Supplies													
Food													
House Supplies													
Utilities (Electric, Water, Trash)													
Cellphone Bill													
Internet Bill													
Travel Home or Other													
Transportation (Around campus & town)													
Entertainment													
Clothing													
Laundry													
Total EXPENSES	0	0	0	0	0	0	0	0	0	0	0	0	0
NET (Income - Expenses)			0			0			0			0	0

Figure 19-6: Your budget.

Listing your income

You also want to list your income on your spreadsheet. You may have multiple sources of income: your college loan, your work and your parents, if you haven't already bled them dry. Put down the amount that you receive each month in another column on your spreadsheet. Your income each month may vary, but the idea is to get a general amount that you can expect to bring in each month. You can then take an average and use that for your income amount.

Tracking your spending

You can also use your spreadsheet to track your spending. Tracking your spending helps you to see how much money you're actually spending on each item and decide what you really want to spend your money on. Keep track by entering your expenses into your spreadsheet. Keep all your receipts and enter them into the spreadsheet. You may be shocked to find out how much the daily coffee is costing you.

You may find it easier to track your spending with an app. Many apps allow you to make an entry each time you spend money. Try out Spending Tracker or Mint from your app store. This can be a lot easier to do than saving your receipts and entering expenses into a spreadsheet later. Also, if you do it at the time of purchasing, you're less likely to forget to enter it in.

Figuring out how to cut back

There are ways to reduce your spending and not cut out all your fun. Maybe you can reduce the amount of money you spend on your phone and Skype more, or instead of going out once a week, invite your friends over for dinner. You could get a bike and save on transport costs or buy secondhand books instead of new ones.

If cutting back isn't an option, you may need to work a few more hours to fill the gap. There are many ways to save money, and the important thing to tell yourself is that you're not losing out; you're staying in control of the money that you do have.

Taking advantage of student discounts

Don't forget about student discounts. Make sure you're registered for everything you can be. Bring your student card with you at all times, and make sure you eat and buy in the shops that give discounts. No need to waste money if you don't have to. Ask your parents for any coupons that they receive for food shopping and keep them with you at all times so you have them when you do go the food shopping.

Keeping your finances organised

Stay in control of your money by keeping organised. If you don't and you forget to pay a bill, you may end up paying late charges. On a tight budget, the last thing you want is to be paying extra money you don't have to. So aim to keep on top of all your bills. Ideally, you want to pay your bills by direct debit so then you never risk late payments.

To keep things organised, get a filing box for all your bills and bank statements. Or, if you receive these online, make sure you create a folder on your computer for each utility and bank statement. You'll need to have all of these handy at a later stage when balancing your budget or working out how much more money you need from Mum and Dad.

Creating a savings plan

If you're lucky enough to have a little extra cash in the pot after you do your calculations, consider creating a savings account. You can use this extra money for weekends at home or planning for the future, for example. Having a savings account is a great habit to get into. No matter how small an amount, saving even just a little each month is a great habit. People who save from an early age are much more likely to be wealthy throughout their lives.

Networking Like a Pro

The old saying, 'It's not what you know but who you know', has some truth in it. However, in modern times, it's essential to have both. Qualifications are fundamental, but having a network of people around you is the key to success. I'm not referring to the old-fashioned nepotism where only friends and family got jobs, but the new world of connectivity, support and knowledge that comes from the people you know.

Networking isn't just about making connections; it's about building relationships and getting to know people well. The more solid your relationships are with people, the more likely they are to think of you when you need them to.

Making connections that matter

In his bestselling book *Never Eat Alone* (Crown Business, 2005), Keith Ferrazzi tells of how he maximised his time by never eating alone and instead always sharing his meals to nurture his relationships. Relationships are the secret to success. Reaching out to others is necessary. Get out of your comfort zone, go to events and conferences and make new like-minded friends. Also reach out to those who inspire you, and get to know people whom you want to help and who may want to help you. In the following sections are some tips on where you can make connections that matter.

You never know who you may need in the future, so be nice to everyone. Many people make rash assumptions about others to be later surprised by their family or other connections. Don't regret how you behaved with people; always be nice to people, even if it's just for the sake of it.

College connections

Getting to know the right people early on is a great strategy as a student. This isn't to say you can't be friends with everyone, but you do want to get to know your lecturers and other important people in your college, such as your student body representative and anyone else that you may need to call on during your time as a student. Forging relationships early on will put you in a stronger position if you need support or assistance later.

Industry connections

Try to look outside into the industry you intend to work in, and make some connections early on. Go to any industry networking events or conferences. This approach will impress potential employers and keep you up-to-date with the latest happenings in your industry. If you don't know where to start, search the Internet or ask your parents whether they have any existing contacts in the industry who may be able to give you advice.

Working as an intern

An internship is a great way to get experience and make connections. Also, if you've spent a couple of months working in an organisation as an intern, you have a much stronger chance of getting a job there when a permanent position does arise.

Always work to the best of your ability and try to make a lasting impression.

Family connections

Too often, people's own families are unaware of what they actually do and what they want to do in the future. Make sure all your friends and family know what you're studying and what you want to do with that in the future. Never miss an opportunity to communicate what you want to achieve in life. You never know whom the people you speak with are connected to.

Social media connections

Create social media connections that matter. Quality is better than quantity. Quantity isn't going to get you a job, but quality may open doors. Here are a couple of things to consider about social media connections:

- Follow the people in your industry on Twitter. Engage with them, comment on their tweets and create relationships online. Don't be a stalker, and don't engage too much or too often. Just keep up-to-date with what is going on and stay informed.
- Be careful about your interaction with social media accounts. You don't want some silly party photos to prevent you from getting your dream job in a couple of years. Ask your friends to refrain from tagging you and avoid posting any photos or posts you wouldn't like your granny to read. You don't want these things to come back and bite you in the future.

Not reinventing the wheel

Having an expanded network can help you with all areas of your life. Think smart. Don't try to do everything yourself. If you have research to do for a project, find out who has done it before you and connect with them. A little bit of guidance can go a long way. People are very often willing to give a younger person a helping hand. Even if you're not a younger person, you'll still find assistance most times you ask.

Finding a mentor

Everyone wants a mentor, and no one knows where to find one. But the truth is, people often have mentors and don't even realise that's what they are. Mentors are people who have more experience than you and are willing to give you their time and attention to help you progress in your career. Chances are, you have a couple of mentors already, but the relationship may not be formalised. So how do you identify your mentors and establish a relationship? Read on!

Finding the right one

Your ideal mentor is someone who has been through the same things you've been through and has come out the other side, preferably successfully. If you're going after a degree in engineering, a social science graduate is probably not the right mentor for you. Go to events that attract the type of mentor you're hoping to find. Ask your ideal person for a coffee date, and ask him or her for advice on something.

Establishing the relationship

After you've found a person whom you'd like to be your mentor, it's probably best not to ask outright, 'Will you be my mentor?' Busy people may see this formal arrangement as too much of a commitment. The best thing to do is to ask for help or advice on a particular situation or project. If the person agrees to that, make sure you're ready when you do meet. Have your questions prepared in advance and commit to taking up as little of his time as possible.

When you finish talking to your mentor, make sure to express how much you appreciate his time. If it went well, ask permission to contact him again, letting him know this advice was invaluable and you'd love to gain more insights. Most people can be charmed into giving more of their time.

Learning to speed read

Speed reading may come in handy to reduce the amount of time you need to spend reading books and papers. Speed-reading software can help you speed up the rate at which you read, and some programmes claim to help you read 40 per cent faster than normal.

The new software methods of speed reading include meta guiding using a pointer and *rapid serial visual presentation* (RSVP) displaying words in rapid succession in order to massively increase your reading speed. You can practise this method and gradually speed up the rate at which the words are presented to you. Some of the current popular tools include Accelerator and Syllable for iOS, SpeedRead with Spritz for Android.

Following are a few simple methods for speeding up reading.

Skimming

With skimming, you don't read every word in the sentence and instead just skim for meaning. Although this method can help you to cover information more quickly, it isn't an effective method for learning. However, it can help you to find where the important information is, so you can focus on that.

Using a pen

One of the older methods of speed reading is using a pen to guide you across the page. This ensures that you're focusing on the right word at the right time and not getting distracted by other words. This method also works by using your finger.

Not vocalising

When you sub-*vocalise,* you hear the word being spoken in your mind. This takes much more time than is necessary, because you can understand a word more quickly than you can say it. You need to turn off the voice in your head and practise not saying the word.

Asking for help

The great thing about college is that you can almost always find people willing to give you a helping hand. Don't be shy, embarrassed or afraid to ask people for help. Most are happy to do so. You can turn to many different people, from professors to students who have already taken the class to students currently taking the same class as you. Have some courage and reach out to all groups.

The first port of call should be your professors. They are the most experienced with student issues. If they can't help you personally, they can point you in the right direction.

Remember that many others have gone before you. Some will have experienced the same challenges you currently face and overcome them. Your professors should be able to connect you with past students.

You can also reach out to the other students in your course and create a study group. This group can help you to discuss ideas and concepts and recommend books and articles to read. A study group is a great way to gain confidence in what you're doing and have a sounding board for writing papers and assignments.

Checking Out Some Clever Tips for Clever Students

Get into good habits early on in your student career. Taking control of your technology and your distractions are habits that stand by you for many years to come.

Taking control of email

Don't make emails a priority in your day, especially if you're a full-time student. Process email once or twice a day, simply to see whether you've received anything of importance from your college or lecturers. You're not coordinating a platoon or working with a team of 50, so if you don't check your email every hour, nobody is going to suffer.

Get this idea into your head early on and avoid the distraction and time wasting many fall into from being a slave to their email.

Switching off to focus

Another habit you should master from the beginning of your time as a student is switching off your gadgets when you're trying to study or complete an assignment. It goes without saying that you should turn off your gadgets in class unless you're using them for taking notes. Otherwise, do yourself and your professors a favour, and switch them off as you enter the class.

Every time you hear a ping or see a message light up your screen, your focus is disturbed. Trying to learn is tough enough; don't make it any more difficult by sabotaging your learning with silly interruptions. You can also restrict your own access to the Internet by using programmes like LeechBlock, StayFocused or WasteNoTime. If you have the courage, you can permanently block time-wasting sites on your computer. Do it if you dare!

Skipping on the TV

Can you spend a year without a TV? Your time at college may be a good time to test it out. TV is a great time waster. You fall down on the sofa after a hard day studying, and hours can go by of unproductive zombie watching. Try to go without a TV, and I can almost guarantee that you'll be much more effective with your time.

Managing Netflix and YouTube

The truth is, with YouTube and Netflix, you really don't need a TV. We have all experienced the joys of Netflix – or, if we're more honest, the problem that Netflix presents. 'I'm going to watch one episode and then get back to studying'. Nobody believes that one. If it's just an episode of *Adventure Time,* one is never enough. Install Netflix at your peril. It's a wonderful, affordable method of entertainment, but students beware.

Using your tablet

Maximise your waiting and travelling time by bringing your tablet with you to catch up on reading or culling your email. You'll have times when you're sitting in a doctor's office or travelling on the bus that you can better use if you have your tablet. If you use a cloud-based storage system, you can have all your files available to you wherever you are.

Make sure you have access to your reading material when you're on the go. Always be thinking about how you can better use your time. The more reading and studying you can do throughout the year, the less intense studying you'll have to engage in before exam time.

Part VI

The Part of Tens

Even productivity experts need a helping hand. Check out `www.dummies.com/extras/productivity` for a list of ten apps that can help to keep you productive.

In this part . . .

- Discover ten ways to focus and get more done.
- Understand ten ways to beat procrastination and become more productive.
- Get the lowdown on ten of the best productivity resources.

Chapter 20

Ten Ways to Focus and Get More Done

In This Chapter

- Discovering ways to get more work done
- Applying mindful techniques for greater focus
- Creating the conditions for success

Learning to focus is a key skill for achieving success in life. Most people find focusing difficult due to constant distraction and information overload. In this chapter, you find some great ways to help you clear your cluttered mind and go for gold. Decluttering, meditating and running all work in different ways to help you achieve the focus of a Buddhist monk.

Decluttering Your Life

Decluttering can have powerful effects on both your work and home lives. Clearing out your cupboards, wardrobes and filing cabinets opens the door for bigger and brighter things.

Physical clutter can affect your mental state. The thought of sorting it all out can be overwhelming, and you may just not know where to start. But remember: when you have less stuff, you need less time to clean and care for that stuff. Downsizing, recycling, donating or dumping – whatever method you choose, you'll feel so much better for it. The physical clutter can inevitably cause stress, anxiety and tension, all traits to be avoided at all costs. Mental clutter affects your brain's ability to function at full capacity. If you can clear your mind of all that you're worrying and stressing about, you become calmer and more focused each day. You are then better able to focus on the right thing at the right time.

Getting It Out of Your Head

Great ideas are no good floating around in your head, nor is your head the place for tasks, chores or responsibilities. Your head is good for having ideas and coming up with plans, but it's definitely not the place for storing things. Going around with too much on your mind isn't a sustainable method of functioning. Here are some ways to free your mind from the mental clutter:

- **Downloading your mind:** A great way to clear the mind is to do a *mind download,* or *mind dump,* which means getting everything out of your head and onto paper or into an electronic note. Dumping everything is the first step in the process. You then need to process everything from every crevice of your mind, which involves adding relevant tasks to your task management system and adding larger and more time-bound tasks to your calendar for scheduling. Head to Chapter 13 for more on task management and Chapter 14 for info about calendar management
- **Mapping your mind:** Another useful way to get it all out of your head is to *mind map* – a method devised by Tony Buzan to help the brain better remember and create in a more creative and visual way. It can be useful when you're feeling overwhelmed or a bit stressed.

  Sit down with a pen and paper and start creating a mind map. In the centre of a page, write the subject, for example 'My Life'. The branches that stem from the subject of the mind map could be all the different areas of your life. In my case, that would be consulting, coaching, speaking, training, family, writing, hobbies and so on. On these branches, write down anything that comes to mind and anything that concerns you that needs attention or improvement. The next step is to decide what you want to do with it. What is priority, and what can be put on hold?
- **Making notes:** Don't leave it up to your mind to remember all the great ideas that you have. If you have ideas, write them down as soon as you get them. Use a piece of paper, a notebook or an electronic notebook, such as Evernote or OneNote. You may want to keep a physical notebook with you at all times like all the great artists and thinkers of time past; Moleskin notebooks are popular for this. If not, Evernote is a great way to capture and retrieve your notes wherever you are and whatever device you have with you. Use tags or keywords to help you retrieve the note at a later stage.

Being Mindful Every Day

Mindfulness, the act of focused awareness on the present moment, has become popular and fashionable in recent times. Mindfulness is about focusing on the here and now to become conscious of what you're doing, when you're doing it. When you focus your awareness on your thoughts, you'll find that you spend most of your day thinking about past and future events. And when you allow past or future events to dominate your present experiences, you rarely have peace.

The practise of mindfulness teaches you to become aware of your thoughts and actions in the present moment. It's a habit you need to nurture because your natural tendency is to stray from the here and now to tomorrow, next week or next month. When you practise mindfulness, you keep calling back your wandering mind to rest on the current moment.

Practise mindfulness as often as you can throughout the day. You don't have to stop what you're doing; mindfulness is about being aware of what is happening now. If you play tennis, don't think about the next move of your opponent or about the scores; instead, think about the ball coming at you and play each point as if it were the only one. If you go for a walk, use the time to notice your surroundings and not think about what you're going to make for dinner or what you'll do on the weekend. If you can focus on the current moment at will, you'll be better able to calm your mind, avoid distractions and focus on what you're working on for longer intervals.

The following lists some benefits of practising mindfulness:

- **Promoting greater focus:** One of the biggest challenges to getting things done occurs when your mind gets distracted. While you try to get one job done, your mind reminds you of ten others that still need doing. You quickly check your email because your mind alerts you to the fact there may be unread emails in your inbox and that if they remain unchecked you may be missing the fact that another big bang is imminent.

  As this thought comes into your head, you then remember that your copy of the Stephen Hawking's *Brief History of Time* is still lying on your bedside locker unopened. You didn't really want to read it; you just bought it because you thought it would make you look clever. Mindfulness jumps in the way of all these mind wanderings and says 'Hey, come back to the present moment and get what needs to be done, done!'

Being mindful . . . right now!

Stop reading and take in your surroundings. Listen to the sounds, and notice how you feel. Are you comfortable in your chair? Or maybe you're lying down. Notice how your body feels. Is it hot, cold or uncomfortable? Do you have any pain in your body? Just notice it. Can you smell food in the background, a candle burning or flowers in the air? Be with the sights, sounds and sensations of the here and now.

- **Managing stress:** Mindfulness not only improves your ability to focus and get more done, but it can also help you to manage stress and anxiety. A lot of stress is brought about by imagining negative future scenarios. If you were to live completely in the present, you wouldn't suffer from stress. The human brain not only has the ability to cast itself into the future but also thrives on doing so. Stressing about future scenarios that haven't happened is a pointless habit, and one that doesn't serve you well. Mindfulness teaches you how to redirect these negative and worrying thoughts back to the present moment and reminds you that the future hasn't happened, and it doesn't control your present circumstances.
- **Ensuring peaceful sleep:** Mindfulness can help with the insomnia that often accompanies stressful situations. If you ever lie awake at night thinking about the bills that need to be paid, bring your focus back to your physical body. Focus on the bed you're lying in and how that makes you feel. Remember that the things that are occupying your mind haven't happened yet. Focusing on the physical here and now can help to quiet your mind enough to help you slip into peaceful sleep.
- **Improving your relationships:** Mindfulness can improve your relationships. When you give focused attention to the ones you love, they feel more valued and loved. We all have friends whom we know don't really listen. This can be frustrating at the best of times. Being listened to is so important for any person of any age. We all need time and attention, and if you can really be with the person in front of you in the time you are together, the relationship will genuinely benefit.

When you come home from work in the evening, dedicate this time to your family. Switch off your phone and gadgets, and really be with the people you love. See how good it makes you all feel.

Redefining Your Goals and Priorities

Do you ever find yourself working furiously on something only to realise you really didn't need to do it at all? This is what happens when you focus on the wrong things. Life can be so busy that little time remains to stop and refocus. It's important to refocus regularly and check whether the goals and targets you had last month are still what you want to focus your attention on this week. Here are some methods to do just that:

- **Go for goals.** Goals help you to know where you're heading. They focus and guide you to the next stage. They motivate and inspire you to achieve more in life. To be productive, the work you do each day must get you closer to reaching your goals. If you spend a day working on something that isn't one of your goals, that was probably time wasted.

Define clear goals, and remind yourself of them daily. If your goals are in clear sight, you're more likely to stay on track and be focused on doing the right work.

- **Use the Eisenhower matrix.** A useful way to understand your priorities is to use the Eisenhower matrix (see Chapter 9 for details). The Eisenhower matrix is a tool that you can use to define your priorities. The tool enables you to identify what is urgent and important in your work and what isn't important and doesn't merit your attention.
- **Practise the Pareto Principle.** The Pareto Principle is another way to identify priorities. The Pareto Principle is also known as the *80/20 rule* and is based on the phenomenon observed by Alfredo Pareto. This principle is widely regarded and used in many areas of life. Most widely known is the sales principle that 80 per cent of your revenue will come from 20 per cent of your customers or 20 per cent of your products or possibly both.
- When you apply the Pareto Principle to productivity, you will notice that 20 per cent of your work will give you 80 per cent of the results. Usually only 20 per cent of what you do is value adding. The 80 per cent is made up of the meetings, emails, administration and other less useful tasks. If you can identify what your 20 per cent tasks are and focus your attention on them, or better yet spend a little more time on them each day, you will see great results.

Getting Some Fresh Air

There will be times when you just can't get it together. No matter how you try, your mind is wandering and your focus is fuzzy. This may be due to many things, but one thing that always works for me is to get some fresh air. It doesn't matter whether it's –2 outside. The fresh air in your lungs will make its way to your fuzzy brain and give it a kick-start. Fresh air can do wonders for your concentration. If possible, go for a little walk and do your best not to think about what you're trying to work on. Practise the mindfulness techniques described earlier in this chapter, and notice the flowers or the grass or the concrete buildings around you.

Using the Pomodoro Technique

A simple method for focusing, the *Pomodoro Technique* encourages you to work in short bursts and take a five-minute break between each Pomodoro. A *Pomodoro* is a 25-minute work period that encourages you to focus and not allow yourself any distractions in this time. If you have a thought or idea, you capture it but get back to work. When you have your five-minute break, you can go to the bathroom, stretch a bit, drink water or make a call, but you get back to work again after the five minutes to start another Pomodoro. You can find out more about the Pomodoro Technique in Chapter 11, or check out `http://pomodorotechnique.com`.

The great thing about the Pomodoro Technique is that it gives you a system to help you run your work time. You know when to focus and when you can relax. The breaks re-energise you: by moving, you're getting oxygen into your blood and avoiding stiffness caused by sitting too long. It is also better for your health not to be sedentary for too long, and it can be a great trigger to drink more water and ensure that you're staying hydrated. There are so many benefits to the system; you just have to give it a go.

Listening to Music with Headphones

When I work from home, I get distracted. The noises of family life regularly break my focus and sometimes make me want to get involved. The way I deal with this reality of family life is to work with headphones. Listening to music with headphones helps me to concentrate and shields me from what's going on around me.

Music can sooth a certain part of the brain that is usually on the lookout for danger, food or other interesting things. With the part of the brain that looks for distraction being soothed and calmed, you can use the best part of your brain to keep working. But not every type of music works as well. Firstly, it has to be music without lyrics and preferably stuff you're familiar with. The better you know a piece of music, the less likely you are to focus on it. You also have to take into account intensity, speed and arrangement – it's probably best to avoid death metal, for example. Websites such as `http://focusatwill.com` can give you the right sort of music to help you focus.

Headphones are also a great way to signal to those around you not to disturb you. Working in an open-plan office can be a productivity nightmare. If people are constantly disturbing you throughout the day, try sticking a pair of headphones on to give them the silent signal 'Do Not Disturb'. You may start a trend and get them all rushing out to buy headphones.

Unplugging from the Distractions

Life is full of distractions, but the reality is that most of them are distractions you can control. You may not be able to do too much about your boss disturbing you regularly, but you can do a lot about your co-workers and the technology distractions that push their way into your life daily.

A very simple way to get in control of your social media and any other electronic communications is to switch them off. Switch off notifications of tweets, posts and anything else that disturbs your focus daily. If someone tweets, you don't need to know right now. Your life will be so much better, calmer and more productive if you have the courage to switch off the notifications. Every time a notification beeps or even shows up on your phone, you allow your focus to be disturbed. It takes 15 minutes to regain your focus to the same level each time you get distracted. In essence, most people rarely work to their full focus.

Pick up your phone, go to the notifications centre, and switch off all notifications from all apps.

You may also be wise to turn off all devices in the evening when you get home from work. This will give you some time with your family to connect and relax.

Exercising Every Day

More and more research is showing that exercise can bring huge benefits. In Tim Ferris's book *The 4-Hour Workweek,* he speaks about a time when Richard Branson claimed he gets an extra four hours of productivity a day from exercising in the morning. Exercise gives you energy – that much we know is true – but it also helps you to focus. Exercise improves blood flow to the brain, helping you to think better and stay focused. Introduce exercise into your life every day. Ideally, a morning exercise session gives you the most benefit. Barack Obama, Richard Branson and many other highly successful individuals all have a morning exercise routine. Improved focus, increased energy, enhanced well-being . . . need I say more?

Exercise produces endorphins, which are said to improve the ability of your brain to prioritise. After exercise, your ability to sort out priorities improves, helping you to block out distractions and concentrate better.

Create an exercise schedule. Plan to get out of bed an hour earlier each day. To do this, you need to go to bed an hour earlier. Start small, and introduce a small amount of exercise each day. A 15-minute run, walk or workout done every day is going to benefit you more than a one-hour run twice a week. If mornings are impossible for you, try introducing a lunchtime workout. This will help you to work more productively in the afternoons.

Remembering to Breathe

The sign above my desk says one thing: Breathe. When I get engrossed in writing or any other type of work, I often forget to breathe. Not the involuntary breathing that keeps me alive (obviously) but the deep breathing that oxygenates my organs and energises my body. Regular deep breaths can help keep you more focused and alert. It also makes you more conscious of your posture when you sit at a desk. When I remember to breathe, it makes me sit up straight to allow the breath to expand my lungs fully. Through the day, I often slump little by little back to a bad posture and limit the amount of oxygen getting into my body. This little reminder above my desk helps to keep me more focused every day.

Stand up and take a deep breath through your nose while raising your arms above your head. Breathe out slowly. Repeat this action three times before continuing to read. Repeat this exercise whenever you think of it during the day.

Chapter 21

Ten Ways to Beat Procrastination

In This Chapter

- Discovering ways to get started and keep going
- Using habits to overcome procrastination
- Scheduling time to get it done

Procrastination is a habit of most human beings, putting off until tomorrow what should be done today. How do you tackle this age-old problem and ensure that the work gets done at the right time? Read on. In this chapter, I give you ten ways to beat procrastination.

Scheduling the First Step

My number-one tip for beating procrastination is to use your calendar. If you think something's important enough, allocate a time for it in your calendar and get it done. Even if you don't know exactly how to carry out a task, putting time in your calendar to focus your attention on it will help you to start making progress. Not sure how much time, attention or work is involved? Schedule half an hour to think it through. You can then do a mind map to help you visualise what's involved. After you put some time into the job, you can see that it's not so daunting after all. You can then start to plan the work you need to do and schedule some time to do it.

The calendar is a powerful way to visualise your work and the time you need to do it. If you're not already set up with a calendar, try using Google Calendar or Outlook Calendar if you work with Outlook. Think about all the tasks and projects you've been putting off. Then schedule some time for each one in your calendar.

Don't overpopulate your calendar. Be realistic, and leave time in your day for interruptions and unfortunate events. Only put work in your calendar that you intend to do; don't fool yourself by planning low-priority work in your calendar that you know you won't do.

Getting Better Goals

Very often people procrastinate about stuff because deep down they're not really bothered about doing it. For example, if you have a goal to write a book on hedge cutting and you just can't seem to get it started, perhaps it's because hedge cutting just doesn't stimulate you as much as you thought. You may need to reconsider your goals and make them exciting and inspiring. Maybe if you set a goal to write a book on motorcycle maintenance, you'll find it difficult to get away from the keyboard. Your goals should move you to action. If this is not the case, it's probably time to get new goals.

As you know, this isn't always possible with work goals. So how do you motivate yourself toward achieving unexciting, unmoving work goals? You have to look at the bigger picture. You have to ask yourself whether you want to continue in the job and what you're prepared to do to continue. If the goal is important for the organisation but tedious or uninspiring for you, you need to buy in to the goal for the greater good – that is, you need your job, you really like your job (just not this aspect) or you see the holistic benefit. Before you get going, make sure there isn't someone else who can do the job or someone you can share the job with. Check that it's still as important as you once thought, and go get started. You may surprise yourself: sometimes things aren't as unpleasant as you may have first imagined.

Eating Frogs

In Brian Tracey's *Eat That Frog!* book, he describes the act of eating a frog as tackling the most challenging or difficult task first in the morning. The 'frogs' are the yucky tasks, the ones you always avoid. They're the ones that make your stomach feel sick or the hair stand up on the back of your neck. Tracey says that you should no longer avoid them, because you need to embrace them and get them out of the way first thing in the morning. The lightness and freedom you feel from ticking the horrible task off your to-do list first thing in the morning puts you in better form for the day. If you can do that, you can do anything. Get those frogs off your to-do list and out of your life as quickly as possible, get into the habit of *worst first* and watch your productivity and happiness soar.

Eating Elephants

I'm sure you've heard the joke, 'How do you eat an elephant? Bite by bite'. This joke has a great moral and one that you can apply in your daily work. Any task that appears to be an elephant can be digested easily enough when you tackle it bite by bite. This can be very useful when a task feels overwhelming, such as your yearly taxes or the garden that hasn't been tended to in over a year.

Break down the large tasks into as many smaller parts as you can. When you see the individual parts, the task will start to look more manageable and cease to put the fear of God into you. When I agreed to write this book, it felt like a mammoth task. An elephant would have looked attractive. No, this was large, hairy and somewhat indigestible. But with advice, I had to plan out all the chapters in advance. I had to spend time thinking about what each chapter would contain and how I would break each subject down into subheadings. What this did was made it manageable and allowed me to focus on only a small piece at a time, in this case, a chapter. By focusing on one chapter at a time, it made the task digestible. By scheduling each chapter into my calendar, it allowed me to see that it was possible to achieve and exactly how I would achieve it.

If you have a large task to complete, take plenty of time to plan it. Break it down and analyse what has to be done. Time spent planning in advance will benefit you massively in the long term.

Creating Positive Habits

The best way to avoid procrastination is to create positive and productive habits to support you in getting things done. To create the right habits, you need to know what, why and how.

- **What needs to change?** Understanding the end goal sets you up for future success. If you have a goal that you're not achieving, you need to reassess whether it's something you really want. If you decide that it is, be clear about the outcome. What will success look like? When you're clear about what a positive outcome looks like, you'll be more likely to stop procrastinating and start taking action toward achieving that outcome.
- **Why do you want the change?** Identification with the 'why' puts you in a more powerful position. If you have a vision and understand how this ties in with your purpose and values, you can connect with an inner drive to make things happen.
- **How are you going to do it?** How are you going to make this happen? The easiest way to change is to create a habit, a routine that will help you to achieve the goals you want to achieve in life. Creating positive habits in your day-to-day life will enable you to stop procrastinating and get more things done.

Using the Ten-Minute Rule

At times, people procrastinate over starting something new because they think they don't have time. One way to overcome this roadblock is to use the *ten-minute rule.* Many years ago when I wanted to write my first book, I complained to a friend, 'I would love to write a book, but I simply don't have the time'. Her reply to me was, 'Ten minutes a day will write a book'. And it did. With this technique, I overcame the fear of getting started and simply committed to ten minutes a day. Of course, those ten minutes often led to periods of 60 minutes or more, but I never let the excuse 'I don't have time' get in my way again.

So what can you do with ten minutes? You can use the ten-minute rule to start many good habits, such as running, writing or meditating. Just think: ten minutes a day is better than no time at all. Doctors will tell you, it's better for your health to do regular small amounts of exercise than to do it all at once.

Try to do your new habit at the same time every day; this will help you to create the habit more easily as you get used to the same routine every day.

Embracing Accountability

One of the most powerful ways to start anything is to become accountable to someone else, preferably a newly found acquaintance or someone you're not too familiar with.

The accountability buddy is the single most effective way to get you off your rear and get started on that thing you've been avoiding. You need to choose someone who will hold you to your commitment. Choose someone who will be willing to check in with you every day and remind you of what you promised yourself. If you've arranged to meet someone to go for a run, you're unlikely to let her down. Get a different accountability buddy for each new thing you need to start.

Learning to Delegate

If you're procrastinating over something, ask yourself whether the task really belongs to you. If a task is sitting in your to-do list for weeks or months on end, try to get rid of it. If you're in the fortunate position of having people to whom you can delegate the task, do so. You can easily check in with them to ensure that the job is getting done, but at least it will have been started.

Delegation is a great way to get work moving. Whether you completely offload the task or just get someone to get started on it, it can be a great way to beat procrastination.

To be an effective delegator, you must have an effective follow-up system. Make sure you have a way to keep track of all the work you have delegated and to ensure that it all gets done.

Dealing with Lingering Tasks

If something has been lying on your to-do list for weeks or months, maybe it's time to be honest with yourself: do you really want to pursue this project, or can you do without completing this task at all? In my experience of working with many senior executives, if things have been lying around on the to-do list for longer than three months, they usually get deleted or delegated. If it wasn't important enough to fit it in over the past three months, what makes it important now? A lot of the stuff people procrastinate on is 'nice to have' stuff. They would like to do it if they had the time; unfortunately, the time never comes. There are four options to handle these types of to-dos:

- **Create a 'someday maybe' list.** If the task is something you want to do and may get around to eventually, you may want to create a 'someday maybe' list or a 'future projects' list, which can hold a list of the nice to do things in the future, someday if you have the time.
- **Schedule it (it's now urgent)!** The other option is to get cracking. If it's something you should get done, stop messing about and get it done. Schedule time in your calendar for next week and actually get the task off your to-do list once and for all. You'll feel amazing as you create that tick.
- **Delegate it.** If you can delegate a task, delegate it. It's better for someone else to do the task than for it to sit in your to-do list for weeks or months. Delegation is a great way to get things done.
- **Delete it, full stop.** If you decide the task is no longer something you need to do, delete it from your list and get back to focusing on the important stuff.

Understanding When Procrastination Is Okay

Believe it or not, there are times when it's okay to procrastinate. Sometimes you need to take your time, be patient and wait. If you always act fast and get things done as soon as they come your way, you're at risk of making the wrong decisions and not giving things the attention they deserve. Procrastination has some benefits – not all the time, but sometimes – and here are some of them.

- **Making better decisions:** Frank Partnoy, the author of *Wait: The Art and Science of Delay,* says that, when faced with a decision, you should wait until the last possible moment to do so. The more time you have to process the decision, the better it should be. He also talks about how gut decision making can be flawed due to the multiple unconscious biases that everyone has.
- **Prioritising better:** If you leave time between tasks, you're more likely to prioritise better. The tasks you're procrastinating over are most likely the ones of lesser importance, unless, of course, it's your tax return – everyone procrastinates over that.
- **Enhancing creativity:** A lot of procrastinators are creative sorts and claim that they need time for the creativity to flow. I do believe you can't force creativity, but you can encourage it to happen by showing up. Delaying for the next big thing is okay, but try to produce something in the interim.

Chapter 22

Ten Best Productivity Resources

In This Chapter

- Checking out web resources to make you more productive
- Reviewing books to help you be more effective

This chapter presents ten great resources – five websites and five books – to help you become the productivity ninja you always wanted to be. Just don't dwell too long on reading about productivity – now's the time to stop learning about productivity and start doing!

Lifehack

Lifehack (`www.lifehack.org`) is one of the web's most popular resources for productivity and life improvements. This site is dedicated to *lifehacks* – advice, resources, tips or tricks to help you get things done more efficiently and effectively. This site's many contributors are writers, bloggers and experts from all walks of life who have tried out and tested many of the tips and tricks on the site.

Zen Habits

Zen Habits (`www.zenhabits.net`) is the blog of Leo Babauta. Babauta is a father of six and author of numerous books. He's a minimalist and advocates simplicity over productivity. His blog is about finding simplicity in the chaos of life. Babauta writes about subjects such as happiness, simplicity, goal setting, getting things done and health and fitness. Previously a smoker and overweight, Babauta changed his life and habits to have a more meaningful life. Along with quitting smoking, he became a runner, is now vegan and has accomplished many impressive deeds in his life.

RescueTime

RescueTime (www.rescuetime.com) helps you track the time you spend on your computer and tells you how productive you are based on the statistics it captures. It allows you to record any activities you specifically want to track and blocks sites to keep you away from online distractions. When you track what you do, you put yourself in a position of power to make changes in the way you do things.

Tracking what you do always leads to more efficient working.

The Pomodoro Technique

The Pomodoro Technique (www.pomodorotechnique.com) is an effective way to focus and get more work done. The basis of the Pomodoro Technique is to keep you focused on tasks by setting a timer for each task. When the time is up, you take a five-minute break before resetting the timer. Using this technique is a great way to figure out how long you need for each task you do. When you know how long a task should take, you're more likely to get things done in the time allocated. Set a timetable for how long you need the next time you do it, and watch how efficient you become.

SaneBox

SaneBox (www.sanebox.com) is a tool you won't want to live without once you've tried it. It automatically prioritises important emails and puts the rest of the junk into other folders for you to review. Okay, so maybe it's not junk, but you don't need to review it straightaway. For example, newsletters and other unsolicited mail often aren't that urgent, so SaneBox helps you focus on what is important by putting them on hold to look at later. SaneBox creates a summary for the less important emails, which you can quickly review to ensure that you haven't missed anything important or interesting.

This is a tool that saves me hours each week – not to be ignored.

'The Power of Habit: Why We Do What We Do in Life and Business' by Charles Duhigg

Charles Duhigg's book on habits (Random House, 2014) is a great opportunity to delve into your habits, why habits exist and how you can change them. Your habits are what determine your success or failure in life. If who you are is determined by your daily habits, it may be a good idea to make sure that these habits are empowering, supportive and positive and not sabotaging your success and happiness. Duhigg explains the different parts to habit formation and how you can, with awareness, change the cycles and create better, more worthwhile habits.

'Getting Things Done: The Art of Stress-Free Productivity' by David Allen

David Allen can be described as *the* guru of productivity. His 2002 book *Getting Things Done: The Art of Stress-Free Productivity* (Penguin, 2001) has become one of the most popular books on productivity in the world. Millions of people worldwide use Allen's Getting Things Done system, or GTD. There has been software created for it, including apps and task management systems, to support the many advocates of his system. His workflow systems allow you to get a handle on what you need to do and organise it in a way that you can actually get it done. Chapter 10 looks at Allen's theories in more detail.

'The 4-Hour Work Week' by Timothy Ferris

The 4-Hour Work Week's subtitle is *Escape 9-5, Live Anywhere, and Join the New Rich* (Harmony, 2009). Sounds wonderful. Timothy Ferris is a wacky experimenter who loves to try out new things that may make his life better. He's a serial entrepreneur who has figured out many ways to make his life easier and get other people to make money for him. This book is inspiring if you can see past the litany of self-promotion and way-out ideas for most normal people.

'Flow: The Psychology of Optimal Experience' by Mihaly Csikzentmihalyi

For more than two decades, Mihaly Csikszentmihalyi studied the states in which people report feelings of concentration and deep enjoyment. His studies point to what makes any experience genuinely satisfying is *Flow* (Harper Perennial, 2008): 'a state of concentration so focused that it amounts to complete absorption in an activity and results in the achievement of a perfect state of happiness'. Flow is about happiness and making your life meaningful.

'Focus: The Art of Clear Thinking' by Valerie Pierce

Valerie Pierce is a modern philosopher and business consultant. In this book (Mercier Press, 2014), she helps you see clearly what you want and develop the willpower, self-discipline and intellectual savvy to achieve it. She describes how to eliminate information overload, transform negative thinking into positive action and think clearly in the moment to achieve your goals.

Index

• A •

• B •

• C •

• D •

• E •

• F •

• G •

• H •

• I •

• J •

• K •

• L •

• M •

• N •

• T •

• U •

• V •

• W •

About the Author

Ciara Conlon is a productivity coach, consultant and speaker who specialises in the areas of personal productivity and leadership development. Ciara's first book *Chaos to Control, A Practical Guide To Getting Things Done* was published in 2012. She has contributed to many publications, including *The Irish Times* and *Tatler* magazine, and has been a columnist for lifehack.org and the journal.ie.

Ciara has a degree in politics and economics from University College Dublin and diplomas in organisational psychology, coaching and IT. She has completed higher diplomas in management and leadership and is currently finalising her master's in business.

Coming from chaos, Ciara transformed her own life by getting organised. Some would describe her as a productivity geek (or maybe freak) as she finds joy from both testing productivity software and organising her sock drawer.

Ciara lives by the sea in Dublin, Ireland, with her husband, three boys and their dog.

You can find out more and reach Ciara through her blog at `www.theproductivityblog.com` or website `www.ciaraconlon.com`.

Dedication

This one is for my angels,

crave knowledge
seek stillness
practice gratitude
and know that you are adored.

Thank you for allowing the mothership to fly.

Author's Acknowledgments

Like all polite authors, I would like to acknowledge those who have helped me get here. Thank you to all the lovely, easy-to-work-with people at Wiley, especially Annie, Chrissy and Jennette. Your professionalism and productivity were impressive.

A massive thank you to Gerry Duffy and P.J. Cunningham who inspired me and held me accountable to my habit of writing. Without you guys, I would never have realised what I was capable of. Thanks to all my friends and family for the ongoing love and support, and to Ockie – now it's your time to shine.

Publisher's Acknowledgments

Executive Commissioning Editor: Annie Knight

Editorial Project Manager: Christina Guthrie

Development Editor: Daniel Mersey

Copy Editor: Jennette ElNaggar

Art Coordinator: Alicia B. South

Production Editor: Siddique Shaik

Cover Image: Mmaxer/Shutterstock